NOW YOU CAN LIVE HAPPILY EVER AFTER

While statistics reveal that millions of couples are facing the possibility of breakup, *Mars and Venus Together Forever* demonstrates clearly and simply why relationship problems are inevitable and offers a host of practical insights and suggestions for developing new skills to ensure more loving and fulfilling unions. . . .

> *For those of you in a great relationship, these skills make it even better. . . .*

> *If you are single, this book will be a revelation. It will give you hope that you can have better relationships. . . .*

> *If you are presently experiencing problems in a relationship, this book will reassure you that you're not alone. . . .*

Mars and Venus Together Forever answers the questions that our parents could not. It points us in a new direction. It promises and delivers the necessary information for creating and sustaining loving and mutually fulfilling relationships. It offers a new seed that, when planted and watered, will grow into a relationship that is not only loving but easy.

Mars and Venus Together Forever

JOHN GRAY, PH.D.

Mars and Venus Together Forever

A Practical Guide to Creating Lasting Intimacy

A New, Revised Edition of
*What Your Mother Couldn't Tell You
& Your Father Didn't Know*

JOHN GRAY, PH.D.

HarperPaperbacks
A Division of HarperCollinsPublishers

HarperPaperbacks

A Division of HarperCollins*Publishers*
10 East 53rd Street, New York, N.Y. 10022-5299

A trade paperback edition of this book was published
in 1996 by HarperPerennial, a division of
HarperCollins*Publishers.*

ISBN: 0-06-104457-1

HarperCollins®, ®, and HarperPaperbacks™
are trademarks of HarperCollins*Publishers.*

First HarperPaperbacks printing: January 1998

This title is also available on cassette from HarperAudio.

Printed in the United States of America

Visit HarperPaperbacks on the World Wide Web at
http://www.harpercollins.com

❖ 10 9 8 7 6 5 4

*This book is dedicated with deepest love
and gratitude to my parents
David and Virginia Gray*

*Their undying love, trust, and encouragement
continues to surround and support me in my
journey as a teacher, husband, and father.*

CONTENTS

Acknowledgments

I thank my wife, Bonnie, for once again sharing the journey of developing a book with me. I thank her for her continued patience and support in helping me be successful as a loving mate and father to our children. I also thank her for allowing me to share our stories and especially for continuing to expand my understanding and ability to honor the female perspective. Her insightful suggestions and comments have provided an important and necessary balance.

I thank our three daughters, Shannon, Juliet, and Lauren, for their love and admiration. The joy of being a parent helps immensely to offset the pressures of a very busy lifestyle. I thank them for their warmth, wisdom, and appreciation of what I do. Particularly I want to thank Lauren for painting the sign in my office: "Please Daddy, finish the book! Hooray!!!"

I thank my father, David Gray, for attending my seminars on relationships. His support and belief in me and my work was and still is immensely helpful. His candid sharing of his successes and failures in his relationships helped me to understand the differences between our generations. Although he didn't know the skills for growing in intimacy, he did his best, and from that I learned that I could make mistakes and still be worthy of love. He is remembered by many as a loving, charming, and generous man.

I thank my mother, Virginia Gray, for the many intelligent and fun conversations we have had on how women and men in her generation behaved and reacted in relationships. Times have certainly changed. I thank her for allowing me to share stories from her marriage and for her persistent accepting and embracing love that surrounds and supports me in everything I do.

I thank all my five brothers and sister for our long discussions into the night at holiday get-togethers. I thank my oldest brother, David, and his wife, Doris, for their keen insight and their appreciation of my new and creative ideas as well as their challenges. I thank my brother William and his wife, Edwina, for sharing with me the more traditional perspectives. I thank my brother Robert once again for his brilliant and spiritual ideas that fundamentally support everything I talk about. I thank my brother Tom for his continued encouragement and pride in my success. I thank him for the many personal conversations when he has shared his insights about men and women. I thank my sister, Virginia, for her openness and loving interest in my life and her candid and discerning understanding of herself as a woman. I thank my deceased younger brother, Jimmy, for his special love and generous spirit. His memory and spirit continue to touch my heart and support me through my most difficult times.

I thank Lucille Brixey for her special and loving support of me since I was six years old. She was always there for me and still is. In her store in Houston, the Aquarian Age Bookshelf, she has displayed my books out front for over ten years. I thank her for always believing in me.

I thank my agent, Patti Breitman, for her helpful assistance, brilliant creativity, and enthusiasm that have guided this book from its conception to its completion. She is a special angel in my life. I thank Carole Bidnick, who connected Patti and me together for the beginning of our first project, *Men Are from Mars, Women Are from Venus.*

I thank Susan Moldow for her wit and editorial clarity, and although she only worked on this book at the beginning, her savvy comments directed and molded its unfoldment. I thank Nancy Peske for her persistent editorial expertise and creativity throughout the whole process. I thank Carolyn Fireside for her editorial contributions. I thank Jack McKeown for his interest and committed support of this project since its beginning and for the support of the entire staff at HarperCollins for their continued responsiveness to my needs.

I thank Michael Najarian and his wife, Susan, for the successful organization of so many seminars. I thank Michael for the many extra hours of creative planning plus the important and insightful feedback he has given to me in developing and testing this material. I thank the many different promoters and organizers who have put their hearts and souls into producing and supporting seminars for me to teach and develop the material in this book: Elly and Ian Coren in Santa Cruz; Ellis and Consuelo Goldfrit in Santa Cruz; Sandee Mac in Houston; Richi and Debra Mudd in Honolulu; Garry Francell of Heart Seminars in Honolulu; Bill and Judy Elbring of *Life Partners* in San Francisco; David Farlow and Juli Ricksecher in San Diego; David and Marci Obstfeld in Detroit; Fred Kleiner and Mary Wright in Washington, D.C.; Clark and Dotti Bartells in Seattle; Earlene and Jim Carillo in Las Vegas; Bart and Merril Berens in L.A.; Grace Merrick of the Dallas Unity Church.

I thank Richard Cohn and Cindy Black and the staff at Beyond Words Publishing for their continued support in promoting and publishing my book *Men, Women and Relationships,* which gave birth to the ideas in this book.

I thank John Vestman at Studio One Recording for his expert audio recordings of my seminars. I thank Dave Morton and the staff of Cassette Express for their continued appreciation of this material and their quality service. I thank Bonnie Solow for her competence and gentle support in producing the audio version of this book as well as the staff of HarperAudio.

I thank Ramy El-Batrawi of Genesis Nuborn Associates and his wife, Ronda, for the successful creation and ongoing production of television infomercials making available audio and video presentations of my seminars.

I thank my executive assistant, Ariana Husband, for her hard work, devotion, and efficient managing of my schedule and office.

I thank my chiropractor, Terry Safford, for the incredible support he provided twice a week during the most intensive six months of this project. I thank Raymond Himmel for his many acupuncture sessions at the end of this project that miraculously healed me of dizziness and exhaustion. I thank Renee Swisko for her amazing and powerful healing sessions with me and the rest of my family.

I thank my friends and associates for their open, honest, and supportive sharing of ideas and feedback: Clifford McGuire, Jim Kennedy and Anna Everest, John and Bonnie Grey, Reggie and Andrea Henkart, Lee and Joyce Shapiro, Marcia Sutton, Gabriel Grunfeld, Harold Bloomfield and Sirah Vettese, Jordan Paul, Lenny Eiger, Charles Wood, Jacques Earley, Chris Johns, Mike Bosch and Doug Aarons.

I thank Oprah Winfrey for her warm and personal support and the opportunity to share freely my ideas on her show before 30 million viewers.

I thank the thousands of participants of my relationship seminars who shared their stories and encouraged me to write this book. Their positive and loving support, along with the thousands of calls and letters I have received from readers, continues to support me in developing and validating the principles of this book.

Particularly for the enormous success of my previous books, I wish to thank the millions of readers who not only have shared my books with others but continue to benefit from these ideas in their lives and relationships.

I give thanks to God for the opportunity to make a difference in this world and the simple but effective wisdom that comes to me and is presented in this book.

Mars and Venus
Together Forever

Introduction

IN THE FIFTIES, when I was growing up, my father secretly confessed to my mother that he was having an affair. What had probably started out as a moment of passion gradually became more serious. He asked my mother for a divorce.

My mother loved my father and was deeply hurt. Instead of sharing her tender feelings by showing him how much she loved and needed him, she became strong. In the most loving way she knew, she said, "If that's what you want, then I will give you a divorce. Let's think about it for a month, and then you decide."

Fate intervened when, a week later, my mother discovered that she was pregnant with their seventh child. With this new responsibility, my father decided not to leave her and the family. My mother was very happy. Nothing more was said about his "other interests." For several years he continued to have affairs in other cities, but they never talked about it.

Though they never divorced, this was a major turning point in their relationship. They continued to love and support each other as husband and wife, but something was missing. The loving romance and playfulness of love slowly began to disappear.

When I became an adult I eventually heard the

rumors of my dad's affairs and asked him about it. His response was "What you don't know can't hurt you." As I persisted in asking more questions, that is all he would tell me.

I realized that this was the way he had justified his affairs. He didn't want to hurt my mother and had rationalized that if he was discreet, she wouldn't be hurt.

To some extent he was right. My mother seemed to be OK with his affairs and never broached the subject or asked him to stop. What neither of them knew was that without monogamy they would eventually snuff out the delicate and tender feelings of affection that attracted them to each other. Like many couples, they mistakenly assumed that it was natural to lose physical attraction and passion after years of marriage.

After my father's death, Mom and I came across a snapshot of him with one of his mistresses. When my mother saw it, tears came to her eyes, tears that were not shed when he was alive. I knew why she was crying.

I could feel her pain at seeing him so open and free with another woman, seeing in his eyes the sparkle they had once shared but which had gradually disappeared from their relationship.

I also felt the personal pain of never having seen my dad so happy. He'd been a loving father, but often moody, angry, or depressed. In this picture, in his secret world, he was charming, helpful, and happy. This was the father I'd longed to know and be like.

When I asked my mother why she thought he had felt the need to stray, she answered, "Your father and I loved each other very much. But as the years passed I became a mother, and your father wanted a wife." I was amazed by how she was so accepting of his infidelity. She told me, "I admired your father for staying. It was a great sacrifice on his part. He had strong desires, but he didn't desert us."

On that day I could finally understand why he had betrayed her: he had stopped being romantically attracted to her and just didn't know what to do about it. He didn't know how to share the responsibilities of a family and also be romantic. He didn't know how to bring back the passion and joy in their relationship. If he had known, he would not have given up and strayed.

I also realized that my mother had done the best she could. She knew too well how to be a loving mother, but was not adept at the art of keeping romance alive. She was following in the footsteps of her mother and her mother's mother. It was, after all, a different world then, with different rules.

In the days of my mother's youth, with the depression followed by World War II, survival was more important than romantic and emotional needs. People just didn't reveal their inner feelings: my mother was too busy raising six and, later, seven children to explore her feelings. Even if she had, she would never have considered sharing her heartaches with Dad, and she wouldn't have known how to unburden herself without making him feel controlled or defensive.

When my father decided not to leave, she was enormously relieved that the family would stay intact. She, like her female ancestors, put the good of her family ahead of her personal needs. My father also put aside his personal needs and honored his commitment to the family by staying married, but, like his male ancestors, continued discreetly to have affairs on the side. Despite everything, my mother assured me that they loved each other very much, and in many ways grew closer through the years.

While my mother's and father's story is common to many people of our parents' and grandparents' generations, we men and women of today want, expect, and require more from our relationships. At a time when the whole basis for marriage has dramatically altered, we no longer mate for survival and protection but for love, romance, and emotional fulfillment. Now, many of the rules and strategies our parents used to keep their marriages together have become ineffective and even counterproductive.

Unfortunately, it could be said that we all have Ph.D.'s in conducting relationships that are just *like* our parents', since we lived with them for eighteen years or more and unconsciously learned how to behave and react from them. For this simple reason, childhood experience heavily influences the quality of our relationships in later life.

Even if our parents dearly loved us, they could not teach us what they did not know. They could not give us solutions to problems that did not exist in their lifetimes. We, their heirs, are pioneers in a new frontier, facing new problems that require new strategies. We not only have to master new relationship skills but must also shoulder the additional burden of unlearning what we learned from our parents. And what are these new lessons and rules? What do we need in order to feel fulfilled?

Women today no longer primarily need men to provide and protect on a physical level. They want men to provide on an emotional level as well. Men today also want more than homemakers and mothers for their children. They want women to nurture their emotional needs but not to mother them or to treat them like children.

I'm not saying that our parents didn't want emotional support; it was just not their primary expectation. It was enough for Mom if Dad worked and provided. It was enough for Dad if Mom managed the house and kids and didn't constantly nag him.

What was good enough for our parents isn't good enough for us. We are no longer willing to make such enormous personal sacrifices. We demand and deserve lasting happiness, intimacy, and passion with a single partner. If we don't get it, many are prepared to sacrifice the marriage. Personal fulfillment has become more important than the family unit.

Recent national statistics reveal that an astronomical average of two out of four marriages end in divorce, and the rate is rising. (In California, the figure is three out of four.) Over 50 percent of America's schoolchildren come from broken homes, while over 30 percent of babies are born out of wedlock. Domestic violence, crime, drug addiction, and the use of psychological medication are at an all-time high. Without doubt, the breakdown of the family is largely responsible for such alarming statistics.

These new problems raise critical questions. Are we to turn back the clock, deny our personal needs, and suddenly make the family more important? Are we to simply endure a marriage that is not emotionally satisfying for the sake of others? While these strategies have worked to ensure our survival in the past, they are not options when our priority is personal fulfillment.

In most cases, the solution is not divorce nor is it self-sacrifice. Instead, the answer lies in learning how to create relationships and marriages that support our personal fulfillment.

There is nothing bad or narcissistic about wanting more than our parents did. The truth is that times have changed, and our values have changed with them.

Now that civilization, to a great extent, ensures our physical survival and security, it also provides us with the physical freedom to be ourselves.

> **No longer motivated by basic drives but by higher needs, we expect more from ourselves and life.**

As a result, we look to our relationships for the emotional support to help us be *all* we can.

In this generational movement toward wholeness, women are developing the masculine side of their natures and men are moving toward acknowledging their feminine sides. Women want to be more than mothers and homemakers; they want to make a difference in the world outside the home. Men also aspire to be more than warriors and work machines; they want affectionate and loving relationships in the home, more time for recreation, and greater participation in child rearing.

The age-old distinction between male and female roles has suddenly blurred, creating confusion and frustration. At this time of transition, getting the emotional support we need from our partners can be difficult.

While statistics reveal that millions of couples are facing the possibility of breakup, *Mars and Venus*

Together Forever demonstrates clearly and simply why relationship problems are inevitable and offers a host of practical insights and suggestions for developing new skills to ensure more loving and fulfilling unions.

For those of you in a great relationship, these skills will make it even better. You'll learn how to smooth the rough edges, iron things out, and bring back the passion of the first few years together. Literally thousands of couples attending my relationship seminars have been delighted to discover a greater mutual passion than they ever felt before. In addition to making a good relationship better, these new skills ensure that your marriage will continue to grow in love.

If you are single, this book will be a revelation. It will give you hope that you can have better relationships. It will allow you to view past mistakes without feeling guilty or bad. It will make it easier to forgive those who have hurt or disappointed you. By clearly seeing others' mistakes with the new awareness that they just didn't know better, layers of resentment will be released. This newfound openness will lighten your heart's burden and allow you to draw the perfect person for you into your life. In addition, you will learn new skills so that you won't unknowingly turn off this special person or create unnecessary problems.

If you are presently experiencing problems in a relationship, this book will reassure you that you're not alone. In many cases, you'll discover that there is nothing wrong with you or your partner. It is simply that you never learned the necessary skills for making a relationship work.

Over and over, I've witnessed couples on the verge of divorce miraculously fall in love again. Through discovering and recognizing their mistakes, they do not feel so powerless and hopeless. Their hearts open up again. Understanding the problem lets them release their blame and begin practicing new skills. As they quickly get results, their relationships are profoundly transformed.

After twenty-three years of marriage, Linda and Daryl were ready to give up and sign their divorce papers. They, like so many couples, didn't really want to split up but weren't getting what they needed from each other and knew of no alternative to divorce. All they knew was that staying in the relationship was like choosing to die emotionally. After they learned new relationship skills, everything changed!

What Linda learned: "I always thought my husband just didn't love me or care enough when he didn't do the things I expected. I felt hopeless, like I would never get what I wanted. When I tried to talk about making things better, he just resisted, and things got worse. Now I know that he was just doing what his father did. I discovered that he really did want to make me happy but just didn't understand me. By learning how to approach him differently, I find he has suddenly become a different person. He listens to me, and I appreciate him greatly. Not only am I happy, but he is too."

What Daryl learned: "So many times I just didn't know what she wanted. When she would talk, no matter what I said it seemed to make matters worse. When I tried to explain myself, she would just get more upset. Now I understand that she basically just wanted to be heard. I have learned to say less and listen more, and it actually works. She is so happy these days that I just want to do more for her. It is kind of embarrassing, but I suddenly feel alive again and I didn't even know I was dying."

To save their marriage, Daryl and Linda had to acquire relationship skills their parents couldn't teach them. Daryl learned the importance of responding to Linda's feelings. Linda learned the secrets of keeping a man happy. As a team they quickly improved their relationship by making *small* but crucial adjustments in their attitudes.

Only after these minor changes are made can the big shifts in the relationship take place. The secret to the effectiveness of the techniques I share is that they do not require radical sacrifice of who we are.

For example, to expect a man who doesn't talk much to suddenly open up and share is unrealistic. With a little encouragement, the same man can easily focus his energies on learning to be a better listener. When approached in this manner, behavioral change is possible regardless of what we learned from our parents.

> **Instead of focusing on what we can't or don't do, this book focuses on what we can do and how to do it.**

Many of the participants in my relationship seminars report amazing results even if their partners couldn't or, in some cases, wouldn't come to the sessions. By learning from their own mistakes and developing new skills for relating, the participants were able to generate dramatic and positive changes on their own.

The same thinking applies to this book. Your partner does not have to read it for you to improve your relationship. The skills I share deal with how you can begin today to get more of what you deserve in all your relationships. Certainly, change will happen faster if your partner does read it. Even if he or she is not interested, the secret of success lies in your learning and using its principles.

So how do women convince their partners to read my books? Men, after all, are very particular about the way in which they are approached. If you hand them the book and say "You need this," it creates more resistance. But if you open the book to sections that describe men and ask your mate if what is written is really true, he may suddenly become interested.

This strategy works for two reasons. First of all, men like to be experts, and you'll be approaching him as an expert on the male perspective. Second, when he hears parts of this book, he will quickly realize that it is not against men nor does it try to change them. It is 100 percent "male-friendly."

In fact, women are generally amazed by the equal attendance of men at my seminars. They can't believe that they're seeing lots of males actually listening, nodding their heads in agreement, even laughing. I point out that men are just as interested in improving relationships, but require practical strategies that don't ask them to become feminine.

Since the enormous success of my previous bestseller, *Men Are from Mars, Women Are from Venus,* thousands of relationships have improved. In the first year, my office heard from over fifteen thousand readers saying that "the book" had saved their relationships. In some of the calls or letters, readers had more questions, practical questions like "What should I do when . . ." or "What does it mean when . . ." or "How do I get him to . . ." or "What should I say when . . ." or "When do I . . . ?" This book is also a response to those questions.

Mars and Venus Together Forever answers the questions that our parents could not. It points us in a new direction. It promises and delivers the necessary information for creating and sustaining loving and mutually fulfilling relationships. It offers a new seed that, when planted and watered, will grow into a relationship that is not only loving but easy.

I offer this book as a collection of jewels, pearls of wisdom and practical gems from which I have personally benefited. I sincerely hope that they work for you as they continue to work for me and the thousands of participants in my seminars. May you always grow in love and continue to share your special gifts.

JOHN GRAY, Ph.D.

CHAPTER 1

What Your Mother Couldn't Tell You and Your Father Didn't Know

ONCE UPON A TIME, untold ages ago, men and women were peaceful partners in a hostile and dangerous world. A woman felt loved and respected because each day her mate went out and risked his life to provide for her. She didn't expect him to be sensitive or nurturing. Good communication skills were not a part of his job description. As long as he was a good hunter and could find his way home, relationship skills were not required for a mate to be desirable. As providers, men felt loved and appreciated by women. While surviving was difficult, relationships were comparatively easy.

Men and women existed in different spheres. They depended on each other in order to survive. Food, sex, children, shelter, and security motivated them to work together because the fulfillment of these basic needs required specific roles and skills. Men assumed the role of provider and protector while women specialized in nurturing and homemaking.

It was a natural separation. Biology had determined that a woman gives birth and hence feels a great responsibility for raising children and creating a home. The man honored and respected her role by agreeing to take such dangerous assignments as venturing into the wild to hunt, or standing guard to protect her and their young. Although men would often be out for days in the freezing cold or blazing sun before making a kill, they were proud of these sacrifices because they honored the female, the life giver. Since the partnership between a man and a woman provided the basics of survival and security, their interdependence generated mutual respect and appreciation.

Now, though, life has changed dramatically. Since we are no longer utterly dependent on each other for security and survival, the rules and strategies of our ancestors have become outdated. For the first time in recorded history, we look to each other primarily for love and romance. Happiness, intimacy, and lasting passion are now requirements for fulfilling relationships.

What your mother couldn't tell you and your father didn't know is how to satisfy your partner's emotional needs without sacrificing your own personal fulfillment. This new agenda can be accomplished only through the practice of new relationship skills.

Times Have Changed

The social and economic changes of the last forty years have enormously affected traditional male and female roles. Women's leaving the home and entering the workforce has diminished men's traditional value to women. Increasingly independent and self-sufficient, contemporary women no longer feel the same need for men to provide for or protect them.

A modern woman charts her own destiny and pays her own bills. When in danger, she can pull out her Mace or call the police. Most important, she now has much more control over when to have children and how many she wants. Until the discovery of the birth control pill, and the widespread availability of contraceptives, women were biologically determined to have children and to be dependent on men. No more.

We are just beginning to comprehend the changes in relationships that have resulted from the widespread use of birth control and the following sexual revolution. We are living in a time of dramatic transition and sexual tension.

In a sense, men no longer have the job they held for centuries. They are no longer valued and appreciated as providers and protectors. Although they continue to do what they have always done, it suddenly isn't enough to make their partners happy. Women require something else, something more than their mothers did.

At the same time, women are overworked. Not only are they mothers, nurturers, and homemakers, but now they are also providers and protectors. They are no longer protected from the harsh and cold realities of the work world outside the home. How can a wife be expected to be relaxed, sensitive, and pleasing to her husband when an hour before she's had to fight a man for a cab? While women today no longer want to wait on a man at the end of a day, men still want what their fathers wanted—to be waited on.

Times have changed, and we have no choice but to change with them. A new job description is required in relationships. New skills must be learned if a man is to feel needed and appreciated by his mate. A new awareness is required of women if they are to continue working side by side with men, then come home to a loving and nurturing relationship. New skills are required to remain feminine and also be strong.

What We Didn't Learn

Our mothers could not teach their daughters how to share their feelings in a way that didn't make men defensive, or how to ask for support so that a man would respond favorably. They did not understand how to nurture a man without mothering him or giving too much. They did not know how to accommodate his wishes without sacrificing their own. They were experts at pleasing their men at their own expense.

In essence, our mothers could not teach their daughters how to be feminine and also powerful. They couldn't teach them how to support their partners and also get the emotional support that they deserved.

Our fathers could not teach their sons how to communicate with a woman without passively giving in or aggressively arguing. Men today have no role models for leading and directing the family in a way that respects and includes their partners' points of view. They do not know how to remain strong while providing emotional support.

We must not blame our parents for failing to teach us things about relationships that they could not know.

Our fathers did not understand how to give the empathy and sympathy that women require today. They did not know the little things a woman requires to be fulfilled. They did not know the importance of monogamy and making a woman feel special. Our fathers simply did not understand women. Without that understanding, the contemporary male cannot develop the skills necessary to get the kind of support he now requires in his relationships.

Our parents couldn't teach us the relationship skills necessary to make relationships thrive in the modern world. Just remembering this—that we could not learn these things from our families—is enough to soften your heart and forgive yourself and your partner for the mistakes you repeatedly make. This gentle wisdom brings hope again.

An Overview of New Relationship Skills

Throughout this book, I will discuss in great detail the relationship skills necessary to support our partners' new emotional needs while getting exactly what we need to be happy and enjoy lasting intimacy and passion. Even if some of the ideas laid out here seem familiar or old-fashioned, they are being presented in dramatically fresh and different ways.

For example, instead of simply advocating that a woman be pleasing to her man, I suggest that she please him by letting him please her. Instead of passively waiting on him, she learns ways in which to get the support she needs.

In a sense, she is still required to help him, but with a new twist: she learns how to help him help her, how to support him in supporting her more, and how to accommodate him so that he will in turn accommodate her needs and wishes.

New relationship skills for a woman require traditional abilities, but with a new twist to ensure that she'll get back what she needs.

I suggest that men continue to be providers but with a new twist. By actually "doing less," a man can learn to provide the emotional support a woman needs. For example, instead of trying to provide solutions to a woman's problems, I suggest that he "do less" and learn to listen with empathy. While "listening with increasing empathy," it actually builds upon his ancient warrior skill of silently waiting and watching.

With the correct understanding, men can become adept in this new skill by using abilities that have taken centuries to develop. Using his warrior skills, he will learn to protect himself constructively when a woman speaks. The new twist is that he learns to defend himself *without* attacking his partner.

Relationships become increasingly difficult when we expect too much of ourselves or our partners. In education theory, to learn something new, you must hear it (and/or apply it) two hundred times. If you are a genius, maybe a hundred and fifty times will do. Mastering new relationship skills is not immediate.

Occasionally forgetting what you have learned is perfectly normal; old patterns and reactions do come back to haunt us. Now, you will understand your part of the problem instead of hopelessly blaming your partner or solely yourself. Changing for the better is sometimes hard work, but at each progressive step it will also become easier, more rewarding, and more fun. And, once learned, these skills will enrich all aspects of your life and your relationships.

Anticipating Setbacks

The most important relationship skill of all is anticipating temporary setbacks and acknowledging the necessity of relearning a lesson until it becomes second nature. This understanding gives us the hope to be patient and the forgiveness to be loving.

**It is imperative that we do not expect
our partners to always know
instinctively what we need
without our telling them.**

Although learning all the new skills may seem overwhelming at times, the process is also very exciting. As you begin to practice new relationship skills, the immediate and tangible results will give you continued cause for hope, encouragement, and support. With your very first step on the journey your parents didn't take, your relationships can dramatically and immediately improve, and gradually, with more practice, keep on getting better.

Through learning these essential skills you can achieve lasting passion, intimacy, and happiness. Passion does not have to dissipate, the happiness shared during the courting process does not have to fade, and intimacy can deepen into a source of increasing fulfillment. In the next chapter, we will explore what women need most, and men really want, if we are to experience lasting intimacy.

CHAPTER 2

What Women Need Most and Men Really Want

THE WOMEN WHO ATTEND my relationship seminars are always amazed by the fact that half the audience is composed of men. They find it hard to believe, but men really are seeking ways to make women happy and are just as interested as women in improved relationships. The problem is that their traditional ways of doing so aren't getting through to the women.

If problems arise at home, the traditional male approach to solving them is to become more successful at work. If a relationship is troubled, a traditional man doesn't take a seminar or purchase a book on relationships; he takes a course or buys a book on business or success. Why? Because from time immemorial, a man could always make his partner happier by being a better provider.

In hunter/gatherer days, this arrangement worked out fine. It worked well enough even for our fathers. For us, however, it doesn't work at all. Today's wives do not leave husbands because they're not being provided for. They leave because they are emotionally and romantically unfulfilled. When a man does not understand a woman's new needs, it is inevitable that she will be unfulfilled. This increased dissatisfaction is also what turns men off. Husbands do not leave wives because they no longer love them, they leave because they can't make them happy. Generally speaking, a man gives up on a relationship when he feels powerless to succeed in fulfilling his partner. Such shared frustration is common because:

Men do not understand women's needs, and women do not understand what men really want or how to give it to them.

By understanding how circumstances have changed for both sexes, we can gain the insight and compassion necessary to master new approaches to mutually supportive relationships.

Why Modern Women Are Unhappy

Modern women are overworked, overstressed, and commonly feel unsupported and overwhelmed with good reason: at no other time in history has so much been expected of them. At least five days a week, they put on a uniform and march into an eight- to twelve-hour battle. When they come home, they feel the need to clean house, make dinner, do laundry, love and nurture the kids, and also be pleasing and happy as well as romantically receptive to their mates. It's just too much to ask of themselves, and it's making them feel split inside.

At work, women are required to behave according to the traditional masculine rules of conduct. At home, they have to switch to being warm, giving, and feminine. It's no wonder women complain that they need a wife to greet them with love and tenderness at the end of the day.

Even a contemporary stay-home mother has a more difficult job than her own mother did because, with most other mothers at work and her kids' playmates at day care, she lacks the traditional company and support of other women.

In the past, a woman was proud to say that she was a full-time wife and mother. Now she may even feel embarrassed when asked, "What do *you* do?" Isolated from the support of other women, she must go it alone, as the value of her commitment is largely unacknowledged by the world.

Still, while women now need more support than at any other time in history, men also miss the ego boost they traditionally received from their mates.

Why Men Are Dissatisfied

Modern men feel underpaid, defeated, and unappreciated. Like women, they are experiencing the toll that a two-career marriage takes.

Years ago, when a man returned to a stay-home wife she could easily show him how much she appreciated his efforts and sacrifices. Happy to care for him because she wasn't stressed out, she asked relatively little in return. Now, abruptly, the home as a male comfort base is under siege.

**At no time in history have relationships
been as difficult for men as now.**

Many men work just as hard as their forefathers, perhaps even harder, but still can't manage to be their family's sole support. Deprived of the strong sense of self that being a sole provider would bring him, on a deep emotional (and sometimes unconscious) level he easily feels defeated when his partner seems unhappy or unfulfilled.

A Man's Primary Goal

When a man loves a woman, his primary goal is to make her happy. Through history, men have endured the competitive and hostile world of work because, at the end of the day, their struggles and efforts were justified by a woman's appreciation. In a very real sense, his mate's fulfillment was the reward that made a man's labor worthwhile.

Today, because women are overworked, they often and understandably feel unfulfilled. Now, at a long day's end, *both* she and her mate are looking for love and appreciation. "I work as hard as he does," she tells herself. "Why is it my responsibility to appreciate him?" Exhaustion now prevents her from giving her man the emotional support he knows he has earned.

To him, her unhappiness signals that he is a failure. "Why should I bother to do more?" he asks himself. "I'm unappreciated for what I do already." The harmful effects of this relatively new pattern are greatly underestimated by both women and men.

When a modern man returns home he
generally faces defeat instead of
victory. His partner's unhappiness
signals that he is a failure.

What Makes Women Happy

Years ago, when most women were full-time homemakers, a woman enjoyed the support of other
women throughout the day. She could break up her
tasks and relax by talking while giving and receiving
in the spirit of cooperation, not competition. She had
the luxury of unstructured time to create beauty in
her home, garden, and community. She cared for others and they cared for her.

This daily routine was conducive to nurturing
her feminine spirit and the love in her heart. Her caring relationships gave meaning to her existence and
supported her through life's inevitable crises.

Women were not expected to shoulder the dou-
ble burden of nurturing relationships and providing
for the family. Men were happy to provide, and able
to be sole providers, leaving their partners free to
perform their tasks while creating and sustaining loving relationships. In the competitive and hard-driving
male-dominated workforce of today, this emphasis
on relationships is greatly missing, and for the first
time in history women are being forced to do without
the support of being in a nurturing and feminine
environment.

Imitation Men

One woman in my seminar expressed her feelings in this way: "I feel like an imitation man. Women in the workforce have no female role models for success. I don't know how a woman can be expected to be strong and assertive and feminine at the same time. I'm losing touch with who I really am."

When women spend their days behaving in traditionally masculine roles, it is tremendously difficult to remain feminine. Working on a very structured timetable, making decisions based primarily on the bottom line and not people's feelings, giving orders when there is no time to share the decision-making, calculating strategic moves to protect herself from attack, creating alliances based solely on profit margins and not on friendship, investing time and energy for personal gain rather than others' benefit, all contribute to the impoverishment of the feminine soul.

The work world does nothing to nourish the female spirit and is dramatically affecting the quality of their intimate relationships.

Women at Work and at Home

Women are affected much more adversely than men by career stress, for the pressures of work outside the home have doubled their load. On the job, they give as much as men do, but when they get home, instinct takes over and they continue giving.

It is hard for a woman to come home, forget the problems of the day, and relax when her programming says, "Cook more, clean more, love more, share more, nurture more, give more, do more."

In the office a woman is motivated to strive by a conscious need to survive, but at home her instincts drive her.

Think of it. Tasks that used to fill a woman's whole day must now be done in a few hours. Along with providing, there is just not enough time, support, or energy to fulfill her biological yearnings for a beautiful, peaceful home and a loving, harmonious, and healthy family. She feels overwhelmed by too much to do.

Whether these instincts come from biology or from watching and identifying with her mother while growing up, they can be very strong. Many times these pressures increase when a woman begins planning for children or has children. While these feelings and pressures are self-induced, they are based on modern physical realities our mothers didn't have to deal with in their efforts to create a home and family. It is not only essential for women to learn new ways of coping, but for men to learn new ways to support their partners.

Men at Work and at Home

Through history, men could tolerate the stresses of the outside world because they would return home to a nurturing and loving woman. All day the male was goal-oriented, but come evening, he either relaxed, played, or was waited on with love. What he didn't have to do was continue working to win his partner's favor.

When a modern woman shares her feelings of having to do too much, a man generally hears it as blame for not doing enough or as an order to do more. Neither message is agreeable to his nature, which is telling him, "OK, you're home. Relax and reap the rewards of your labor."

For men, the home has traditionally been a vacation spot. For women, it is a major hub of activity.

Giving Requires Receiving

Men are wired to give their all to work, then come home and receive. To a great extent women are built to give and receive at the same time. They love to give but need to be fueled simultaneously: when they give without receiving, they tend to give more and eventually feel overwhelmed, empty, and resentful.

It follows that a woman who spends her day in a competitive, masculine workplace does not get the emotional support she would if she were in a more feminine, nurturing environment. She gives and gives at her job but doesn't receive validation and support. She comes home burned out, but instead of relaxing, she continues to give.

This is an important difference between men and women. When a man is tired, he will generally have a strong tendency to forget his problems and rest and relax. If he is not getting the support he needs, then he will tend to stop giving more. If he gives at work without getting back, then particularly when he gets home he feels ready to relax and receive for a while, or at least take some time for himself.

On the other hand, when a woman feels unsupported, she feels responsible for doing more and begins to think of or worry about all the problems she doesn't have the energy to solve. The more overwhelmed she feels, the more difficult it is for her to relax and put off the chores that just can't be done, and really don't have to be done right away.

When she feels overwhelmed, it is difficult for her to determine what really needs to be done and what can wait. In some cases, the expectations her mother had about how a home should be kept instinctively come into play. The more overwhelmed or unsupported she feels, the more these instincts come up. In a subconscious way she may be trying to live up to the standards of housekeeping and entertaining that were appropriate back when every wife was a homemaker and had the time and energy to do it all.

Particularly when a working woman cannot afford outside help for chores at home, she may begin to feel that she is just not doing enough. Instinctively she feels that she has to do more, yet realistically she can't do it all. It is as though she is gripped by out-of-date social programming that expects her to do it all at home.

In some cases, just as a woman feels responsible for doing it all at home, a man is socially programmed to feel that it is all her responsibility. Just as it is difficult for her to relax and do less, it is equally difficult for him to find the energy to help out. Understanding this pattern can bring more compassion between the sexes:

A man's programming assures his job is done when he returns home, while hers is pushing her to do more.

Scott and Salley

Scott works full-time to support his family, while Salley, his wife, works part-time, balancing her roles as mother and homemaker. When Scott returns home, he seems to ignore her unless she asks for something and then he seems to be a little irritated by her requests. Then, when she distances herself from him at dinner, he doesn't understand why.

When asked about her feelings, she says, "I resent that he doesn't even ask me about my day or care about me. He doesn't even offer to help me. He sits on the couch while I do everything for him."

Scott says, "I sit on the couch to relax from my day. If I ask her about her day, all I hear is that she does too much and that I should do more. I need to relax when I get home. I don't need another boss. If she is doing too much, then she should just do less."

Salley says, "And you think I don't need to relax from my day? I can't relax. Someone has to make dinner, clean house, and take care of these kids. Why can't you do more or at least value what I do?"

Scott then looks at me and says, "See."

In that one word he means "See, this is why I don't listen to her when I get home. If I did, she would have me doing more and more. I can't open myself to that."

Salley resents the fact that her partner doesn't offer his help, while Scott is turned off because he gets the message that what he has done is not enough. On the one hand, she wants to feel seen, cared for, and supported, while on the other hand, he wants to feel acknowledged and appreciated for his work with the recognition that he earned the right to relax in his home. The solution to this problem is to first recognize that no one is wrong or to blame. Then, through applying new skills, the pattern can be changed.

Scott's suggesting that Salley do less is like telling a river to stop running: giving is an innate expression of the loving female nature. What women today need most is not to curb their loving tendencies but to receive more nurturing in their relationships with men. To expect Scott suddenly to have the energy to do more is equally unrealistic. That would be like telling a river to switch directions.

By understanding what both really need, a new solution begins to emerge and come into focus. As we will see, men and women can learn new skills of communicating that require very little from men and provide a lot for women. Both partners can learn to practice new skills that don't require more effort but result in feelings of emotional support for the woman and appreciation for the man.

As a woman feels more emotionally supported in the relationship, she will find a peaceful center within herself where she is not so driven to do more. She will gain a more relaxed perspective of what can or can't be done, and what really has to be done in light of her limited resources of time and energy. Likewise, as a man begins to feel more appreciated when he returns home, slowly but surely he will have more energy in the home as well. More important, he will immediately be able to give his partner the empathy and understanding she needs to continue being able to give of herself.

Contemporary women do not need to curb their loving impulses. They need more nurturing in their relationships with men.

Why Women Burn Out

Today, while men are away working, women are also away working; modern women don't have the time, energy, or opportunity to support each other as their mothers did. A modern woman will give and give, but because she is not feeling supported, she commonly returns home feeling burned out.

In addition, when a woman is dependent not on a man but on her work to survive, her tendency to give freely is also restricted. If a women gives to make money, her support is not "freely offered." This manner of conditional giving further disconnects her from her femininity.

Working women are required to be overly masculine. They are no longer supported in expressing their femaleness through mothering, working together in cooperative and nurturing relationships, gathering (shopping), and homemaking. This tipping of the balance toward their masculine aspect is rapidly creating female burnout and dissatisfaction throughout the modern world.

The women of ancient days didn't burn out because their work environment nurtured their female nature. Women today burn out because they are not being sufficiently nurtured in their jobs.

It is not how much a woman does but the quality of her relationships and the support she receives that determine the difference between burnout and fulfillment.

Learning from the Wisdom of the Past

Traditionally, women felt proud of their biological roles, since mothering was highly honored, respected, and even considered sacred. In some cultures a woman was seen as being closer to God than a man, for she alone had been given the power to create life. Women were honored as the mothers, and men gladly became warriors, willing to risk their lives to provide for and protect the mothers of their children.

Going back just to my mother's generation, it is easy to find women who felt very good about themselves as mothers. I remember once as an adult asking my mother if she had liked being a mother. Her immediate response was, "Well, John, I still am a mother, and I still love it. I feel so fortunate to have seven beautiful children."

I was surprised that she so strongly and proudly identified herself as a mother even after her children were grown. I felt fortunate that she hadn't had to go to work and had truly enjoyed being a full-time mom with a husband to support her.

Most mothers today do not often have the luxury of full-time parenting. Having kids *and* having a job mandate a very difficult list of duties requiring new skills that your mother definitely could not have taught you. Without these strategies, the juggling of motherhood and career amounts to a tortuous trek through uncharted territory. Contemporary women considering motherhood are understandably hesitant.

While I am in no way suggesting that we turn back the clock and encourage women back into the kitchen, it is important that we understand what we have given up. As we stride forward on our quest for a new and better world for both women and men, we need to keep in mind the wisdom of the past and use it wherever applicable. Contained in that ancient wisdom are certain elements that are essential for female and male contentment. We should never lose touch with the ancient truths that have always enhanced female and male fulfillment.

Through understanding them, we can more effectively map out fresh approaches to relating that fulfill our instincts while allowing us to move ahead to new goals and dreams.

A Woman's Work Is Never Done

I remember a very telling conversation on the subject of contemporary motherhood. While I was signing books in a bookstore, three women and my wife were sharing stories about how difficult it is to be a mother today. When one woman disclosed that she was the mother of seven, another immediately gasped in admiration and sympathy.

"I only have two children," she said, "and I thought I had it bad. How do you do it?"

A third mother added, "I have only one child and that wears me out."

"I have three children," said my wife, "and I thought that was a lot. I can't imagine how you handle seven."

"Whether you have one, two, three, or seven kids, you give them everything you have," the mother of seven replied. "You only have so much to give, and every mother, no matter how many children she has, gives it all."

Suddenly the other three mothers realized that they were in effect doing the same job. They were each giving everything they had to give to mothering. They were following the ancient wisdom.

This insight completely changed my relationship with my wife. Before, when she complained about doing so much, I assumed she would never be happy until she learned to do less. Now I realized her doing too much was not the problem because she would always do all she could. Instead, I began to focus on finding ways to nurture her female side as she gave and gave. Not only was she happier, but because she felt so much more supported, she could indeed relax and do less.

Overgiving Is Not Dysfunctional

Giving too much becomes a problem only when a woman is not adept in getting back the nurturing support she needs to continue giving. Many popular books label women who give too much as "codependent" or dysfunctional when in many cases they are not. They are just following their healthy feminine instincts to give freely of themselves.

A woman's natural inclination to give unconditionally becomes problematic only when her business and personal relationships do not nurture her in return.

The more focused, responsible, competitive, and aggressive she is required to be at work, the more difficult it is for her to reconnect with the softness of her femininity when she gets home. It is then more difficult for her clearly to feel her needs. A woman will return home and continue thinking about the needs of others.

When a modern woman gets home she generally doesn't have the energy her mother had for domestic work. Instead of looking forward to and enjoying some nice "downtime," a woman, to various degrees, is driven to do more and can't relax. Although she instinctively feels she has to do more, she doesn't have the energy. This combination of feelings makes her feel suddenly exhausted and dissatisfied with her life.

The Nurture Cure

If an exhausted woman is given a big dose of nurturing, I assure you that she will get a second wind and not only more effectively cope with her need to act but actually enjoy it. When a woman feels exhausted, it is because she is not nurturing her female side.

When a woman's female side is nurtured, her body begins to function naturally, and her exhaustion magically lifts.

This does not mean that women today don't need more help around the house. It is important that a man understand that modern women do require more support in the home. It is, however, also equally important that a woman understand that in some cases her expectations of what needs to be done in the home are unrealistic, given that they may be based on standards set by a generation of women who had more time for housework. While it is not fair to place those expectations on her male partner, it is also not fair for a man to ignore her legitimate need for more emotional support.

While the resolution of this problem will be different in every situation, the ability to resolve this potential conflict is based on mutual understanding, patience, and compassion.

What a Man Can Do

Through allotting an extra twenty minutes three or four days a week, a man can do wonders to nurture a woman's female side. Not only will she be happier, but he will begin to get the appreciation and acceptance he needs when he gets home. No matter how over-worked or exhausted she feels, he can, with a small amount of concentrated attention, focus his love and caring in ways that make a big difference.

Unless he comprehends the importance of nurturing a woman's female side, he may mistakenly leave her alone or try to persuade her to do less. Neither approach works, and may actually alienate her.

Quite commonly he might say any of the comments listed here, thinking he is being helpful when he is really making matters worse.

He Mistakenly Says:	**She Hears:**
1. *He says:* "You take on too much."	1. *She hears:* "You don't leave enough time for me."
He really means: "You deserve more support."	She thinks: "He doesn't value all that I do and just wants more."
2. *He says:* "You shouldn't worry about that."	2. *She hears:* "What you are worried about is really not that important."
He really means: "I care about you and I am here to support you if the problem gets worse."	She thinks: "He doesn't care about what is important to me."

He Mistakenly Says:	**She Hears:**
3. *He says:* "It's not that bad."	3. *She hears:* "You are once again making a mountain out of a molehill. You are an alarmist, overreacting to the problem."
He really means: "I trust that you will handle it. You are quite competent and capable, and I am sure that you will work it out. I believe in you."	She thinks: "He doesn't care about my feelings. I am not important to him."
4. *He says:* "You expect too much of yourself."	4. *She hears:* "You shouldn't be upset with yourself, you are always getting upset for no good reason."
He means: "I think you are wonderful, and you give so much of yourself to others. I appreciate what you do, and I think you deserve a lot more support than you get. I understand if you have less to give me today."	She thinks: "He doesn't understand what I am going through and why I feel so bad. Nobody understands what I am going through."

He Mistakenly Says:	**She Hears:**
5. *He says:* "If you are going to complain about it, then just don't do it."	5. *She hears:* "You are being too negative. Anybody else would be able to do it, but you can't."
He means: "I care about you, and I don't want you to do what you don't want to do. You already do so much, you deserve to relax more."	She thinks: "He thinks I only care about myself. He doesn't understand how much I do for others."
6. *He says:* "If you don't want to do it, then don't."	6. *She hears:* "A loving person would be happy to give more."
He means: "You already give so much, I don't expect you to do more. You deserve to have more of what you want."	She thinks: "He thinks that I am selfish and that I am not entitled to relax and give to myself."
7. *He says:* "You don't have to do so much."	7. *She hears:* "What you're doing is unnecessary and a waste of time."
He means: "What you do is already so supportive that I don't expect you to do more."	She thinks: "If he doesn't value what I do, I will never get the support I need in return."

Simply trying to understand what her feelings are and what she goes through with some empathy or sympathy, and not making any of these comments, can have a tremendous nurturing effect on a woman's female side.

An overworked woman, with neither the time nor the opportunity to nurture her female side, may not even be aware of what she's missing; consequently, she may not know how to recapture her femininity. To do so, she needs a healthy dose of "relationship." Anything a man can do to nurture her female side will assist her in releasing her cares.

A man can skillfully respond when a woman feels overwhelmed by addressing the female side of her being, which cries out for nurturing.

Through addressing this female side of her being, a man can respond compassionately and skillfully to a woman feeling exhausted and overwhelmed. Through clearly delineating her male and female aspects, he can effectively work at steering her toward "feeling like herself again."

A Perfect Fit

A woman can most successfully cope with the stress of experiencing nonnurturing relationships in the goal-oriented work world by coming home and experiencing a loving, caring, and cooperative relationship. The most important element of a nurturing relationship that she is generally missing at work is non-goal-oriented conversation. Through "talking" in a non-goal-oriented way, without having to get to the bottom line, without having to solve the problem, a woman is gradually released from the domination of her masculine side.

Talking in a nonlinear, unedited, emotional way is especially beneficial when her listener understands that by articulating her problems, she can put them aside.

That a woman can forget the problems of her day by remembering them is a concept foreign to most men, who generally banish the problems of the day by not talking about them. To bring them up in conversation, a man would have to address himself to solving them.

While it is important to men to *not* talk, it is equally important to women *to* talk. This apparent incompatibility is actually, we will find, a perfect fit.

When a woman needs to talk, it is really not necessary for a man to talk. In fact, if he talks too much, it can actually prevent her from opening up. When he thinks too much about what he is going to say, his mental focus shifts away from her.

Any man will listen when he is approached in the right way. Telling a man "You never listen to me" or "We never talk, we should talk more!" is definitely taking the wrong tack. Such comments only make a man feel blamed, attacked, and defensive.

Any man can learn to listen if he is approached in an appreciative, welcoming manner.

How to Get a Man to Listen

An approach my wife uses is simply to ask me to listen. She'll say, "Oh, I'm so glad you're home. I've had such a day. Would this be a good time to talk about it? (pause) You don't have to say anything. (little pause) I'm sure I'll feel better if I can just talk about it."

By inviting me to listen in this way, she gives me what I really want—a chance to make her happy—and she gets what she needs most—the opportunity to talk, share, and nurture her female side.

When women support their male partners in supporting them, everybody wins. With practice, sympathetic listening can eventually become easy for a man. Paradoxically, what women need most from men can be given with a minimum of effort.

Although listening in this special way is a new requirement for men in relationships, it is a talent we have spent thousands of years preparing for. Since the ancient hunter's major task was to watch and listen silently, men are good at it. Once he acquires the knack of applying this traditional talent to listening to his mate, a man can give a woman the special, focused attention she finds so wonderfully fulfilling.

The Art of Listening

The art of listening to a woman does not entail solving problems or offering advice. Conversely, a male listener's goal should be helping his partner regain her feminine/masculine balance.

This new job description clarifies his goal and

thus guides him to watch and listen while giving her the sympathy she craves, not the solutions.

> **Men must remember, a woman talks
> about her problems not to solve them
> but to nurture the female side
> of her psyche.**

To develop skill in listening, a man needs to recognize that when a woman is upset and seems to be demanding solutions to her problems, it is only because she is still operating primarily from her male side. By not responding with solutions he assists her in finding her female side; she will then eventually feel better. Men are easily tricked into thinking that if they can give solutions women will then feel better.

Remembering this is particularly helpful when a man feels a woman is upset with him. To explain why she shouldn't be so upset with him only makes matters worse. Although he may have disappointed her in some ways, he must remember that her real complaint is that she is not being heard or nurtured as a woman.

> **When his partner is upset with him, a
> man needs to remember that she has
> temporarily forgotten how wonderful
> he is. To remember, she needs
> to feel heard.**

Then she will be capable of, and eager to bestow on him, the appreciation and acknowledgment that he has earned.

What Men Really Want

These days, when a man gets home, his wife not only is overwhelmed but is generally needy. She may have love in her heart, but he doesn't see it.

Deep in his soul, a man expects his woman to acknowledge and appreciate his efforts and in some measure be fulfilled by them. When she does not seem happy to see him, something very significant begins to happen. His tender but passionate desire to please her, protect her, and provide for her is dampened and is eventually snuffed out.

Men don't generally pinpoint what is happening inside themselves because they are more concerned with trying to make women happy. Yet the more a woman acts and reacts from feelings of unhappiness, something inside a man switches off. When his hard work seems to count for nothing, his life and relationship lose all magic and meaning for him.

Remember, what a man really wants is to make his partner happy; if he loves a woman, his primary goal is her fulfillment. Her happiness signals to him that he is loved. Her warm responses are like a mirror reflecting back to him a shining image.

**When a woman is unhappy,
a man may feel like a failure and may
eventually give up trying to fulfill her.**

Understanding Our Differences

This understanding of what men really want does not imply that a woman doesn't care about her partner's happiness as well. Certainly, when a woman loves a man, she wants him to also be happy, but note this crucial difference between men and women:

A man can be stressed out from a day at work, but if his partner is happy with him, he feels fulfilled. When he senses her appreciation for his labor, his stress level dissipates; her happiness is like a shower that washes away the stressful grime of his day.

However, when an exhausted woman returns home to a happy man, he doesn't make her day. It's great that he appreciates her hard work to help support the family, but it doesn't in the least diminish her unease. As we have discussed, she needs to communicate and feel some nurturing support before she can begin to appreciate him.

**A man thrives on appreciation because
it directly nurtures his male side. A
woman thrives on communication
because it directly nurtures
her female side.**

By understanding and honoring that men thrive on appreciation and women on communication, we gain the knowledge and the power to create mutually fulfilling relationships.

Even if you read only this chapter and apply these insights, your relationships will change forever for the better. To utilize this new understanding most effectively, we will explore a new job description for both partners in a relationship in the next chapter. Just as we must update our skills in business, so also do we need job retraining in our relationships.

CHAPTER 3

A New Job Description for Relationships

THE REASON THERE ARE SO MANY problems in relationships today is that we just don't understand each other. Men, in particular, don't understand what women need to be happy, and women don't know how to communicate their needs in a language that men understand. Old relationship skills are no longer effective, and are many times counterproductive. With an updated understanding of modern pressures and needs we can begin to formulate a new job description for relationships that can nurture and support both men and women.

Old relationship skills required men to be effective providers and protectors while women learned to be pleasing and accommodating. If strictly observed today, these old skills would go from being the solution to being the problem. When modern men focus on being better providers and protectors, they only burn out, working more and spending less time sharing in their relationships.

Let's look at a playful example of how times have changed. When men were hunters, it was much easier to have relationships. It used to be fine if a man was late getting home. When he eventually did return home, his wife was happy that he was still alive.

The harder and longer he worked, the more she felt taken care of. Now, when he is late it is taken as a sign that he doesn't care, and he is in the doghouse. Our fathers had a much easier time in their relationships; not only were they not rejected but they didn't even have to remember to call home.

On the other hand, women didn't mind being pleasing and accommodating to a man when he came home because he was generally very tired and went to sleep. Now, with men spending more time at home, women begin to feel as if they give more than they are getting in return. From this playful perspective, our mothers seem to have had it much easier when men spent more time away from home.

When modern women focus on being more pleasing and accommodating, they end up feeling like martyrs who sacrifice their own needs to ensure harmony in the relationship. For women, practicing old relationship skills today is like setting a time bomb. They gradually become so overworked that they explode, feeling resentful, overwhelmed, and unsupported. Although they love their partners, it is hard to *be* loving. Men, seeing that their mates are not happy, assume that they have failed as providers and, in time, withdraw completely.

The only antidote to despair and divorce is the application of new relationship skills based on new job descriptions for both men and women.

Our Parents Never Told Us It Would Be Like This

If a woman is unwaveringly pleasing and accommodating according to the old ways, her man will never get the message that she needs a different kind of support. A man generally doesn't have a clue as to what a woman really needs on an emotional level. He is too busy feeling the pressure to be a better provider. When a woman complains, he hears it simply as her wanting more, which implies that he isn't giving enough. Not knowing what to do, he will just withdraw. Feeling unappreciated, a man who uses old relationship skills commonly reacts by doing less. He figures that if this isn't enough, then why bother trying to do more.

New relationship skills are imperative for women today to get what they need from men.

No wonder so many contemporary women feel so hopeless about men.

In previous generations, women could focus on being pleasing, accommodating, and nondemanding because men were well trained and knew their jobs. Women didn't need to ask for help or learn how to communicate their wishes to men because men received a clear job description from their fathers and their culture. A woman did not need to instruct her partner; instead she could focus on appreciating his efforts and forgiving his mistakes.

Doing Less but Supporting More

When a woman shares her frustrations of the day, a man hears her wanting him to solve all her problems. For men, the thought of having to do more is many times a strong message that they are not doing enough. Feeling unappreciated, it is difficult for men to find the energy and motivation to do more.

When a man hears that he is not required to solve her problems or do more in the home, but is primarily needed to listen when she wants to talk and be supported emotionally, then when she talks he can relax and begin to really listen.

When a woman gives a man the message that he can do less and support more by listening, he will slowly but surely begin to have more energy and will automatically begin offering to help out. When a man truly understands a problem, an inner energy then emerges to assist him in solving it. When he is told he is the problem and must do more, he feels little energy and is very resistant.

While women want men to do more, men want to feel that they are doing enough. The most successful approach in a relationship is to focus first on creating good communication, where a man can feel appreciated for being empathetic, sympathetic, and understanding. As he begins to listen more and is appreciated for supporting her in this way, he will almost magically begin to do more.

To get what they need from their men, women must learn how to communicate needs and desires without demanding or finger-pointing. In most cases, as we will discover, a woman can be made happier by a man who is actually doing less because he is supporting her differently, according to new rules which are infinitely more effective. When a man understands this truth, his motivation to do things differently greatly increases.

Part of a man's frustration is that when a woman wants more he mistakenly assumes that he has to do everything she needs. He does not know that as long as he is taking small steps toward helping her around the house, coupled with better communication, she will be immeasurably happier.

As both partners begin successfully to give and receive the support they really need, they will happily give increasingly more. He will give her more of what modern women most need and appreciate. She will give him more of what men really want.

Today, we can detect a definite generational shift away from rigidly defined gender job roles and toward wholeness.

B.B.C.—Before Birth Control

To discover the behavior patterns that nourish femininity and masculinity, let's return for a moment to the world of the male provider and his nurturer mate. Religion and social convention encouraged differences between men and women, particularly through assigning specific roles. This division of labor held steady for millennia, well into our parents' time.

The hunter's day was filled with risk and danger and was primarily focused on the single task of successfully protecting the home and bringing home the kill. The life of his family depended on his competence, assertiveness, aggressiveness, and skill. Men evolved in specific ways to cope successfully with the pressures of "men's work."

A nurturer's day was a flow of repetitive and detailed tasks that sustained her children, her family, and her community. The life of her family depended on her ability to communicate, negotiate, accommodate, and cooperate. Women also evolved in specific ways to cope successfully with the stresses of "women's work."

Today, the lines dividing men's work and women's work are dramatically fading. This shift away from rigidly defined gender roles provides greater freedom, but it also generates new stress. With a greater understanding and respect for how our ancestors coped with stress, we can be better equipped to support each other during this transformation.

How Our Ancestors Coped

On a very basic level, our brains and bodies have, over the millennia, developed specifically to deal with the unique stresses of traditional men's and women's work. Although modern lifestyles are rapidly dispensing with those roles, evolution has yet to catch up and produce new coping mechanisms.

Chief among the traditional female coping mechanisms is communication. For the nurturer women of long ago, talking in a non-goal-oriented way, while giving and receiving sympathy, was essential to peace of mind and generated feelings of security and belonging. Years ago, women with children were much more vulnerable and were dependent on the goodwill of others. Before government welfare programs and expanded legal rights and educational opportunities, women had to rely on others for security and safety. If her husband left her or died, a woman depended on her family and community to take care of her, so she had to maintain strong relationships with those around her. Talking connected her to her support network and made her feel secure. When a modern woman today is upset and begins talking, she is automatically connecting with that time-honored feeling of security.

Why Women Need to Talk About Problems

As a common practice, nurturer women shared their problems with each other not directly to ask for help but to share sympathy and community. Problem solving was secondary to the exercise of the cooperative spirit.

Women supported each other unconditionally, without being asked and expecting nothing in return. This cooperative sharing strengthened relationships within the community and ensured a woman's and her children's survival should she be widowed.

Talking about problems, sharing feelings, and articulating desires became a feminine ritual to create greater intimacy and express loyalty to the community. Today, when a woman goes to a counselor, she is seeking out that same support. Most counselors and therapists, it should be noted, are trained to listen attentively rather than focus on problem solving. Hence, the process offers tremendous support for women in coping with day-to-day stress.

Through talking and feeling heard in therapy, women come to feel nurtured, and the weight of their problems lifts. Once able to relax and proceed at a more easygoing pace, they can begin to deal with their problems.

When Men Offer Advice

Men instinctively don't understand this and, unlike therapists, are not trained in how to support feelings effectively. When a woman talks about her feelings, he assumes she is seeking his help to solve her problems and instinctively responds to her feelings by offering help or advice.

Take a fireman, for example. When he receives a call, he must get the size and location of the fire as quickly as possible and then do something to put out the fire. Asking a lot of extra questions and offering empathy is not part of his job description.

Imagine this scene. A fireman receives a call and responds by saying, "You have a fire. How awful. How does it feel? Really." Obviously, this kind of empathetic response would be out of place.

When a man becomes restless while listening to a woman it is not because he doesn't care about her. It's because every cell in his body is saying: If there is a fire, let's get out of here and put it out. If there is a problem, he wants to do something about it and not just talk about it.

Modern men need to understand that modern women need, more than anything else, the opportunity to talk about their feelings without focusing on solving the problems that cause them. By responding with empathy, sympathy, and understanding, he makes sure that her female side is nurtured so that she can throw off her feelings of being overwhelmed.

**In a practical sense, by just listening a
man frees a woman to forget the
urgency of her problems and remember
what a great guy he is.**

When a woman is unhappy and talks about
problems, a man must remind himself that it is not
him but modern culture that demands she must bear
the stress of having two full-time careers—homemaker and wage earner—at once. Remembering that
he is not the prime source of her frustration helps
him to not feel blamed when she is unhappy. This
awareness frees him to sympathize with her rather
than defend himself.

How Men Cope

Men commonly cope with stress differently. For
instance, by working at achieving a simple goal like
driving the car, or hitting a tennis ball around, teeing
off, or shooting hoops, a man sorts out his thoughts
and concerns, clarifies his values and priorities, and
develops a plan of action. It gives him a sense of
security.

Remember, a hunter's survival is ensured by
moving quietly and then striking. Through his hunting—or problem-solving—skills, his family's security
is ensured. It is the subconscious hunter, buried deep
inside the contemporary man, who feels secure when
he lobs a paper ball into the wastebasket across the
room.

If a man can put his feelings into action, he

begins to feel more in control. By simply pacing back and forth when he is frustrated, he can find the same relief a woman might feel through talking. Through understanding this vital difference, men and women can more effectively support each other.

Silently Sitting on a Rock

Traditionally, men have dealt with their problems by silently and patiently thinking up solutions. Ancient hunters would sit on a rock and silently search the horizon, looking and listening for their prey, or looking across the plains at their target, studying its movements and planning the attack.

This process of sitting, waiting, scheming, and planning allowed him to relax and conserve energy for the inevitable chase. Focusing on the solution kept his mind off the fear of being attacked or of missing his target, and when he achieved his goal he returned home a happy, stress-free man.

Women cope with stress through sharing in nurturing relationships, men by solving problems.

Why Men Watch TV

When a modern man comes home, quite commonly he sits in his favorite chair and either reads the newspaper or watches TV. Like the ancient hunter who needed to recover from the stress of his day, he instinctively finds his rock to sit on and begins gazing off into the horizon.

Through reading or listening to the news he is, in effect, looking out over the world or scanning the horizon. As he picks up the remote control and begins searching through the stations, or turns the pages of his paper, he is once more in control: he silently and swiftly continues his hunt.

As he assumes this ancient posture, he becomes more comfortable. Feelings of security automatically begin to emerge. Feeling in control, he is able to most effectively cope with the stress of not having immediate solutions to the problems of his life.

Through this instinctive ritual he is able temporarily to forget his problems at work and is eventually ready for the relationship.

When Women Don't Understand Men

When men today attempt to fulfill their need to be solitary, the modern woman commonly misunderstands. She mistakenly assumes that he wants her to initiate a conversation. She thinks he is waiting for her to notice that he is distressed, and that he wants her to ask him what is bothering him. She does not realize that he really wants to be left alone.

When she persists in asking, he becomes increasingly annoyed and sends her what he thinks are clear messages to leave him alone, but she misinterprets his cues. Here is a common pattern.

She Says:	He Says:

1. *She says:* "How was your day?"

   She means: "Let's talk, I'm interested in your day, and I hope you are interested in mine."

2. *She says:* "How did your meeting go with your new client?"

   She means: "I will keep asking you questions so you know that I really care and I am interested in your day. I hope you will be interested in my day. I have a lot to say."

3. *She says:* "Did they like your proposal?"

   She means: "I suppose it must be hard to talk about it, so I'll ask a more neutral question to get us started. It's OK if you don't open up right away. I am here for you, and I am interested. I know you

---

1. *He says:* "Fine."

   He means: "I am giving you a short answer because I need some time alone."

2. *He says:* "It was OK."

   He means: "I am trying to be polite and not reject you, but would you stop bothering me with more questions?"

3. *He says:* "Yes."

   He means: "Look, I don't want to talk right now. Would you just leave me alone? You're bugging me. Can't you tell I want to be alone? If I wanted to talk I would talk."

She Says:	**He Says:**

will really appreciate it,
and then you will want
to hear what I have to
say."

4. *She says:* "What's
wrong?"

   She means: "I can see
that something hap-
pened that is upsetting
you. You can talk to
me. I will listen, I care.
I'm sure that by talking
about it you will feel
better."

4. *He says:* "Nothing's
wrong."

   He means: "Nothing's
wrong that I can't deal
with alone. After a while I
will forget my problems
and then be available for
the relationship. So would
you just ignore me for a
little while and then I will
be much more open and
interested in you. I just
need to shift gears to get
back home."

5. *She says:* "I can tell
something is wrong.
What is it?"

   She means: "I know
something is wrong, and
if you don't talk, it will
get worse. You need to
talk!"

5. *He says nothing and
walks away.*

   He means: "I don't want
to get mad at you, so I am
just walking away. After
a while I will be back,
and I will not be mad at
you for annoying me."

How Women React When Men Don't Want to Talk

Inevitably, when a man resists conversation and a woman doesn't understand his need to be alone to recuperate from the day, she will have a variety of misinterpretations and begin to panic. These are some of the ways in which she may then react:

She Thinks:	She Reacts:
1. She thinks there is some big problem in the relationship and he doesn't want to be with her.	1. She reacts by feeling rejected, and to clear things up insists on discussing their relationship.
2. She thinks he doesn't trust her to care about his feelings.	2. She reacts sympathetically by asking lots of questions and trying to show that she cares. Eventually, she feels frustrated when he resists her loving attempts to help.
3. She thinks he must be angry with her.	3. She reacts by feeling inadequate and confused.
4. She thinks he doesn't want to talk because he is hiding something that might upset her.	4. As a result, she does get upset worrying about what it might be.

She Thinks:	She Reacts:
5. She thinks he is selfish and only cares about himself and not about her.	5. In reaction, she doubts his love for her.
6. She thinks he is trying to punish her by withholding his love and attention.	6. She reacts by getting angry back and withholding her attention and love.
7. She thinks he is dissatisfied with her.	7. She reacts by feeling unappreciated for all she does for him.
8. She thinks he is just lazy.	8. In reaction, she feels resentful because she is giving so much more than he is.
9. She thinks he has lost interest in her.	9. She reacts by feeling ignored, isolated, and powerless to get what she needs. She may also begin to feel unattractive, boring, and unworthy of love.
10. She thinks he has a deep fear of intimacy brought about by his dysfunctional past and that he needs therapy.	10. She reacts by feeling powerless to ever get what she needs until he is healed.

She Thinks:	She Reacts:
11. She thinks he is hiding something from her.	11. She reacts by feeling afraid that she has done something bad or that he has done something bad.
12. She things she got involved with the wrong man.	12. She reacts by thinking other men are not this way and longs for a more sensitive and talkative man.

In each of these examples, the woman's reaction is based on a misunderstanding. If a woman is to support a man in coming back to the relationship, her new job description requires her to understand this difference and accept his need for space. As we will continue to see, this doesn't mean that she must sacrifice her need for conversation. What is required, however, is a new sense of timing.

Why Men Pull Away

When a woman learns the skill of temporarily postponing her needs and allows a man the time he needs to shift gears from his work life to his home life, she creates a fertile ground for him to find his love for her and then act on it. As he grows accustomed to this support, he begins to anticipate it. At this point, just the thought of returning home begins releasing his stress. The more he gets this kind of support, the less he needs to pull away from his mate.

Without this new relationship skill a woman unknowingly prevents her male partner from successfully making the transition from work to home. Through her demanding more of him or reacting negatively to his need for private time, he may never relax enough to come back into the relationship. If the downward spiral continues, it can actually hinder a man from contacting his loving feelings. He may even believe that he doesn't love his partner anymore.

> **When a man arrives home to a needy woman, he continues to pull away.**

The more he feels pressured to talk or be "in relationship," the more he needs to back off to relax. He can most effectively forget the demands of his job when he feels no pressure or demands from his mate.

When a man returns home to a nondemanding woman, he feels free to take the time he needs to relax. He can then automatically shift gears and give his partner the love she deserves.

Literally thousands of women who have applied this relationship skill report that this single insight has magically transformed their relationships.

> **When a man is not expected to give more, he automatically wants to.**

When Men Don't Understand Women

When a woman is emotionally distressed, a man mistakenly assumes that if she is to feel better, she needs some solitary time just as he does. He will tend to ignore her and give her lots of space because that is precisely the kind of support he would want. To ignore her, though, is the worst thing he can do.

Even if he asks her what is bothering her, he may misread what she really needs. Again, let's look at a common pattern.

Tom says to Mary, "What's wrong? You seem upset."

Mary says, "Oh, it's nothing." Mary is silently saying, "Nothing is bothering me, unless of course you really care. Then you will show me by standing here and asking me more questions."

Tom says, "OK," and walks away. He is silently saying, "It's OK if you don't want to talk about it. I understand if you want some space. I'll support you by acting like everything is OK. I trust that you can handle it."

Tom actually thinks he is being supportive and has no idea that he has just failed the test. Most men think like Tom, but almost any woman would instinctively understand that when Mary said, "Nothing's wrong," she really wanted him to ask more questions and draw her out. When a woman says "Nothing's wrong," something usually is, and she needs to talk about it to a listener who is interested and cares. She wants to be asked questions that will eventually help her to open up.

Let's look at some other common ways in which men misunderstand women.

1. He asks: "Do you want to talk about something?"	1. She says "No" but really means "Yes, and if you really care, you will ask more questions."
2. He asks: "Do you want any help?"	2. She says "No, I can do it" but really means "Yes, and if you really want to help, then watch what I am doing and join in."
3. He asks: "Did I do something wrong?"	3. She says "No" but really means "Yes, and if you care to make things better you will figure out what by asking more questions."
4. He asks: "Is everything OK?"	4. She says "Yes" but really means "No, and if you want to work it out, then you will ask more questions about what might be upsetting me."

In each of these examples, the woman is testing to see if it is safe to talk about her feelings. If he understands her hidden meaning, then she is assured that she can share her feelings and that her needs will be supported.

Without a clear job description of what he is supposed to do at such times, few men have a clue and just walk away thinking they are being helpful.

When Women Talk About Feelings

After feeling neglected for some time, when a woman does eventually talk about her feelings a man will again misunderstand. Commonly, he misinterprets her complaints and assumes that he is required to be a better provider instead of hearing that she really needs more attention and nurturing at home. Let's look at some common examples.

She Complains:	He Misunderstands:
1. When she complains about the house, she is really only wanting to share her frustrations and be heard.	1. He thinks that he has to earn more money for a bigger house before she will be happy.
2. When she complains about her job, she is really only wanting to share her day and reconnect with her partner.	2. He thinks that he has to make more money so that she doesn't have to work, and only then will she be happy.
3. When she complains about having to do housework, she is generally sharing her feelings of being	3. He thinks that he has to either provide a maid or become one for her, and only then will she be happy.

She Complains:	He Misunderstands:
overwhelmed and is asking for help if he has the energy.	
4. When she complains about the weather or other problems with no solution, she is generally seeking a little sympathy for what she has been through.	4. Emotionally, he begins to feel as if he has to earn more money so that they can move to a better climate before she will be happy.
5. When she complains that he works too hard, she is wanting him to know that she misses him and would love to spend more time together.	5. He thinks that he now has to make more money so that he doesn't have to work so hard, and then she will be happy.

In every case, when the woman is distressed the man feels on a deep instinctual level that he has to work harder to be a better provider. This instinct to succeed more at work causes him to be less present in the relationship. When he does become more successful, or when he does exert himself to solve her problems and she is still unhappy or unfulfilled, he feels ever more intensely the frustration of not being able to make her happy. To cope with this frustration he begins to turn off his romantic feelings of caring about her fulfillment.

Why Men Don't Commit

This same principle applies to many single men. When they don't attract the woman of their dreams, they begin to feel as if they have to make more money. Instead of recognizing that they need to work on relationship skills, they may focus too much on their careers.

Some men give up on the thought of marriage because their particular talents make it seem unlikely that they will earn big money, or they feel that they'll have to sacrifice themselves too much to make a large salary. Some men may have the woman of their dreams but are afraid to commit because they don't make enough money.

Jackie and Dan are a very dramatic example of this. They had been living together for nine years. She wanted to get married, but he didn't. He assured her that he loved her, but something inside was stopping him from getting married. He claimed that he just wasn't sure. Then, one evening while talking about a movie they had seen, she happened to say, "I'd love you even if we were always poor."

The very next day, he went out and bought the ring.

All Dan needed was a clear message from Jackie that he didn't have to make a lot of money to successfully provide for her happiness. Then he could make the commitment. Like most men, Dan was able to commit to the relationship when he felt his ability to provide for a woman was enough to make her happy.

While all men are not as obsessed with making money, they do need to feel confident that they can provide for a woman's happiness before making a commitment to marriage. New relationship skills help a man realize that, regardless of how much money he makes, he can provide emotional support and a woman will be much happier.

Why Men Become Preoccupied with Work

When a man experiences the stress of thinking that his family is unhappy, he instinctively focuses more and more on succeeding at work. He focuses to such an extent that he doesn't realize how much time he is away. For him, time may pass very quickly, but while she is waiting for him to come home it passes much more slowly. He doesn't realize that in modern times, his presence at home is at least as important to her as his success at work.

The more work stress a man experiences, the more he focuses on solving problems. At such times it is extremely difficult for him to release his lock on the problem and bring his full attention back to relationships. He can become so focused that he forgets everything else and unknowingly neglects his wife and family.

It is as though he is looking through a tunnel and only takes in what is relevant or useful to achieving his goal. He doesn't realize that he is not listening or responding to the people he loves because he is so utterly focused on solving his problem. At such times, he has temporarily forgotten what is really important to him. He does not recognize that he is pushing away the people he loves the most.

When a Man Ignores His Family

When a man withdraws from intimacy to focus on his work problems, it is hard for a woman to recognize it as an automatic reaction. She views it as a deliberate act of coldness and indifference because for a woman to focus on work issues and ignore her family would require a deliberate decision on her part and, in most cases, would also signal that she just doesn't care.

When a man is focused on his work, he doesn't just decide to ignore his family. He truly forgets. He doesn't decide to forget picking up his daughter at school, it is an automatic by-product of increasing his focus on solving his problems at work. It is not a sign that he has stopped caring. If anything, it is a sign that he does care but is just not adept at coping with his stress.

This same tendency to focus on one thing and forget everything else causes a man to procrastinate about doing things he really is willing to do. Many times a woman will ask a man to do something he really intends to do, but then he forgets. Since it is actually hard for her to forget, she makes the mistake of assuming that he is deliberately trying to get out of a chore by putting it off.

A man today cannot simply make a kill as his ancestors did and then come home to celebrate. His life is much more complex. It may take months to finish a deal and make a killing. During that time his mind is consumed. He thinks at work, at home, and in his sleep. He can remember every detail required to achieve his work goals, but he then forgets to bring home the milk no matter how many times his wife reminds him.

Shifting Gears from Work to the Relationship

A man's tendency to be absorbed in his work not only is counterproductive for a woman, but it is also counterproductive for him. Until a man can apply new relationship skills and directly nurture a woman's feelings, his instincts will urge him back to his work when she is upset or unfulfilled.

There are basically three ways in which a man is able to shift gears between work and the relationship. To various degrees, all three are simultaneously required.

1. Success

The more successful a man feels when he leaves work, the easier it is for him to forget his problems and enjoy his relationships. A successful day at work makes him feel that the hunt is over and he can now return home and more easily relax. When a man is not succeeding as much as he would like, or as much as he thinks he should, then the next two ways become more important.

2. Distraction

To forget the problems of his day, he distracts his focus from work to sitting on his favorite rock and watching TV, reading the paper, listening to music, going to the movies, or any other easy and nonde-manding activities requiring focus.

Another practical way for him to shift gears through distraction is to work out, focusing his mind on exercising his body. This can be vigorous activity or even something as easy as going for a walk. To free his mind from solving problems at work, he just needs a new challenge that requires focus.

A man forgets his real problems by focusing on other problems he can easily solve or problems he is not responsible for solving. Playing games, fiddling or tinkering with things, cheering on teams, playing sports, and watching the news are the most common stress reducers. When he mentally solves the world's problems or figures out how to get his team to win, he feels competent again and confident about facing his real-life problems.

Without a hobby, a man may not be able to disengage himself from work and can become overstressed.

Indulging in a hobby allows him to forget the really pressing and important problems.

To encourage or expect a man to be in his female side and talk about his problems in many cases goes against his nature. In some cases, talking about his day before he is relaxed may increase his stress by bringing his awareness back to work, with all its frustrations, disappointments, and worries.

First, a man needs to forget his problems and then he feels as if he has something positive to offer. He will then automatically remember what is most important to him—his wife and family or the desire to have one. This shift in awareness to what is really important to him is also essential for him to recharge.

3. Appreciation

The third means to shift gears from work to the relationship is to return home anticipating the support of his partner. A woman's accepting and appreciating love is something he begins to look forward to. To anticipate this support makes him feel that he is a success even if he didn't achieve his goals at work.

The very thought of returning home to a loving partner can wash away much of a man's stress. Then, if he still needs to take some alone time, he won't need to retreat nearly as much.

On the other hand, when a man anticipates arriving home to an unhappy partner, he becomes even more consumed with his work. It is then harder for him to release the pressures of his job.

In my relationship with Bonnie, there are a variety of little things that I can do when I get home to ensure that I get this appreciation. Without much effort at all when I get home, I can find her, give her a hug, ask her about her day, and listen for a few minutes, and I am certain of being appreciated. The more I feel her appreciation and love welcoming me home, the less I need to distract myself from work when I get home. In addition, I tend to acknowledge and recognize my success each day so that I can more easily leave the problems at the office.

A New Job Description

It becomes easier for women to understand the extra time a man needs to be open to the relationship if we compare it to a different arena in which she requires more time to open up. For example, to enjoy sex after a stressful day, most women will strongly relate to feeling the need for more time, attention, conversation, and romance first.

In a similar way, it is as difficult for a man to open up to a relationship when he gets home as it is for a woman to open up to sex after a long, stressful day. A man needs more time and space and lots of appreciation to make the shift from office to home.

By correctly understanding a man's tendency to focus and forget, a woman can be more forgiving, accepting, and appreciative. She does not take it so personally when he is withdrawn. This accepting awareness, combined with new relationship skills for communicating, gives her new power not only to get what she wants but also to support a man in letting go of his stress and opening his heart.

Likewise, as men begin to understand women, they can apply the new skill of providing emotional support and not focusing primarily on physically solving women's problems. A man can learn to listen when his partner speaks without it causing him to feel that he is being required to do more. By learning these new relationship skills, men happily discover that without having to change who they are, or do a lot more, they can support their mates much more.

Emotional Role Reversal

When a woman is more on her masculine side, and her female side is neglected, an emotional role reversal occurs. She begins to function from the needs of her male side, not her female side. While most modern women can easily recite a litany of valid work- and relationship-related problems and injustices, often the real culprit responsible for their general dissatisfaction is this emotional role reversal.

For women to feel happy in relationships, they need to regain the balance of their male and female sides. Both men and women need to work together to assist the woman in coming back to her female side.

A man's new job description requires him to assist a woman in finding her feminine self again after a long day's work.

The Problems of Emotional Role Reversal

The stress of switching back and forth from the masculine to the feminine side every day has an invisible but devastating effect on lasting romance, passion, and intimacy. Just as a ball rolling downhill gathers speed, so a woman continues to spiral further into frustration if there is no conscious intervention to relieve this stress. Without an understanding of this underlying dynamic, a man's logical attempts to solve partnership problems can be disastrously counterproductive.

When emotional role reversal occurs and a woman is more on her male side, then she automatically feels a greater need to solve problems. It is not enough for her to do what she can do and then relax through talking about everything that is not done. Instead, she feels a strong pull to solve all the unsolved problems before she can relax.

At those times when she feels a need to solve

problems, a man can best support her by listening. I remember when I first recognized the symptoms of emotional role reversal in my own marriage but didn't have a clue about correctly supporting my wife.

Bonnie and I had just returned home after playing a really enjoyable tennis game.

"I can't wait to take a nap," I told her.

"That sounds so good," she agreed. "I'd love to take a nap."

As I was walking up the stairs to our bedroom, I noticed that she wasn't behind me and called, "Aren't you coming?"

"I'd love to," she called back, "but I can't. I have to wash the car."

How could she make washing her car more important than taking a nap on a day off? I thought to myself. At this point, I realized we definitely were from different planets.

I did not suspect that she was stuck on her male side and locked into solving her problems. I did not know that nurturing her female side with some conversation would assist her in releasing her burdens and responsibilities. Without an understanding of how I could support her in relaxing, I continued upstairs and instantly dozed.

I woke refreshed and was looking forward to a romantic evening—until I went downstairs and discovered Bonnie in a bad mood.

I casually said, "You should have taken a nap. I feel great." This comment did not go over big.

She responded icily, "I have no time for naps. I still have to do laundry, help with the kids' homework, clean up the house. And I still have to make dinner."

Not realizing that she needed to talk, I continued

trying to solve her problems by suggesting we go out for dinner.

"You don't understand," Bonnie insisted, "I have food in the refrigerator that needs to be cooked. And Lauren still hasn't finished her school project."

I said, "This is the weekend. You should be relaxing."

"I can't relax," she said. "You just don't understand!"

At this point I was also in a bad mood. Whatever romance I had inside me quickly dissipated. Bonnie was even more upset because I didn't listen sympathetically, and I was ticked off because she had rejected my solutions.

Now, when Bonnie is feeling overwhelmed, our conversations sound quite different. Instead of feeling rejected or defensive, I know just what to do. She needs to talk to come back to her feminine side, and she needs my help to do it. This is an example of a conversation we might have when Bonnie is overwhelmed and having difficulty switching to her feminine side:

John: "What's wrong?"

Bonnie: "I don't know, there's just too much to do."

John: "Oh."

Bonnie: "I don't have enough time."

John: "Tell me about it."

Bonnie: "I still have to do laundry, and dinner isn't even started."

John: "Hmmm."

Bonnie: "I was supposed to take Pearl to the dentist today and I completely forgot."

John: "What did you do?"

Bonnie: "Oh, I don't even want to think about it."

John: "Hmmm."

Bonnie: "Pearl was so worried, she thought something terrible had happened. (pause) I never forget things like that."

I said nothing, just took a deep breath and shook my head back and forth.

Bonnie: "It worked out OK, though. We just rescheduled another time."

John: "That's good."

Bonnie: "I don't know what to do about dinner. I haven't planned anything."

John: "Hmmm, I don't know either."

Bonnie: "Do you mind eating leftovers tonight?"

John: "Sounds good to me. What do we have?"

Bonnie: "Oh, I don't know. I really don't feel like making anything."

John: "Let's just go out to eat, and then we'll have some time left for us."

Bonnie: "Great!"

What a difference a few years of practice makes! Without my knowing how to support Bonnie with the new relationship skill of nurturing conversation, we would probably just argue, eat leftovers, and go to sleep frustrated and turned off.

Why Women Need More Talk

When, over the course of a relationship, women don't feel free to talk, they disconnect from the natural happiness that comes when their female side is nurtured. Even more distressing is the fact that, as they lose touch with their female side, they may also lose the awareness of what they need. All they know is that "something is missing," and generally, the man in their lives gets blamed.

The more a woman disconnects from her female side, the less receptive she is to a man's support. Meanwhile, her partner feels frustrated because he can't fulfill her and feels powerless to change things.

To cope with the added stress of leaving the home to work, today's woman has a much greater need for partnership support. When she gets home, she needs to talk more.. She needs the security of being able to open up and share feelings that may not always make sense or be related to the bottom line. She needs to feel that someone understands what she's going through and cares about her.

This is what happens when a man tries to "solve" a woman's problems:

Anatomy of a Misunderstanding

1. She claims "You are not listening" or "You don't understand."

2. He explains that he was too listening or he couldn't have offered such a great suggestion.

3. She continues to insist that he's not really listening to her and that he doesn't understand her problem.

4. He begins to feel frustrated and tries to prove that he does understand and that his solution is the right one.

5. They begin arguing.

He thinks she is saying that he doesn't understand the problem or that his solution is the wrong one. What she is really saying, though, is that she's not getting the empathy or sympathy she craves. When she says "You don't understand," she really means "You don't understand what I need from you. I just need you to listen and empathize."

Men don't readily know how to respond to work-stressed women because they never saw their fathers do it. In most cases, our mothers spent their days nurturing their feminine natures through communicating with other women. I don't remember ever hearing my mother complain to my dad that "we never talk." By the time Dad came home, she had already talked enough. However, women of our generation don't have this luxury. They are required to be mindful of the time and always to get to the point when talking. They are pushed toward maleness.

One comedian put it this way: God gave women an average of six thousand words a day and men two thousand. Quite commonly, by the end of a workday they have both used two thousand words. When she comes home she still has four thousand left. No wonder she feels neglected. She wants to talk, but he has already spent his allotted two thousand words.

While this is a fun way of understanding the problem, the problem is very real.

The lack of communication in relationships is the number one reason contemporary women are dissatisfied.

Literally thousands of relationships dramatically improved in an instant as men began to understand the female need to be listened to.

Remember, when men talk about problems, they are generally looking for solutions. Most of the time, however, a man looking to recover from the day doesn't want to talk. The calm he achieves through not talking, women achieve through talking.

In simple terms, a man needs to remember that even when an overwhelmed woman shares a list of problems that demand solutions, the only one that has to be solved immediately is her need to be heard by someone who is not trying to talk her out of her feelings or solve all her problems.

Women must remember that when men don't listen it is mainly because they don't understand why "feeling heard" is so important to women.

By recognizing that the working world prevents women from nurturing their female sides and finding happiness, men can at last begin to make sense of the feminine need to be heard. Men really do want to make their partners happy, it's just that until now they haven't understood how.

A man can more easily endure the lack of feminine values in the workplace because he has from time immemorial come home from work to a female in order to find balance. But since women rarely work outside the home in a nurturing feminine environment, and they do not have a female to come home to, it is much harder for them to find balance.

Finally, women don't know how to communicate their need for support. Either women expect men to be mind readers and know their needs, or they let their needs build up until they are resentful and then demand more. Neither approach works.

Why Women Don't Like to Ask

Women are wanting more from relationships, even they don't know exactly what they need. In our parents' day, if a man loved a woman he would do what she wanted without being asked.

That is because what she wanted was also what his father taught him to do and her mother told her to expect. He learned from his father how to be a good provider. She didn't have to teach him. Each day he focused on being a better provider. He was not expected to be a domestic helper, and she was not expected to be stressed out and overwhelmed.

When Men Are Self-Motivated

When a man loved a woman according to the old ways, he would provide for her and would willingly give up his life to protect her. That was his most precious gift to her. He did not rely on her to tell him what to do. If he loved her, he motivated himself to provide for her. That self-motivation expressed the extent of his love.

Now women want things our fathers were not required to do. If a woman is to receive a new kind of support, she is required to educate her partner about her needs and to ask in pleasing ways for more.

Having to ask is not easy for women. If she has to ask, then it doesn't feel as if she is being loved. In addition, she really has had very little exposure to a woman asking for what she wants in a way that works. For this reason, I recommend first improving communication, and then beginning to practice the art of asking for more. Once there is good communication and a man begins to understand her feelings more deeply, he will automatically understand her problems better and will slowly but surely do more.

For centuries, the sign that a woman was loved was her not having to ask. Now, when a man appears to a woman as if he is not motivated to support her needs, it weakens her self-esteem and humiliates her. She feels that she is not worthy of his love.

In a similar way, when a man feels that he is unfairly being asked for more, he may not feel that his self-esteem is weakened, but he certainly doesn't feel like giving more. When he returns home from work, he will feel increasingly lifeless and lethargic.

To Ask or Not to Ask

It used to be that the squeaky wheel got oiled. Today, however, the squeaky wheel gets replaced. Asking for more can easily begin to sound like nagging. Men hate to hear it, and women hate to do it. Without understanding how to assist a man in taking the time to listen to her feelings, a woman is left with only two alternatives. She can become a martyr and settle for whatever she gets, or she can try demanding and nagging for more.

Neither alternative will work. To get the love and support she needs, it is crucial for a woman to focus on what is most essential. Ask him to listen, and gradually, over time, as he understands her feelings better, she can begin to ask for more physical support.

> To sustain love and good feelings in a
> relationship, it is vital that a woman
> learn to express her feelings and needs
> in a way that can work for both
> her man and herself.

I am in no way suggesting that women not express themselves, but I am saying that if they want to be heard and respected, new relationship skills and new job descriptions are definitely required.

What to Expect

When approached in the right way and at the right time, men are happy to do more. With a few months of good communication without demanding anything, and several doses of appreciation, any man will be willing to do more. A man's idea of "more" and a woman's may be dramatically different.

> Men can give more only in
> small degrees.

It is unrealistic to expect a man suddenly to be motivated to do 50 percent of the housework if he has been used to doing much less. Likewise, if he is the quiet type, it is not probable that he will immediately open up and share his feelings.

It is equally unrealistic for a man to expect his female partner to greet him at home with great appreciation and feel fulfilled when she has also spent all day working. These unrealistic expectations create unnecessary resentment and alienation in both men and women.

Both women and men can get the support they need, but it doesn't happen overnight.

As women begin to accept the fact that they can ask for and get more without having to nag or complain, they give up their resistance to giving a man the daily appreciation he requires. They assume full responsibility for communicating needs, confident that they can get them fulfilled. They don't expect men to know what they need instinctually, but patiently and persistently appreciate what they do give and gradually ask for more.

Adjusting Our Expectations

Just as a woman needs to adjust the expectation that a man will automatically listen to her feelings and will equally share all domestic duties, so also a man must adjust his expectation that a woman will speak in a loving, pleasing manner, make no demands of him, and be fulfilled when he gets home. In essence, women need to release the expectation that men will do everything they want, and men need to release the expectation that women will always be loving and happy.

Through practicing his new relationship skills,

instead of feeling annoyed by her feelings of discontent he can begin to see them as opportunities to make her happier. When a woman is not getting the support she wants, she can see it as an opportunity to take the responsibility for getting what she needs. She can view it as an opportunity to practice expressing greater power, but in a feminine way. This is generally something her mother could not tell her.

When a woman is unhappy and talks about problems, a man doesn't have to feel blamed. He can reverse this pattern through understanding her real need to share. When she claims to feel a lack in the relationship, he realizes that it is not because of his deficiency (although it may always sound that way) but because our modern culture doesn't sufficiently support her feminine side. This frees him to truly consider and feel her feelings rather than defend himself. It also greatly clarifies what he is required to do.

When a woman is disappointed by her partner, instead of taking it personally she can reverse the pattern and recognize his loving intent and willingness to support her more, but in small steps. Through adjusting her expectations she can eventually connect with the grace of her feminine spirit, which does not demand perfection but seeks to love and embrace life just the way it is. She realizes that it is not personal but that he was not trained by his father's example in how to fulfill a modern woman's new needs.

In the next chapter, we explore how to apply these skills by understanding how men and women are different.

CHAPTER 4

How Men and Women Think and Feel Differently

WITH AN AWARENESS OF HOW men and women think and feel differently, we are freed from the tendency to try to change our partners at those times when we are not getting what we want. With a greater level of acceptance and understanding, love flourishes and we get what we want from our relationships.

Through understanding our historical and evolutionary development, we can take what is useful from our past and update it in ways that do not reject our genetic makeup, and can expand or stretch ourselves to be more of who we can be.

Trying to ignore differences only creates more confusion and frustration between the sexes. The generalizations I make about men and women are certainly not true for everyone at all times, but they are true for a lot of people. When they do not apply to your situation or experience, just set them aside like an outfit that others may buy but that you don't. What is most important is that when the differences do show up, you will have positive and useful relationship skills for coping with them.

Understanding these broad categories of differences helps you to accept them in a noncritical way, and then assists you in working *with* them instead of against them. I have found that these differences begin to show up even more when couples begin to have intimate relationships; in some cases, differences become more pronounced when the couple has children.

Brain Differences

In recent years, a multitude of scientific studies has clearly indicated many differences between men's and women's brains as well as in the way they use them. While these studies do concretely show differences, it is still too soon for scientists to know exactly what these differences mean.

In general, women tend to use both sides of their brains simultaneously, while men use one side or the other. This means that a man tends to use either his left brain language skills or his right brain spatial problem-solving skills. A woman uses both at the same time.

Studies have revealed that some women have much more corpus callosum, or connective tissue, between the two hemispheres of the brain, which would account for a woman's tendency to use both sides of the brain simultaneously. Even though some women do not have more connective tissue, MRI brain scans reveal that these women still have a tendency to use both sides of the brain simultaneously. While some men may have more corpus callosum than some women, these men still use only one side of the brain at a time, while the women use both. The impact of this difference is staggering.

While we eagerly wait for more studies that will reveal how men and women use their brains differently, what has already been discovered can dramatically assist us in understanding some of the great mysteries between the sexes.

Bodies, Brains, and Hormones

During the course of evolution, men's and women's bodies, brains, and hormones have become specialized to best support their different roles and activities. A man, for example, is most efficiently wired to cope with strong emotions by silently problem solving. As a hunter and protector in the jungle, he adapted to his role and coped with strong feelings of fear, anger, and loss through silently problem solving. By planning his strategies to protect himself and his family, he was most effectively able to cope with his feelings.

Women, on the other hand, have adapted to their role of nurturer and have learned to cope with feelings and problem solving primarily through talking and sharing with others in the family and community. Not only does this reflect a woman's tendency to use both sides of her brain at the same time, but repeatedly in scientific testing women show an advantage when it comes to left brain language skills. Men have an advantage when tests require right brain spatial skills.

That talking is an integral part of femininity makes perfect sense when we learn that the female brain is organized in a way that allows her to communicate feelings more efficiently. Females' extra connective tissue, which comprises billions more neuroconnectors between the feelings and the language center of the brain, allows little girls to develop language skills before little boys do. Most commonly, at an earlier stage of development girls will use many more words than boys. This difference is repeatedly validated in the testing of children.

While a girl's brain is developing to express her communication abilities, a boy tends to develop his spatial skills. Spatial skills, for example, help us to determine how far to throw a ball, or where to run to get help and how to get there. The development of spatial skills allows a boy to "do something about it" when he is emotionally distressed. Spatial skills for him are an integral part of problem solving.

As any parent knows, at an early age a girl's impulse is to talk, sometimes without thinking, while a boy's impulse is to act, sometimes, as well, without thinking. When a girl feels supported in talking without the fear of rejection or loss of love, then she is eventually able to grow the neuroconnectors that allow her to feel, speak, and think at the same time.

As an adult, when she is upset and is not thinking clearly, she will instinctively want to talk to someone who will just listen. This support helps her to reconnect her thinking to her feelings and make sense of the situation to determine what to do. When a woman is distressed, she seeks out help in the form of someone to listen to her articulate her feelings.

On the other hand, when a boy feels safe to act without fear of abusive punishment or the loss of love, he has the freedom to act, make mistakes, and then think about what he did and correct his behavior. This self-corrective mechanism allows him to learn from his mistakes. Eventually, he can grow the neuroconnectors needed to feel and then think before acting.

When a man is upset and not thinking clearly, he will instinctively want to move around. He may simply pace back and forth just to satisfy his urge to do *something* before he has figured out the right thing to do. Any simple, mindless activity will help him to express his feelings of wanting to do something while he is trying to use the right side of his brain to figure out what to do.

Just as spatial skills are required for playing games like basketball, soccer, and football, they are also required for the hunter to stalk his prey, accurately throw a spear, and then find his way back home. When we consider how long men have specialized in being the hunters and protectors, it is no wonder that our brains are organized so differently.

A man must think about feelings before he talks about them, while a woman can feel, talk, and think all at the same time.

While a woman may be quicker to speak out about her feelings, a man will tend to act more quickly to solve a problem. While she will want to explore a problem more fully through talking, a man will be restless to do something about it. While neither approach is necessarily better, the best approach is when we work together.

From the dawn of time, a man's ability to throw spears was essential for his survival, just as a woman's ability to talk and form relationships was responsible for her survival. It is no wonder that our brains developed so differently, with a woman able to communicate her feelings more efficiently, while a man's pattern is to detach from his feelings to consider a problem and its solution.

Different Brain Maps

We can visually imagine that as a girl's brain develops, billions of neuroconnectors are mapped out from her emotional centers to the talking center in the brain. In a boy's brain, other priorities are operating. The right side of the brain, required to shoot arrows, hit a target, and then find the way back home, develops first. Eventually, a boy does develop his language center and a girl develops her action center, but the way we use these centers as adults ends up being very different. As a result of this different order of development, a man's emotions are more tied into action problem solving and not talking, while a woman's emotions are more tied to communication and then problem solving.

A man's brain first develops billions of neuroconnectors between his emotions and his action center. When he is emotionally charged or upset, he generally wants to do something about it. Finding a solution is his priority. Certainly, a woman will also act to solve problems, but because of the way her brain develops, her initial tendency is first to talk about it.

A woman has billions of neuroconnectors between her feelings and the talking center. In a sense, she has superhighways connecting her feelings to speech. When a man attempts to put his feelings into words, he needs to first think about what he wants to say. For him to express his feelings in words, there are no freeways and he has to take winding back roads.

First he has the feeling, then he wants to do something, then, in analyzing the feeling and what he can do about it, he decides if it is useful to talk about it. He then has to move over to the left side of the brain and begin formulating the words for these feelings. After he talks and new feelings come up, the whole process then has to start over. This is hard for a woman to understand because, as mentioned before, she tends to feel, talk, and think all at the same time.

Boys Will Be Boys and Girls Will Be Girls

This difference in brain development is most commonly seen in various childhood behaviors. One study revealed this difference in a very dramatic way. In the experiment, a mother was asked to enter a room where her toddler was already sitting. In the room, the mother was separated by a glass wall from her child. She was instructed to stand in front of the glass wall with a neutral expression. The results of this experiment showed a very clear difference in the way boys and girls responded.

If the toddler was a boy, he would see his mother, become distressed that she was not holding him, and begin crawling to her. When he arrived at the glass wall, he would attempt to push it over or try to climb over it. Eventually, his mother would reach over the wall and pick him up.

When the toddler was a girl, she would see her

mother and, like the little boy, she would become distressed that she was not being held. Instead of crawling to her and trying to overcome the glass wall like the little boy toddler, the little girl would make eye contact and then cry out. The boys consistently expressed their feelings through action, while the girls expressed their feelings verbally.

Male and Female Cognitive Development

At a later stage in the brain's development for both boys and girls, the logical or cognitive centers begin to develop. At this stage of development, billions of neuroconnectors are made to the cognitive or thinking parts of the brain. Again we see this development reflected in common male and female tendencies.

When a woman is upset, her first tendency is to talk about it; then as she continues to talk, her cognitive abilities set in and she can think about what she is saying and feeling and thus *sort it out*. She starts out in the feeling part of the brain, then she travels to the communication part, and from there she goes to the thinking portion. This is her most natural route because this is the order in which her skills developed. Gradually, over time, she develops the ability to feel, talk, and think at the same time.

For a man, his process of dealing with feelings is different because his skills developed in another order. First his feeling center develops, next his action center, and then his thinking. When he is upset, his first tendency is to do something about it. Action leads him to clearer thinking. Gradually, he develops the ability to feel, act, and think at the same time.

Because of these significant differences in the way our brains develop, men and women behave and communicate differently. Men use communication primarily as another tool to express their thinking in order to achieve some goal or solve a problem. Women use communication for this reason as well, but they also depend on communication as a way to connect with their feelings and to clarify their thinking. Communication has a much greater significance for a woman.

In a similar way, action is more significant to men. Action is like a pump that activates the thinking part of a man's brain. Women also use action as a way to solve problems, but for men it is much more. Action is the most significant way for a man to find mental clarity and to express his feelings.

How Men Deal with Feelings Differently

When a man puts his feelings into action, he is able to sort them out. Simple, goal-oriented activities like sports allow him more fully to activate the thinking part of his brain and more effectively to deal with emotions.

A close male friend of mine was given the very terrible news that his daughter had cancer—which I knew about from my wife before he called to tell me. After a normal exchange of greetings, he announced that he had bad news, then paused.

"I already heard from Bonnie," I said to spare him having to go through the bad news again.

After another pause, he asked me if I was free to play some tennis. I said I was, and we arranged to meet at the neighborhood courts in a few minutes.

When I told Bonnie where I was going, she understood perfectly and told me to give my friend a hug for her.

During the game, when my friend and I changed sides or went to the net to retrieve balls, we'd exchange a few words. Then we'd play some more, then talk some more. For him, playing tennis—something he did well and enjoyed—allowed him an opportunity to express his feelings about what had happened. Talking was how he could sum up his ideas and then receive my feedback and support. But the way he connected with his feelings in the first place was by playing tennis.

In focusing his attention and energy on keeping the ball in the court, he was able to contact and express his frustration at not being able to remove the cancer: when he hit it long or wide, he was connecting with the pain of not being the perfect father and reflecting on possible mistakes he had made; when the ball stayed in, he connected with his desire to do the right thing and be the best father he could. By connecting with his desire to beat me and win, he fueled his desire to beat this cancer and save his daughter.

After the game, sitting on a bench by the court, we explored different ways of supporting his little girl through the coming ordeal. Throughout our conversation, he automatically connected with and occasionally expressed his fears of losing his daughter, along with his deep feelings of love for her. At this point, I gave him a hug from me, followed by the one Bonnie had asked me to send him.

This story has a happy ending. My friend's child was successfully treated, and today is fine.

How Men Receive Love Differently

It is through his actions that a man can most directly connect to his feelings, and it is through acknowledging and appreciating his actions that he feels most loved.

**Direct appreciation of a man's
decisions and actions and forgiveness
of his mistakes is the most direct
route to his heart.**

This acceptance frees him to most effectively experience the fullness of feeling loved, and in return become more loving. Women do not instinctively understand this because their feelings are directly connected to the brain's talking—not acting—centers.

Women mistakenly give the kind of loving support they themselves want without intuiting a man's needs. When a man is distressed, women think they are being very loving by trying to get him to talk. They do not instinctively realize that the best thing they can do is lovingly to accept him by giving him lots of space and then, when he is directly supportive, to respond warmly in a way that says they are glad to have him in their life. With this new awareness of how men feel loved, women can begin to focus their support in ways that matter most to their mates.

How Men Cope with Stress

In prehistoric times, there were those occasions when a hunter did not return home with the kill. To cope with the strain of not having adequately provided, he developed strategies for shifting his focus from critical problems to less important ones that he could handle successfully.

Men became experts in temporarily forgetting their real problems by focusing on lesser ones. They came to depend on hobbies, sports, or any other activity that would distract them from thoughts of providing. Today's men, following in ancestral footsteps, likewise rely on distractions like hobbies to relieve the pressure generated by a bad day at the office.

A hobby is a freely chosen activity that a man performs in his spare time. While making very few personal demands, it's challenging because it requires skill. Although a hobby has little real-world importance, it matters to a man's peace of mind and ultimately supports his competence and skill in solving problems of significance.

In order to function fully as a stress reliever, a hobby or activity must be one at which the man can easily or enjoyably do. Even if he feels down because he didn't accomplish what he wanted to at work, beginning to do something he is good at makes him feel more in control. This transition prepares him for reconnecting with his partner.

• Competition and Sports

Competitive sports allow a man to redirect and channel his aggression. They enable him to express his frustration at not being able to solve real-world problems. Instead of killing his prey or potential enemies, he focuses on beating the other team or player.

The male instincts that are required to
hunt, kill, and protect find free
expression in sports.

By releasing his focus from work
through a seemingly unimportant
activity, a man gradually remembers
what is most important to him—
his love for his wife and family, and
the desire to be there for them
and with them.

• Hunting, Fishing, Tennis, and Golf

If a man can't solve the problems of work, he can
still stalk game or bring home some fish. This is why
hunting and fishing are such important leisure activities. After a successful outing, somewhere deep in his
male spirit he feels he has solved his problem and can
now relax and receive his partner's love and support.

Tennis and golf are also perfect distractions to
relax through doing. Two men feel much more at
ease being together and occasionally talking if they
are also doing something.

• Movies

Many men enjoy going to the movies because the
images are bigger than life and allow them to shift

focus by absorbing their attention. Through identifying with the characters on the screen, they are temporarily released from their personal problems. Action movies are particularly helpful for a man with a sit-down job; suspenseful thrillers for a man with a routine kind of job; violent movies for one who has to be loving all the time. At the movies, men connect with feelings that their "day jobs" don't allow them to feel or process.

• *Reading or Watching the News*

When a man concentrates on world problems, his own suddenly seem smaller. He is able to relax because he does not feel any immediate responsibility for solving these problems. They are out of his control.

• *TV and Fire Gazing*

Contemporary man's most common leisure-time activity is watching TV. Most women don't understand this at all. Some women hate a man's watching TV because it gets all his attention. But while TV is a recent invention, watching it is the contemporary form of an ancient ritual.

While visiting communities so primitive that they didn't have TV, I noticed that at dusk, while the women were occupied in talking and performing tasks, the men were sitting silently in a circle gazing into a fire.

Fire gazing is the most ancient and potent of male stress reducers. When men today stare into the TV, they are, in effect, mindlessly looking into the fire. It allows men to redirect their focus, stop think-ing, and just relax. This relaxation rejuvenates the body, releasing the stress and tensions of the day.

How Men Can Accomplish More by Doing Less

One of my most relaxing activities is watching the news. It is relaxing because these are not problems I feel I have to solve. Once I really realized that I didn't have to solve my wife's problems for her to feel bet-ter, then listening to her became as relaxing as listen-ing to the news. And even better, she appreciates me for it and the TV doesn't.

Most men do not realize that by actually doing less in a relationship, they can support themselves and their partners much more. By learning to listen to a woman's feelings in a sympathetic way and focusing less on solving her problems, not only can he make her much happier, but he can also relax. Although the end result is enhanced mutual ease and support, it will take some extra start-up effort to excel at this new relationship skill.

It is common for a man to hear a woman's feel-ings of unhappiness after a hard day's work and con-clude that he must do more to make her happy. When he does more and she is still overwhelmed, he naturally feels frustrated and unappreciated and eventually stops giving. Pleasing an overwhelmed woman becomes an impossible task.

When a woman is overwhelmed, she needs *emo-tional* support. In most cases, she first needs to talk about her feelings with a partner who understands and sympathizes with her. Then and only then can she appreciate his physical efforts to solve her problems.

Doing more so that a woman will have
less to do is not the answer to making
her happy.

The way to support a woman best is to nurture
her female side so that she doesn't feel an urgency to
do everything now. Men do not instinctively realize
that her overwhelming feelings are not "fixed" or
illuminated through helping her solve her problems.
To support her, a man needs to remember that her
overwhelming feelings are released only through nurturing conversation.

As we discussed in chapter 3, a woman's work *is*
never done. There will always be more to do.
However, by learning to initiate conversation and listen respectfully, a man can free her from the urgency
to do it all now. From this centered and loving perspective, she can then accomplish what is humanly
possible in a more relaxed manner.

Men Who Do Too Much

When a man focuses on solving problems for his
partner rather than providing initial emotional support—despite the fact that his efforts and actions are
indeed motivated by love and caring—he will make
matters worse by doing too much. Let's look at some
common examples.

Tom, like so many men, was frustrated by hearing his wife, Sharon, complain about having too
much to do. His way of dealing with the problem
was to attempt to divide domestic responsibilities

along guidelines that she agreed were fair. Though this scheme seemed like the answer, it brought them to the verge of divorce.

They came to me for counseling as a last chance to save their marriage. Tom began by complaining that even after he started doing half the work at home, Sharon still wasn't happy. "I can't stand it anymore," he told me. "I'm willing to do more chores if it makes her happy. But if she's still going to be unhappy, I'm through."

Tom made the classic mistake of expecting Sharon to be happy by solving her problems. What he didn't know was that Sharon would always need to talk about her feelings; no matter how many problems he solved for her, there would still be problems she felt compelled to talk about.

As it turned out, Sharon was every bit as dissatisfied as Tom. When he began doing more chores, she felt as if she'd lost the right to complain. At this point, he had become so supersensitive that whenever she was overwhelmed or upset, he would automatically shake his head and either sulk or criticize her for being negative.

In their sincere attempts to solve the problem, they had unknowingly made it worse. Look at how it went:

1. Because he was doing more at home, Tom expected Sharon to be happier.
2. When she occasionally felt overwhelmed, he felt even more frustrated and unappreciated.
3. Now she couldn't freely talk about her feelings because it upset Tom too much.
4. In time, Sharon began to feel more and more overwhelmed.

5. The more she had to control her feelings, the more urgent her need became to identify and solve problems.
6. It was now impossible for her to relax and enjoy her life and relationship.

Doing Less but Supporting More

Through acquiring new relationship skills, Tom and Sharon were able to find a creative solution to their dilemma and save their marriage. Tom's new job description would not include doing more at home and trying to solve problems, but listening and comforting Sharon. He would practice giving nurturing support.

Sharon agreed to practice appreciating Tom for what he did at work without demanding more at home. She would focus on asking him to listen to her feelings while making sure that he knew how much she appreciated his emotional support. As he got better and better at listening to her feelings, he would eventually be able to do more without expecting her to always be happy or appreciative. They solved this common problem in two stages.

Stage One: No Solutions

Initially, they both agreed that Tom wouldn't try to *do* more for her but would focus just on listening.

He practiced being sympathetic to her feelings while making sure that he did nothing to directly solve her problems. Sharon had already given him the clear message that he was already *doing* enough, and that the only request she was making was to share her feelings.

With this dynamic in place, Tom was able to listen to Sharon without becoming frustrated. He was amazed by how effective just listening was. Sometimes she would simply say, "Thanks for listening, I feel much better." At other times she would say, "I feel so much better now. I love being able to talk like this with you. I feel relieved to know I can." With this kind of feedback, it wasn't long before Tom was able to understand what was truly required of him by his wife. Not only was it sometimes pleasurable to do but it was actually easier than trying to solve her problems.

Sharon, on the other hand, was amazed by Tom's attentiveness when he knew nothing except empathy was required of him. Tom said he now felt as free as when they'd first met. He didn't feel responsible for Sharon's problems or take them personally. Since he didn't *have* to do more, he found himself naturally wanting to do more. After several weeks of successful practice, he suggested they start stage two.

Stage Two: He Offers Help

Tom was to continue listening as before but now was able to offer help in problem solving by doing more for her—in very small increments.

I recommended that Tom start by listening to Sharon's litany of problems and offer to help solve the easiest. He was surprised to learn that he was not expected to solve her toughest problems. What she needed from him was to feel that she was not alone in dealing with her problems. In fact, Tom discovered that

by offering to do several small things, he gave Sharon
more support than trying to tackle one big problem.

**When a woman is convinced that she is
not alone in coping with and solving
life's problems, she feels
deeply comforted.**

Without feeling pressured to solve her problems,
not only did Tom become a better listener but—using
his own feelings as a gauge—he learned to regulate
how much he could give without expecting his mate
to be happy all the time.

When he felt frustrated that his partner was not
happy, he recognized it as a signal that he was giving
too much, not that she was asking too much. Sharon
loved this. No longer feeling responsible or protective
of Tom's feelings, she could freely share her emotions
and talk openly with him about her life. A deep, feminine part of her being was at last being nourished.

Over time, Tom began to give more and do more
as he felt appreciated for his efforts—not because he
was trying to get rid of her negative feelings but because
he truly sympathized with her needs and wanted to
help. He realized that most of the time, she really just
needed to talk. Tom was able to rewrite his job description successfully because he was properly prepared.

Preparing a Man to Listen

Whenever a woman shares overwhelming feelings, a
man tends mistakenly to feel frustrated or blamed.

Amazingly, it only takes one simple statement to prepare him properly so that he can avoid feeling blamed and be an attentive listener. I myself went through the gradual process of learning that problem solving was not what my wife needed or wanted from me. I remember how Bonnie cleverly applied new relationship skills to help me support her better.

In the first years of our marriage, Bonnie would occasionally feel overwhelmed and complain about what had happened at work.

Each time I would listen for a few minutes and then offer her what I thought was sage advice: "If you don't like your job, why don't you just quit? You don't have to put up with that!" She would proceed to tell me what else had happened to bother or stress her. I would then tell her again that she should change jobs. I would point out why she should quit, and she would defend her job. After a while, I didn't even want to listen. I kept thinking, Don't keep complaining about something if you're not going to do something about it.

She felt as if I didn't care about her feelings and was too controlling. We argued frequently.

Then one day she tried something new, which changed everything. She told me, "I'd like to talk about my day, but first I want you to know that I love my job and I don't want to quit." Then she proceeded to complain. It was amazing. Every time she paused, I wanted to say, Why don't you just quit that job? but I couldn't because she had already answered it by saying that she loved her work. Having nothing to say, I listened without speaking or solving.

I had been prepared.

Then she proceeded. After a while I truly saw that without any solutions on my part Bonnie was indeed much happier. Preparing me for what she was about to say made it much easier for me to listen.

A woman can prepare a man to listen by letting him know in advance what it is that she needs. This allows him to adjust his instinctive expectations to learned expectations. For example, when a man has worked hard or was particularly successful that day, his instinctive expectations are much higher. When she talks about her problems, he fully expects her to respond favorably to his solutions and doesn't relate to her need to communicate feelings and talk about problems as a way to feel better. He instinctively feels that as a result of his actions that day she should be happy. Without some preparation from her, it is easy for him to be frustrated.

Success and Relationships

When a man begins to realize that he has gone about as far up the ladder as he is going to go, and his partner is still complaining, he despairs of ever receiving the support he wants most. As he was moving up, there was always a little voice in the back of his head saying "When I get a little more successful, she'll appreciate me. When I make a little more money and take her on that vacation, she'll be happy." But when he finally levels out at a fixed income, it becomes very hard for him to handle her unhappiness. This stress is relieved when he understands what she really needs, and that it is not about how much money he makes or whether he can solve her problems.

Women and Wealth

Women also have new hurdles to overcome when their partners become better providers so that they no longer have to work. A woman who doesn't have to work is expected to be categorically happier, not only by her husband but by everyone she knows. However, it is the lack of nurturing relationships that creates unhappiness in women, not the lack of wealth. A woman who doesn't have to work each day also needs to be emotionally nurtured.

As any well-off person can tell you, money does not eliminate problems. If anything, it makes life more complex. The greater the wealth, the more momentous the decisions about spending it, using it, and protecting it.

Money doesn't prevent women from feeling overwhelmed.

If a man can use his money to create more time away from work to spend with his wife, and also be understanding of her daily frustrations and problems, then money can help a relationship. Generally, however, making a lot of money without ruining a relationship takes a disciplined and conscious effort on both the man's and woman's part. He must strive to listen and she to appreciate him.

Women feel overwhelmed when their daily relationships are not nurturing to the feminine spirit; it has nothing to do with money. Greater wealth may either assist her in, or prevent her from, finding more nurturing. Since women with money tend to get less sympathy, they are frequently overwhelmed.

Not only are less well-off women disinclined to respond sympathetically to her problems, but a wealthy woman's husband becomes increasingly intolerant because he instinctively believes that money should buy her happiness.

For all of the above reasons it is essential for a wealthy woman to learn how to support her male partner in giving her the support she deserves. Sometimes all it takes is just a few well-chosen phrases to prepare him to listen to her feelings. When he is able to listen and understand what she goes through, she can more easily give him the appreciation he needs.

The Contrary Role of Wealth

Jeff is a successful lawyer, and Teresa is a wife and mother who doesn't have to work. For the first ten years of their marriage, they were in love, and their relationship flowed. When Teresa expressed feelings of unhappiness, Jeff could be understanding because although he was working long hours, they didn't have a lot of money. When she complained, he could be sympathetic because he appreciated her sacrifices. He also felt that one day he would be a success and have lots of money, which would finally make her happy.

So he prospered, but as women have done for centuries, Teresa continued to talk occasionally about her problems. Now, however, he couldn't deal with it and took it personally. He felt he was still not doing enough, and that no amount of money would ever be enough to satisfy her. Whenever she complained about her day or wanted more from him, he felt that she wasn't appreciating his hard work.

In counseling, Teresa would insist that she didn't care about the money, the cars, or the house. She wanted Jeff's love.

I immediately asked her to take a brief break because I could feel Jeff react to those words with a desire to attack. "I know how you feel," I told her, "but I also know how that must sound to Jeff. Money is his most precious gift to you. He has worked hard for it. Let's find another way to share those feelings without rejecting him. While I understand that you want to feel loved, do you also appreciate the lifestyle he provides for you?"

"Well, of course," Teresa responded. "Jeff is a great provider. In that sense I feel very lucky."

"Good," I told her. "Now this time, before you share how you feel, first prepare him by letting him know how much you appreciate all he does give you."

Teresa needed only a slight shift in direction to make everything she said clear to Jeff. This is what she told him:

"I want you to know that I feel so lucky to be married to you. You work so hard, and you provide me with so many comforts that my friends don't have. Some of my friends don't even know if they can pay their rent this month. I also have a lot of other feelings. I miss you. I would like to spend more time with you. I feel like your clients get the best of you, and when you get home you are too tired for me. All these years I have looked forward to being able to spend more time with you. In the past, you had to be busy so we could survive, but now I would most love the luxury of spending more time with you."

Jeff was able to hear her this time without getting defensive and suddenly became much more cooperative. I explained how important it was for women to feel heard and have their feelings validated. Jeff learned that it was normal for his wife to have emotional needs, and that overwhelming feelings were perfectly appropriate for her to experience.

Jeff gradually learned to listen without feeling as if Teresa didn't appreciate what he was providing for her. This took a lot of practice and patience, but they both did successfully rewrite their job descriptions through the use of new relationship skills.

Teresa learned to be playful about their learning experience, and Jeff greatly appreciated it. Sometimes before sharing difficult feelings, she would prepare Jeff by saying things like, "I am really happy that we have so much money! I love it, and it really makes me happy. I also had an awful day, would you take a few minutes to just listen? You don't have to say anything, and I will feel better!"

Over time, Jeff became a much better listener, and without Teresa having to demand it, he started spending more time with her. As communication improved, she became much less overwhelmed and happier to see Jeff at the end of a day. Gradually, he began to do more to help, but most important, he focused on learning to listen without feeling responsible for solving Teresa's problems.

How Women Unknowingly Turn Men Off

Quite commonly, a man gets turned off to a woman because he doesn't understand a woman's need to talk about feelings and problems. While she thinks she's just making conversation and letting him know that she is open to him, he misreads the situation and feels that he could never make her happy and decides to not get involved.

A limousine driver I had occasion to speak with put it like this when I asked him about women and relationships. He was thirty-two, single, and experienced. He claimed he had had seven relationships that he considered "special." I was curious to discover what went wrong. After we talked for a while he said, "I think I'm jinxed. I'm only attracted to women with psychological problems."

I laughed and then said, "Let me see if I can guess what happened. In the beginning these women were very warm and pleased by you. You felt really good about yourself when you were with them. You cared for them and wanted to make them happy. Then, as each relationship progressed, they would begin to talk about problems. It seemed as if no matter what you said, they just came back with more problems."

"Yeah, that's right!" he exclaimed. "How did you know?" I assured him that these women did not have psychological problems. As I explained to him why women feel overwhelmed and what they really need, he—like most men—began to feel relieved and expressed a renewed interest in pursuing the relationship he was just ending.

While this is a nice story, there are still millions of men out there who don't understand how to react when a woman talks about her feelings. If women are to stay feminine and share their feelings, it is essential that they learn the advanced relationship skill of preparing a man to listen to them.

Many times it takes only one sentence to remind

him in a playful way that she appreciates his listening, knows it must be hard to listen, and that she really doesn't need him to say anything or do more to make her feel better.

Once a woman masters the art of preparing a man to listen, she will begin to experience a new freedom of expression in her relationship, whether she is starting a partnership or is already involved in one. And, as with all new relationship skills, it only requires a small shift that doesn't involve changing who you are.

Successful Giving and Receiving

Without becoming overworked himself, a man *can* learn to be more effective in supporting his partner. At each step, her appreciation will motivate him to do more. It will not entail a major sacrifice nor will he feel controlled.

Men *want* to be the providers, they *want* to take credit for a woman's happiness, and they thrive on feeling successful in making a difference. They just need to feel appreciated for it. This is the kind of love and support that a man craves most from a woman.

Men and women complement each other in a very magical way. Men thrive on successfully caring for their partners, while women thrive when they feel cared for. Certainly, women also love to care for their male partners but primarily need to feel cared for themselves. I have never heard a woman say "My partner completely ignores me, but I still *love* giving to him." In a similar way, men need to feel cared for but primarily need to feel successful in fulfilling their partners.

Why Couples Break Up

In listening to hundreds of couples on the verge of parting, I hear the same message over and over. Women say they give and give and are tired of giving and not getting back. They want more.

A man's discontent is similar but different in a very significant way. Men say "I give and give, but no matter what I do, it is never enough to make her happy." This is because his condition for fulfillment is primarily based on fulfilling her needs. When she is happy, he is happy.

Men who don't want to give more simply are not feeling sufficiently appreciated. Before asking him for more, a woman must convince her partner that he is already doing enough. To read him a list of what he is doing wrong only creates more resistance. Appreciating what he does do, however, and making specific requests in small increments, is the key to getting more.

This simple approach of man as giver and woman as receiver does not mean that men don't need women or that women should not give. Women will always give, and men will always be happy to receive. That is not the problem. The problem is that women give too much and feel overworked, while men give only what their fathers gave and expect to receive the same measure of support.

Why Women Feel They Give More

Women today feel they give more, and in return expect men to give back more. It is not that the man gives less. He is giving what men have always given. Through understanding the problem without blame, both men and women are motivated to solve their share of the problem.

To solve this basic problem we must first recognize that it is not really about how much more she does. Instead, it is about what she is not getting in order to be fulfilled. As we have explored, the real need that women have that is not being fulfilled is the need to be heard.

As men learn how to provide emotional support through using new relationship skills, then and only then will women begin to feel greater warmth and appreciation. Then, as a woman truly feels more centered and appreciative, a man is naturally motivated to gradually do more in the home.

Just as a weight lifter gradually builds muscle by slowly increasing his weights, a man can and will do more and give more at home to nurture his partner if it is a gradual process.

Once a man experiences his woman's appreciation, his resistance to doing more melts away. Instead of feeling like a child controlled by his mother, he begins to welcome her requests for more.

In the next chapter, we will explore how men can use ancient warrior skills to duck and dodge when they feel verbally attacked in conversation. By putting a new spin on old skills, they can easily learn to listen to a woman without getting upset with her. After focusing on skills that men can use, we will then focus on new skills that women can use to communicate so that men will listen and truly understand.

CHAPTER 5

Masculine Skills for Listening Without Getting Upset

TO GIVE A WOMAN THE EMOTIONAL support she requires, a man needs to listen in a new way, using new relationship skills. When she is upset, his most powerful means of assisting her in feeling better is to listen without getting upset that she is upset. To do this successfully, he does not have to make major changes in himself. Instead, he is required only to reconnect to his ancient warrior skills.

By learning to duck and dodge what he hears as blame, mistrust, and criticism, a man can gradually learn to listen patiently and not get shot to pieces. Through listening in a skillful manner so that he is not hurt by her words and feelings, he will begin to hear her calmly.

While he is perfectly capable of mastering this relationship skill, it is not as easy for him as women assume. His mate's conscious assistance in this process can greatly speed up his progress.

We have already discussed that hearing a woman talk about problems is particularly hard on a man because he either is inclined to offer solutions that she doesn't appreciate or feels blamed for what is bothering her.

If a man simply practices listening passively for more than ten minutes without clear guidelines, and without doing something to make his mate feel better or at least defend himself, he will become increasingly frustrated and upset.

Even if she does not intend to attack or blame him when she talks about her feelings, he may feel that she does. Merely listening is too inactive for him. It is as if he is standing in front of a firing squad. When she begins to talk, he wants to either fight back or put on a blindfold.

Instead of allowing himself to be wounded by his partner's words, a man can practice the new relationship skill of ducking and dodging. When he feels under attack, he can actively support her by not taking it personally. He is superbly equipped to do this because protecting himself from harm is the most basic of warrior skills. If he has survived this long, with a few adjustments he can begin applying his skills in conversation.

Emotional Self-Defense

The instincts that sent warriors boldly into battle to defend themselves and protect their loved ones come into play when a modern man tries to listen to a modern woman. To prevail, he must learn to duck and dodge.

A modern man is required to be a warrior but now must defend himself without retaliating.

Ducking and dodging require new mental strategies for correctly interpreting the situation. Instead of reacting to blame and criticism, a man learns to hear the correct loving message in her words and responds in ways that diminish friction and conflict. Ducking and dodging allow a man to keep his cool and respond respectfully to a woman's need to communicate.

When he listens to a woman *without* ducking and dodging, he will be repeatedly assaulted by her words and begin to feel blamed, criticized, unacknowledged, misunderstood, rejected, mistrusted, or unappreciated. No matter how much he loves her, after about three direct hits he will no longer be capable of listening to her in a supportive way. War breaks out.

When a man is struck by a woman's words, it is much harder to restrain his ancient warrior instincts to intimidate, threaten, or retaliate. Once these defensive responses are triggered, he will attempt either to change her mind through arguing or protect her from his own aggressive reactions by emotionally withdrawing. However, through new relationship skills of listening without getting struck, he can easily sidestep provocative reactions.

Women Still Want to Be Protected

Although modern women are independent and assertive, their female natures still seek out strong men who can provide protection. They still want to be protected, but in a different sense.

Women now look to men to provide the emotional climate in which they can safely explore and express their feelings. When a man can listen to a woman's feelings and allow her to articulate them without responding negatively, she is not only very appreciative but more attracted to him as a result.

Through ducking and dodging, a man will avoid getting upset along with his partner and will create a new dimension of protection for the woman he loves. This new ability and strength not only helps her but ensures that he too will get the love he deserves.

Security is the most important gift a contemporary man can give a woman. In hunter/nurturer societies, that security was primarily physical. Today, it is emotional as well.

When a woman feels secure enough to share her feelings with the man she loves and he can listen without being wounded, the relationship will thrive.

Buying a Computer

I'll never forget the day I first discovered this truth in my own marriage. Before then, even knowing that women needed to be heard and feel understood, I didn't realize that safety was an even more important element to them.

On the last day of the year, I decided to buy a new computer. I had put off this decision for a long time but finally decided to do it on New Year's Eve so that I could take it off that year's taxes. When I mentioned this to Bonnie, the force of her reaction stunned me.

"*Why* do you need to buy a new computer?" she demanded. "You already have one."

Although I didn't like being "questioned," I paused to consider her request, then began to explain by simply saying, "Well, for a lot of reasons."

By saying as little as possible, I was again able to "duck" and avoid getting hit by her inevitable emotional response to my gut reactions. If I hadn't ducked, we would have clashed. By doing so, I prevented the situation from escalating into a full-blown fight.

"What's wrong with the computer you already have?" Bonnie persisted.

I again paused, then observed, "You seem upset. What's the matter?"

"Have you researched the market?" she persisted, not answering my question. "How much is this computer going to cost?"

Although she was again asking me demanding questions, I knew Bonnie was upset and needed to talk. If I started giving complicated explanations of why I needed a new computer, not only would she continue to be upset but I would become upset because it would feel as if she didn't appreciate my explanations.

Men should duck answering a woman's direct questions if they are provocative, turn the conversation back to her, and keep their responses to a minimum to draw her out.

Here's how it went:

John: "I think before we talk about the computer

we should first talk about how you feel. I want to understand what you are feeling and why you are upset."

Bonnie: "Well, I am upset. Whenever you want something, you just go out and get it. I don't know why you have to get another computer. Yours works fine. If we are going to spend money, there are other things we could spend it on."

John: "OK, what do you think we should buy?"

Bonnie: "It's not that I have this all thought out. It's just a feeling. I feel like you get what you want and I get seconds. Maybe I am mad that you want so much more than me. When I want something, it doesn't seem so important."

John: "What do you want?"

Bonnie: "I don't know. But it feels like everything we do is for you and not me. We always do what you want to do, and you always get your way. I'm afraid I will not get what I want."

John: "I can understand that feeling."

Bonnie: "We have been waiting six months to redo our floor. Our couch needs to be recovered. I still need a kitchen cupboard. There are so many things we need to spend money on in the house and you are buying a computer. It just feels like you don't care about me. You are going to buy what you want, and that's it. What I have to say doesn't matter at all."

As the conversation progressed in this way, I was vigorously ducking and dodging. As I continued to hold back and not retaliate, I realized that I could only take so much more.

John: "I really want to understand your feelings *and* it really is hard for me. It's starting to sound like you're saying I'm this selfish person. Don't I do anything nice?"

Bonnie (softening): "Of course you do. I don't mean to upset you. I just have a lot of feelings coming up. I really appreciate you trying to listen. Just the fact that I could talk about my feelings without you getting upset with me makes me feel so loved."

She then burst into tears, and I gave her a loving hug.

The Importance of Safety

At that moment I realized how important it was for Bonnie to feel safe enough to express her feelings. When I share this story in my couples' seminars, women repeatedly get misty-eyed relating to Bonnie's feelings.

**The freedom to express emotions safely
with their mate's help is vital to
women. Men inevitably express
surprise at how much women
need to feel safe.**

When a man seeks an intimate partner, he wants primarily to be needed and appreciated. When a woman seeks a mate, a man's ability to protect her is a key job requirement. This is a very primal feeling directly connected to her emotional well-being.

Down through the centuries, women have looked to men for protection because it was crucial to their family's survival. This protector role carries over into our generation of relationships, but now, as we've said, it is more linked to emotional security.

Emotional security guarantees that a woman is safe to share her feelings without invalidating argument and interruption from her man. It is the force that frees her to be herself.

It means that she can talk without worrying about hurting him and without reprisal. It means that she can be in a bad mood without her mate's holding it against her or ignoring her.

The Emotional Freedom to Be Herself

Women are under such constant pressure to be loving and sweet that the freedom to be themselves is the greatest gift a man can give them. Even if he doesn't really understand her feelings, the attempt to do so calmly makes her feel powerfully supported.

Sometimes a woman doesn't understand her own feelings until she freely talks about them. If she doesn't have to worry about her man's losing control or withdrawing his love, she is doubly relieved and deeply grateful. Even if she remains upset *with him* after receiving this support, it becomes much easier for her to draw deep from her loving center the strength to forgive and forget.

When I wanted to purchase a computer, through sharing her automatic feeling reactions my wife was able to process emotions—not just about the computer—that had been building up steam over time. By verbally sorting them out, Bonnie was able to shed her emotional resistance and support me.

Generally speaking, when anyone, male or female, has a strong emotional reaction, it is to a combination of many elements, not just the subject at hand.

The Right Time for Problem Solving

After taking Bonnie in my arms, I began to address her questions. Now that she felt heard, it was time to put aside emotions and concentrate on problem solving.

"I've been researching this computer for six months," I began. "It's a great deal. And if I buy it today, I can claim a tax write-off this year. But I've got to get to the store before they close.

"I understand you want things for the house," I assured her. "When I get back, why don't we sit down and plan what *you* want? Sound good?"

"Sounds good," she answered with a smile.

So I got my computer, and Bonnie got refinished floors. Most important, we both got the satisfaction of knowing we had somehow spoken each other's language, fully communicated, and grown together in love.

It's All in the Timing

Timing is essential when offering solutions. I personally discovered that I became most upset with Bonnie when she continued to be emotional or argumentative after I offered suggestions. As a man, I believed my most valued gift to her was to provide a solution. It was like offering my most precious jewel and having the woman I loved reject it.

Gradually I learned that when a woman is upset, she rarely has the ability to appreciate solutions. This is because what she needs then is to be heard, not fixed. In some cases a solution makes matters worse by minimizing or even invalidating her feelings.

Blaming Bonnie for not appreciating my solutions when she is upset and needy would be like blaming a hungry lion for biting my hand after I put it in its mouth. Although I can understand intellectually that there are times when my wife can't fully appreciate my solutions, it still feels like rejection.

The art involved in offering solutions is first to make sure a woman is receptive to attempts to help.

By offering a solution before a woman is ready to hear it, a man is setting himself up to feel rejected—significantly decreasing his ability to continue listening without getting more upset.

Once he is hit, he will almost inevitably be struck again, with each successive emotional blow growing more and more painful. After the third strike, it is advisable to take time out to cool off, think things over, and then resume the conversation when you feel more centered.

The Inner Mechanics of Ducking and Dodging

To some women, the above dialogue might sound like John Gray is this loving guy who can hear his beloved wife because he loves her so much. The truth is that I do love her with all my heart, but in the computer incident, we avoided getting into an ugly argument and a clash of wills because I have spent years practicing the skills of ducking and dodging, and Bonnie has supported me in that process.

In the beginning of our marriage, Bonnie and I would often fight and argue because in essence we weren't speaking the same language. Now, after rewriting our job descriptions and practicing new relationship skills, communication is much, much easier.

When conversations repeatedly turn into fights, one or both partners will eventually begin to close up, and passion will start to fade. When men begin to understand this, they are motivated to listen more. However, without becoming agile at ducking and dodging, it's a hard row to hoe. Men attending my seminars are uniformly grateful for advice on ducking and dodging and always ask for new tips.

Let's revisit "the computer incident," but this time noting the inner reactions and reflexes exercised as ducking and dodging that allowed me to patiently listen and give my wife the consideration and support she deserved. This description of what it takes to be a good listener may astound women and assist them in being more appreciative of what a man goes through. An in-depth understanding can help her to be more accepting and patient when he needs to take a time-out and not talk for a while.

Preparing to Dodge

Before even mentioning the computer, I have to prepare myself for Bonnie's resistance, because every instinct in my body is telling me she'll disapprove. For starters, she doesn't have the same appreciation of electrical gadgets and gizmos that I do.

Her resistance is making the conversation much harder for me to start. In some ways, I feel like a child or a subordinate asking permission. I don't feel very manly; in fact, I feel like a weakling.

I am able to overcome my resistance by reminding myself that I don't need to get her approval, but that I am supporting her by respecting her need to be included in the decision. To feel respected, she needs me to seriously consider any opposition or suggestions she might have.

Although the computer is a purchase exclusively for me to use, Bonnie is my equal partner in life and deserves to be included in any major financial decision. For her to feel equal, she needs me to take her emotions into account.

I plan my words carefully with an eye to keeping them as brief as possible to give her room for whatever reaction she needs to have. After all, I've spent six months working through my resistance, weighing the pros and cons of a new computer—why shouldn't she have some resistance as well? With this preparation, I begin the conversation.

The Importance of Containment

John (casually): "For several months I've been thinking about buying a new computer. I know just what I want, but I also want to include you in the process. How do you feel about it?"

Bonnie (shocked): "*Why* do you need to buy a new computer? You already have one."

I pause and consider her question. Before answering, I "contain" my gut reaction and practice the relationship skill of ducking and dodging. While taking a calming breath, I remind myself, It is OK for her to be upset. It doesn't mean I can't get what I want. I don't need to get upset back. Let her talk. This was a quick duck.

Bonnie: "What's wrong with the computer you already have?"

John: "Hmmm."

At this point I quickly dodge and reassess the situation by thinking that although it sounds as if she is trying to control me, she is not. She is not saying I am wrong for wanting a computer nor is she acting like my mother and telling me I can't buy one. I don't need her permission, but she deserves my consideration.

However, she is upset and needs to talk before she can be more supportive. This may take twenty minutes. It is crucial that I relax, get comfortable, and let her explore her feelings out loud. Although it will sound like blame, it is not. I must not take it personally.

While I am doing my best to dodge, I still feel

like shouting, "How dare you tell me what to do! Why do you have to get upset because I want to buy a computer?" Fortunately, I appreciate the wisdom of containment and duck by not indulging in expressing my gut reaction.

Women Don't Demand Agreement

Men don't realize that an emotionally upset woman is not demanding agreement or submission from him. She just wants to be considered. He mistakenly assumes that he has to fight to be himself when she only wants to feel heard, not stop him or control him.

A man does not instinctively understand this because he is so much more goal oriented.

> **When a man is upset and he talks, then his goal is to get his listener to agree with him so that some problem can be corrected.**

When a woman is upset, she first wants to talk about it and decide later what she thinks should happen. A man mistakenly assumes that he has to give in to her feelings and sacrifice if he wants to please her. He mistakenly concludes that he has to agree with her point of view before she can feel OK again. If he doesn't agree and doesn't want to give in, he feels driven to point out the deficiencies in her argument to get her to agree with him.

Through understanding this difference, a man can contain his tendency to argue when a woman is emotional. When I use my brains instead of my guts, I can easily duck and dodge. This does not mean that I should disregard my gut reactions. They are inevitable. What is required in a relationship is that men control their instincts when they are feeling blamed or attacked and not retaliate.

Certainly there will be times when a man is struck by her words and gets upset. It's only to be expected. A woman can handle a man being upset if he can contain his negative reactions and respond respectfully. As long as he contains his feelings and doesn't lose control by dumping them on her, it counts as support. However, one loose derogatory zinger can undo twenty minutes of attentive support.

When emotions are involved, it is important for men to think before they act. Whenever I contain my reactions and use my brain to respond, both Bonnie and I win. Otherwise, we both lose. I may win the argument, but I will eventually lose her trust.

What Women Admire in Men

A woman admires a man if he has the strength to control his emotions and the sensitivity to consider the merits and validity of what she is saying. He doesn't have to put his tail between his legs and do whatever she wants.

A woman admires a man if he has the strength to control his emotions and the sensitivity to respectfully consider her point of view as a valid perspective.

Women are turned off by passive and submissive men. They don't want to be the boss in an intimate relationship. They want to be equal partners. If a man respects a woman's primary need to be heard, she will respond by becoming equally respectful of his wishes.

Dodging the Challenge

Back to Bonnie and me and the computer. As the conversation continues, she says in a mistrusting tone, "Well! Have you researched the market? How much is this computer going to cost!!?"

I am now livid and silently feel inside, Who is she to doubt my competence? I don't need her telling me how much money to spend on a computer. I don't need another mother!

Before these emotions become real, I make sure to nip them in the bud by remembering my goal—to provide a safe place for her to share whatever feelings she has.

I find it useful to always keep my objective in mind. I need to remember that I am not trying to win a court case. Instead, I am trying to give my wife nurturing support at a moment when she has little to give me.

If I were a litigator, my objective might be to immediately invalidate her credentials. Not only would I attempt to discredit her competence, but I would establish my own competence in the field of computers. After all, I used one and she didn't; in addition, I used to be a computer programmer. How could she dare challenge my authority?

This kind of approach in conversations creates immediate conflict and friction. It may convince a judge, but if a man uses such tactics in his intimate relationship, he'll end up using them next in divorce court.

The worst move a man can make in discussions with a woman is to invalidate her feelings.

Rather Than Be Right, Do the Right Thing

When a woman is emotional, any attempt on a man's part to explain the correctness of his point of view invalidates her feelings. Instead of trying to be right, I attempt to see what is right with her feelings. This way, she will in turn be able to be more supportive of me.

To remain supportive in our conversation, I need to remember that Bonnie isn't intending to discredit me. Interrogation is an automatic reaction when women don't feel safe enough to share their feelings. So, instead of responding, I dodged the missiles of mistrust and remembered that she was caught in the middle of a process and was really not intending to be derogatory about my competence.

Rather than feeling challenged, I have learned to interpret my wife's questions as a plea for me to "hear" her.

When women become emotional, they generally ask questions as a sign that they need to be questioned themselves so that they can explore their feelings.

Bonnie's doubt and fear were less about my competence than about whether or not I was interested in her feelings. This doubt was valid, because on a gut level, I didn't want her to interfere. But on a heart and head level, I do care about her and did want to give her the respect she deserves.

Now let's get back to our dialogue.

The Prime Objective

In response to Bonnie's questions, I reject arguing from my guts in favor of realigning myself with my prime objective, to support and be supported back.

John: "I think that before we talk about the computer we should first talk about how you feel. I want to understand what you are feeling and why you are upset."

This kind of steady focus is required if arguments are to be minimized. Even if a man is practicing new relationship skills and intentionally not solving a woman's problems, her questioning can catch him off guard. Suddenly he is giving answers instead of asking more questions.

The more a man says, the more there is for a woman to question, and the more upset he will become. The more words she speaks, the more heard she can feel and the more appreciated he will be. The technique to remember here is to delay answering questions by asking more questions. Answer her questions by asking her to talk more.

A man will always be tempted to defend his point of view. He instinctively feels that if he could only share *his* understanding of the situation she would feel better. In truth, she will feel better only when he shares in her understanding of a situation. When a woman feels understood and validated, she can relax. Otherwise she feels she has to fight to be heard.

Delayed Solutions

At this point in the computer conversation, I am restraining myself from offering Bonnie solutions. I do not explain that as a writer, I am as dependent on my computer as a cowboy is on his horse. That I love computers and can certainly afford one. That my extensive research has made me certain this model and price is the best deal around. Or that because it's a business write-off that I could use this year, I'm actually saving money by buying it today. But all of these arguments are futile until I first find out what is really upsetting her.

If she wasn't upset and needing to talk when I told her about the computer, she would simply have said, "Really. You want another computer. What kind of features does it have?" As she listened for a while, quite naturally she might say, "What is it going to cost, what do your magazines say about it," et cetera, and I would discuss it with her.

On this day, however, she isn't responding in such a cheerful way. To avoid making things worse at such times, I have learned never to get logical and try to have a solution-oriented technical conversation.

When a woman is upset, it is extremely difficult for her to appreciate a man's explanations, or indeed his entire rational approach.

Ducking the Generalizations

To my question about her feelings, Bonnie replies, "Well, I am upset. Whenever you want something, you just go out and get it. I don't know why you have to get another computer. Yours works fine. If we are going to spend money, there are other things we could spend it on."

When she acknowledges that she is upset, my inner voice goes: Yes! Now I can get her to talk about it, and soon she will feel better. Be careful, John, don't correct anything she says, silently listen. Remember, feelings are not to be taken literally. They are poetic expressions to indicate one's passing emotions. They are not intended to be taken as factual statements. Nor are they about me.

Whenever Bonnie begins to use incorrect statements or make sweeping generalizations, I relax because it is a clear reminder to me that we are not having an intellectual or factual conversation. She is expressing the need to feel heard. When she eventually feels heard, the resistant feelings pass away.

Most men fear that if they don't correct a woman's statements, she will continue holding on to them as fact. This is true in court but not in a relationship. In a courtroom, if she said, "Whenever you want something, you just go out and get it," I would be required to point out the incorrectness of her statement. I would defend myself by reminding her of all the things that I want that I don't get. I would point out to her all the times I had sacrificed my wishes for her. While this may be the way the wheels of justice turn, it will not work in an intimate relationship.

Explaining that I also make sacrifices—such as

waiting six months to buy the computer—would only confirm that I didn't understand her general feelings. It would also stimulate her need to talk about her sacrifices. Before we knew it, we would be arguing about which of us sacrifices the most.

Ask Friendly Questions

As the computer conversation continues, Bonnie completes her comments by saying, "There are other things we could spend our money on." She pauses. This is my opportunity to be civil and ask what she thinks we should buy.

When she pauses, I have a choice. I can ask a question in a friendly or at least neutral tone to draw her out more. Or I can undo everything I have accomplished by asking something condemning like "How can you say that?"

What most men don't understand is that the more a woman feels the right to be upset, the less upset she will be. If a man doesn't criticize her for being critical, or blame her for blaming him, he gives her an opportunity to release any criticism or blame she may be harboring.

Why Men Argue with Feelings

Men assume that an emotional woman is inflexible in her thinking. They don't realize that at such a time, when a woman talks about her feelings she is not making conclusions or expressing fixed opinions.

When a woman shares negative emotions, she is generally in the middle of the process of discovering what she feels to be true. She is not stating an objective fact.

She talks to "discover" the range of feelings within herself—not to give an accurate description of objective reality. That's what men do. Instead, she is more concerned with discovering and describing what is going on in her subjective, inner world.

Meanwhile, I'm waiting for Bonnie to answer my question about what *she* feels we should buy instead of the computer, but she's still in the midst of discovering what her feelings are. Finally, she tells me, "It's not that I have this all thought out. It's just a feeling. I feel like you get exactly what you want and I get seconds. Maybe I'm mad that you want so much more than I do. When I want something, it doesn't seem so earthshaking."

I realize that "It's not that I have this all thought out" means she's still talking feelings, not facts. But even with her help, I'm still struggling to dodge and duck from feeling criticized and unappreciated. Inwardly, I'm fuming.

How can you say you get seconds? I silently demand. I do so many things for you. I work hard so that you can have practically anything you want. How do you have the nerve to even suggest you're not important to me! Although these are my true gut reactions, I thoroughly appreciate how counterproductive it would be to express them.

If I were to "tell her what I think of her," it would only be to try to convince her that she is wrong or is being very unfair. I would succeed only in invalidating her feelings and confirming her doubts and mistrust. But by listening without attacking her, I am giving her the time and opportunity to talk more, remember the good things about me, and let go of the negative comments *on her own*. Despite my resentment, I'm convinced that she soon will.

When a woman has a chance to share her feelings freely, she begins to feel more loving. Sometimes she may realize how wrong, incorrect, or unfair her statements sounded, but in most cases she just forgets them as she begins to see things from a more loving perspective.

It's hard for men to relate readily to this mood change because it's foreign to their natures and they just can't fathom it. When a man is upset and talks with the person who is upsetting him, he tends to remain upset unless that person agrees with him in some significant way or until he can find a solution. Simply listening to him and nodding your head in sympathy is not enough if he is really upset.

After a woman shares a negative feeling, a man mistakenly takes it as her "final" conclusion and thinks she is blaming him. He doesn't know that her feelings will change if he just lets her talk them out.

Why Men Feel Blamed

Quite commonly in counseling, a woman will share her feelings and a man will feel attacked and blamed. This is how it goes:

He says: "You're blaming me."
She says: "No I'm not. I'm only sharing my feelings."

He then says: "But your feelings tell me you *are* blaming me. When you say you feel ignored, you're saying I'm not attentive. When you say you don't feel loved, you're accusing me."

She then says: "No I'm not. I'm just talking about how *I* feel. I am not saying something about *you*."

He says: "Yes you are! I'm the only one you are married to."

She says: "I can't talk to you."

He says: "There you go again blaming me for how you feel."

Without some intervention, they will go on arguing until they give up in frustration.

Men must understand what is really going on inside a woman when she sounds blaming. On the flip side, a woman can make communication much easier by appreciating why her partner imagines that she is blaming him.

As men begin to comprehend the female thinking and feeling process, they will see that from the woman's viewpoint, she really isn't blaming them.

For years I couldn't comprehend this when I was listening to my wife. It was really hard to dodge when I felt repeatedly blamed. While she shared her feelings, I would feel an urgent need to argue with her. Then one day all that changed. It was a realization that occurred while I accompanied her on a little shopping excursion.

As I observed my wife shopping, I noticed a striking difference between us. When I shopped, I found what I wanted, bought it, and got out as quickly as possible, like a hunter making a kill and hurrying home with it. Bonnie, however, was very happy trying on many outfits.

When she finally settled on a shop that interested her, I was relieved and parked myself in a chair by the dressing room. She was very excited about several outfits. I was very excited because not only would she be happy but we could finally leave. How wrong I was!

Instead of simply buying an outfit or two quickly, she took what seemed like years trying on each one to get a feel for it. As she preened in the mirror, she made comments like, "This one's sort of cute, isn't it? I'm not sure though. Is it really me? The colors are good. I really love the length."

Finally she announced, "No, it's not me." This scene was repeated with outfit after outfit. Sometimes before changing out of one, she would say firmly, "I like this one."

After forty-five minutes of this, we left without her buying anything. To my surprise, she wasn't the least bit frustrated. I could not ever imagine putting that much time and energy into the hunt, coming home empty-handed, and still being happy.

How to Dodge Blame

As I reflected on that incident, I realized that this was the key to understanding why a woman sounds blaming when she claims she is not.

You see, an overwhelmed woman talks about her feelings the way she shops. She is not expecting you to buy a particular feeling any more than she is necessarily going to buy it herself. She is basically trying on emotional outfits to see if they fit. Just because she takes a lot of time trying on an outfit or testing an emotion doesn't mean it's "her."

> **Women who share their feelings are not committed to those feelings but are in the process of discovering what really fits. Just because a woman says something, it doesn't mean she's going to take it home and wear it forever.**

Now, in the spirit of fairness, when my wife seems to blame me I pretend that we're shopping and she is just beginning to try things on. It may be an hour before we actually "leave the store," but only then can I know what she finally believes.

Negative Feelings Are Not Permanent

It is easier to dodge a woman's resistant feelings and not feel blamed if a man remembers that her feelings are not permanent and that she is just trying them on for size. If he argues with her, she will become defensive. Having to protect herself prevents her from getting immediately to the place where she can return her negative feelings to the rack and "buy" more positive ones.

Women speak negatives out loud to discover the positive, loving, and more accurate picture of what happened. Even if some mistake was made by the man, as she lets go of negative feelings, she is able to see the bigger picture and remember all the good he does as well.

Articulating negatives helps women accept men and love them just the way they are without expecting or even depending on them to be perfect. To find real love that does not demand perfection, a woman needs a man's support so that she can express her feelings without being held accountable for every word she utters.

Feelings need to be expressed in a free and fluid way if a woman is to find the love in her heart.

Feelings Are Not Facts

When a man expresses a feeling, it is more like a fact—something he believes to be true but doesn't have a lot of objective evidence to back up. This is not what a woman means when she shares her feelings. For women, feelings are much less about the outer world and more about their *experience* of the outer world. For women, feelings and facts are very different animals.

Bonnie's comment that "It feels like everything we do is for you and not me. We always do what you want to do and you always get your way" sounded like a critical comment about me. I heard her saying "You are selfish and you only care about yourself. You don't care about me. We only do what you want to do." I dodged by remembering that her feelings were not facts about me. When I can remember this, it helps her to remember it. I also felt assured because I knew that when a woman can expand, dramatize, or intensify her feelings about a situation and feel heard, she eventually can and will begin to see the positive facts more clearly on her own.

How to Duck Criticism

To duck Bonnie's criticism I needed to remember that she really didn't intend her words to be a statement of fact. Her feelings were not a final critical statement about me and my actions. Translated into a language I could understand, she said:

"Sometimes when I am emotional and not thinking clearly, like right now, I forget what a wonderful guy you are and all the times you are there for me and begin to feel *as if* everything we do is for you and not me. It is *as if* we always do what you want to do. I feel *as if* I can't ask for what I want because you don't care. I know you really do care, but this is how I react *sometimes,* particularly when, like today, you really want something. When you really want something, you are so clear about it that it feels *as if* we are not partners anymore, and no matter what I would say, it wouldn't count. I really know I do matter to you, but these feelings do come up. Your consideration of my feelings would make me feel really good right now. Would you reassure me that I do count and that you do care about me by listening to my feelings?"

To expect her actually to say all that is unrealistic. It would go against her feminine nature to be extremely rational, logical, and objectively accurate when she is in the process of exploring, sharing, and releasing negative emotions.

**A man who doesn't demand masculine
pinpoint accuracy from an emotional
woman allows her to reach objectivity
with greater love, trust, acceptance,
and appreciation.**

To dodge criticism successfully, a man needs to remember that all feelings are temporary. By listening to a woman's negative emotions, he allows her the opportunity to discover her positive feelings as well. In return, a woman can help *him* duck and dodge by making supportive comments. These comments we will explore more thoroughly in the next chapter.

Feelings Change

Another tip for successful dodging is to remember that negative feelings can shift 180 degrees in just a few minutes without a man's saying anything. If a man reacts in a negative way to a woman's negative feelings, she doesn't feel understood and must continue explaining those feelings before she can move on. Reacting in a negative way only prolongs the process.

It is not a contradiction—in fact, it's perfectly normal—for a woman to say in a single conversation "I feel like you only care about yourself" *and* "You really are a very caring person, you give me so much support."

Once aware of a woman's inherent flexibility, a man can relax and listen instead of focusing on how to change her mind. When a man doesn't know how to dodge, he resists by "spilling his guts," which in turn forces a woman to lose her flexibility and become closed, rigid, and righteous.

Disarming by Asking More Questions

Whenever a man asks a woman questions, he sends her the *disarming* and soothing message that he cares and that he is there for her. By asking questions or making statements like "How can I help you?" or "Tell me more," he releases her from feeling she's fighting an uphill battle. You'll find a list of "disarming" questions in chapter 7.

You win by asking more, you lose by talking about your gut reactions.

The secret of supporting a woman who feels upset or overwhelmed is to help her work through her feelings by getting her to speak more words—negative or positive, accurate or inaccurate, defensive or vulnerable. The more words he can hear and dodge, the more she will feel heard and seen, which will shift her attitude back toward love.

Bottom-Line Advice for Men to Support a Woman

Remember, if a woman doesn't have to focus on getting a man to listen to her, she can do what is most natural for her—talking and shifting her *own* attitude. To support her in feeling more loving and accepting, here is some bottom-line advice for men:

1. When you suspect she is upset, don't wait for her to initiate the conversation (when you initiate, it takes away 50 percent of her emotional charge).
2. As you let her talk, keep reminding yourself that it doesn't help to get upset with her for being upset.
3. Whenever you feel an urgent need to interrupt or correct, don't.
4. When you don't know what to say, say nothing. If you can't say something positive or respectful, keep quiet.
5. If she won't talk, ask more questions until she does.
6. Whatever you do, don't correct or judge her feelings.
7. Remain as calm and centered as possible, and keep a lock on your strong reactions. (If you lose control and "spill your guts" even for a moment, you lose and have to start all over at a disadvantage.)

Just as ducking, dodging, and disarming are all fighting skills, so also is delivering. In a real fight, a man needs to wait and watch for the right moment to deliver his punch and make contact. In a loving conversation, a man needs to apply this same skill. He needs to watch and wait for the right moment to deliver a word or phrase of support that will end the battle.

In a loving conversation, a man needs to apply the warrior skill of delivering.

During the computer conversation, after hearing many of Bonnie's feelings I waited for her natural pause to ask her what she wanted. By supporting her in expressing desire—even if she doesn't know yet what she wants—I open her to feeling my desire to support her.

Asking her what she wants doesn't mean I have to give up what I want. It does mean that I will have to expand my awareness to see how I can support her wishes as well as mine. It shows her that I consider her needs as seriously as my own. This kind of equal respect is a soothing ointment that nurtures her wounded female soul.

What It Means to Understand Feelings

To illustrate my next point, let's again return to the computer conversation. As Bonnie expresses her feelings, I am waiting to deliver another supportive statement to assure her that I'm on her side. After she says she's afraid she can't get what she wants, it's easy to support her.

I say, "I can understand that feeling."

By saying I understood, I didn't mean that I agreed with her fear. I was not saying "Yeah, you should be afraid of never getting what you want. You are married to a real selfish guy!"

By saying "I understand that feeling," I was really saying "I understand what it is like to feel afraid of not getting what you want. I have certainly felt that way at times in my life. It is painful and uncomfortable."

During an emotional conversation, a man needs to be alert and ready to offer simple gestures of his support, like nodding his head in agreement, giving her a hug, or making sympathetic sounds.

The Importance of Eye Contact

When women are upset, they want to be seen. Unlike men, they don't want to be ignored or left alone. The most important thing a man can do is to notice when his partner is upset. When she feels seen, she can more directly see herself and more efficiently explore her feelings.

When a man listens, his basic tendency is to look away in order to think about what is being said. It is hard for women to understand this difference because when they talk about their feelings with each other, they instinctively deliver their support by lots of eye contact.

If a man simply stares into a woman's eyes when she talks about feelings, his mind will start to go blank and he will space out. Without understanding that a woman needs more eye contact than he does, a man tends to look away to figure out what his partner means or how he is going to respond.

Learning to maintain eye contact not only delivers a very important kind of support but also helps a man to check his reaction to attempt immediately to offer a solution to her problems. The trick for a man is not only to remember to do it, but to do it without going blank.

This can be accomplished if he looks in a special way. Instead of staring, he should first look in her eyes for two to three seconds. Then, when he would naturally turn his head and look away, he should instead look to the tip of her nose. After that, he should look at her lips, then her chin, and then her whole face. Then he should start over.

This procedure keeps him looking in her direction and yet frees him from spacing out or going blank. It can also be relaxing because it is something else he can do instead of passively doing nothing.

Cold Fronts

When I notice a cold front coming from my wife's direction, my old approach to making her feel better was to assume that she needed space to be alone. After a while I would notice that it was getting colder and colder, and the chill was definitely directed toward me. I would grumble to myself that I didn't deserve Bonnie's cold shoulder and inwardly begin getting furious. Eventually we would negatively interact and sparks would fly.

Once I understood more about women, I no longer sat around ignoring my wife when she was cold and getting angrier as she grew more distant.

It eventually occurred to me that by giving her more space, I was only making things worse. I finally realized that Bonnie didn't want more space but wanted more contact and attention. Most of the time when I was feeling the cold front, it was not even about me—she just needed to talk in order to warm up. But when I didn't notice and come over to touch her and ask questions in a caring manner, it just made her more cold and distant. So, even though her feelings weren't initially about me, they soon became so.

Now I cope with cold fronts by preparing myself to put on a warm jacket and fly straight into the storm. By touching her and initiating a conversation, I know she will eventually warm up to me without my having to do anything else but dodge, duck, disarm, and deliver.

How to Warm Up a Cold Woman

Now when I sense a coldness coming from Bonnie, I immediately go up and touch her.

If she doesn't pull back when I make physical contact, I know that her distress is not about me. If she does pull back, I realize that I'm going to need to duck and dodge a lot more, but I also know she'll get back to loving me even more.

I touch not only to defuse her anger, but also to check the temperature. If she is really angry with me, I find out and ask the appropriate questions. If she isn't, I simply relax from needing to duck and dodge. To initiate conversation, I ask her how her day was or if she's upset with me. A complete list of questions to ask are detailed in chapter 7.

In most cases, a woman will respond to these questions with "Oh, it's not you. There is just so much going on," and will then continue to talk. Even if she *was* a little upset with her mate, she will quickly tend to dismiss those feelings because he's initiated the conversation. When she feels supported, she can be very generous with her love.

If an overwhelmed woman says "It's not you" before she begins talking about what's bothering her, it's much easier for a man to listen.

What to Do When She Is Angry with Him

When a woman is angry with a man, the most powerful message he can send her is that she has a right to be angry, that it is safe for her to be angry, and that he wants to understand what he did to upset her so that he can stop doing it.

When I touch Bonnie and she remains cold or pulls away, the most important thing for me to remember is not to be hurt or offended by her rejection. Since I'm testing the temperature, I am prepared for a possible rejection. If I were not prepared, I would instinctually react with anger.

Let's look at another example. One day I was feeling a cold front that had been building for several hours. I truly had no idea what it was about. The old me would have reacted by feeling unappreciated and unfairly denied. Instead, I knew how to quickly nip it in the bud by giving her a chance to talk about it.

When I touched her, she immediately pulled away. But instead of stalking off, I summoned up my relationship skills and didn't take her action personally. I continued to stand there, and look in her direction, wondering what was bothering her. As it worked out, it took at least fifteen to thirty seconds for her to even realize that she had rejected me. Since I didn't react negatively, it was easy to rebuild trust.

I now knew for certain that she was angry with me. To protect myself from feeling hurt by her anger and blame, I was careful not to ask a question like "Are you upset with me?" or "Did I do something wrong?" To protect myself from getting hurt, it was best to at least start out with a question that didn't directly link me to her anger.

The Power of Gentle Persistence

The most effective neutral question to ask at times like this is: "Do you want to talk about something?" If the answer is no, it is easy to dodge because deep inside I can easily understand her not wanting to talk.

I say, "I really want to understand what happened." Again I am careful not to open myself up to much of her anger.

She pauses and says, "There's not much to say." That tells me that there is a lot to say. I begin preparing myself to duck and dodge.

My objective is to gently persist in my goal of being there for her. By holding my ground without demanding more, I earn her respect, and she gets the message that I really care.

When women don't want to talk, it is generally because they don't feel safe, don't feel you care, or feel that you won't understand. This resistance can only be overcome with gentle persistence.

Bearing that in mind, I say, "Is it something I said or did?"

Her response is a deep inhalation and a long sigh, indicating that she really doesn't want to talk about it.

I say, "If it is, I really want to know," then, after pausing, "If I hurt you, I want to know what I did so that I won't do it again."

At this point she opens up and gently replies, "The other day when we were talking, you answered the phone right in the middle of what I was saying. Afterward, you didn't even ask me to finish the thought. I felt really hurt."

I say, "I'm sorry, that was insensitive of me." Although a surge of explanations come up, I quickly push them away and reach out to touch her shoulder. This time she receives it.

Bonnie proceeds to talk about her feelings, and after a while we feel very close again. I would never have known how to do this years ago. How could I? Nobody ever taught me. But now that I am "working" according to a new job description based on new relationship skills, I know better.

What It Takes to Duck and Dodge

Once you've mastered the elements of these new relationship skills, it only takes a few moments to discern how to use them. It's similar to hitting a tennis ball or golf ball—a lot of practice goes into developing the swing, but once learned, it's practically automatic.

Learning to listen is similar to learning any new skill. When you first drive a stick shift, for example, the mechanism seems very complex. After practice, though, a seasoned driver doesn't even think about shifting because the process becomes a series of reflex actions.

For a man, learning to listen attentively without getting upset or frustrated when a woman is upset is definitely a new and difficult skill. However, with a lot of practice it can easily become second nature.

If Only Our Fathers Had Known

If a man could have repeatedly observed his father listen to his mother hundreds of times while growing up, he wouldn't need intimate job retraining. But because our fathers and mothers did not know about new relationship skills, all of us have to learn these techniques.

In future generations, when our children have a chance to grow up watching their parents model these communication skills, they won't have to work on them so hard in their relationships.

Until that time, if men are to learn this important skill, the assistance of women is invaluable. In my own experience, the element that has helped me to learn most quickly is my wife's cooperation and support. By not expecting me to be perfect and by letting me know when I was helpful, she made my way easier.

In the next chapter, we will explore advanced relationship skills that women can use to assist men in being successful listeners. By drawing on ancient nurturing skills, they can learn how to love and nurture a man without mothering him. Women will learn to apply the skills of unconditional love that are so natural to women, while at the same time making sure that they get the love and support they themselves need.

CHAPTER 6

Feminine Skills for Talking So a Man Will Listen

WHEN WOMEN ADDRESS men as they have always talked to other women, men either don't get it or just stop listening. It is as if women were speaking a different language that men tend to misunderstand. A woman can greatly assist a man in learning her language by making a few small but significant changes in her communication style.

By learning to pause and prepare a man before sharing her feelings, a woman immediately begins getting the kind of support she most needs.

**By making clear up front how she
wants him to support her, she can relax
and share her feelings without having
to worry about upsetting him
or losing his attention.**

This formula for talking so that a man will listen can be as simple as saying the following phrase:

"You don't have to say anything or do anything, I just need to talk about my feelings in order to feel better."

Through first pausing and then preparing him in this way, he doesn't feel an obligation to offer suggestions or think up solutions to make her feel better. Instead of focusing on attempting to solve her problems while she is talking, he can relax and really listen. By doing less, he can actually give her the emotional support she is really looking for.

Talking in a logical and focused manner is primarily how men communicate and business is done. For eight hours each day to varying degrees, a working woman is required to express herself in this way. If she limits herself to talking "Male," a man may listen more, but it pulls her away from her femininity.

When a woman gets home, her first priority is finding the balance to be feminine again. However, if she abruptly begins talking "Female" and tries to share her feelings without clear guidelines, it will inevitably ruin her intimate relationships. Eventually, she will either give up on men or close down the feminine part of her that needs to talk. Both such courses are disastrous to her happiness and fulfillment.

To relax and connect back to her warm, loving, feminine feelings after being combative, competitive, efficient, and goal oriented during the day, a woman needs the freedom, permission, and support in her relationships to communicate her feelings in a non-goal-oriented, nonlogical, nonaccurate, and nonrational way.

To recuperate from her day, she needs to freely expand through expressing her feelings. If she is always editing them to make sure they are correct, accurate, and presented in a logical manner, she stays in her male side. Without understanding what a woman requires to nurture her female side, men become overly frustrated with a woman's need to talk in a feminine way.

A man does not instinctively know this because his male side is nurtured when he talks in a focused, direct, clear, logical, and goal-oriented manner after a lot of silent thought, consideration, and deliberation. He doesn't realize that to demand this focused approach from his partner is counterproductive and will inevitably prevent her from being feminine.

A New Dilemma

The contemporary woman is faced with a new dilemma. Either she trains herself to talk like a man and loses a part of herself as well as an essential source of happiness, or she disregards a man's resistance and lets it loose. In response to her free expression of feelings, he stops listening, and she eventually loses his love and support. Since neither approach works, it's fortunate that there is another way.

Traditionally, women didn't depend on men for nurturing conversations, nor were they required to talk like men throughout the day. If a woman had to be more linear when she occasionally talked with a man, it was OK because she had the whole day to talk in an expanded female style.

Women today have a much greater need to talk in a "Female" way with their male partners because they are deprived of it at work.

The need to communicate with men is a new challenge for both women and men. By applying new feminine skills, a woman can greatly assist a man in listening to her feelings. Once a man is prepared, a woman can relax and let go. This is the secret. By her saying a few words, a man can be conditioned to effectively deal with her different style of communicating. Even if her words would normally sound critical and blaming to a man in "Male" language, even if he is not yet good at ducking and dodging, if he is prepared correctly he can even handle a direct hit.

The Great Houdini

My favorite example of a man's need to be prepared comes from the life of the great Houdini.

The magician Harry Houdini offered the challenge that he could get out of anything. He was an escape artist. He became famous for getting out of chained boxes, straitjackets, bank safes, and jails. The second challenge he made is less well known.

He made the challenge that anyone, no matter how big they were, could punch him in the stomach and he wouldn't be hurt by it. He could take any punch.

One Halloween night during the intermission of his magic show, a young college student came backstage and asked, "Is it true that you can take any punch?"

Houdini said, "Yes."

Before Houdini had a chance to prepare himself, the student gave him a quick jab. It was that quick punch that killed the great Houdini. He was rushed to the hospital but died the next day.

Like Houdini, a man can handle a woman's verbal punches if he is prepared and can, in a sense, tighten his stomach muscles so that he doesn't get hurt. If he is not prepared, then he is overly vulnerable and can easily be hurt.

There are a variety of ways in which a woman can prepare a man so that he can hear what she is saying without getting bruised. In this chapter I will suggest some that may be appropriate for you and some that may not be. As time passes, other ways of preparing may feel more appropriate as you and your mate grow into them.

Trying on Different Outfits

Treat these suggestions as if they were different outfits that you might like to wear. Try them, see if they fit, and if you like them, then check them out with your partner to see if your partner likes them as well. Take your pick.

I suggest the following examples as a springboard for developing other expressions as well. Once you get the hang of it, it will become a natural way of supporting the person you love most in your life. Eventually you will find yourself integrating these advanced relationship skills into all your relationships.

Giving a Man His Job Description

When a woman talks, a man commonly does not know what is required of him. Listening is difficult for him because he misunderstands what is expected or what she is really saying in her language. If he is not skilled in ducking and dodging, the more he *cares*, the more he will feel hit by what sounds like criticism in "male talk."

> It is much easier for a man to duck and dodge in the business arena because he does not interact with such an open caring of others. In his romantic relationships, he is much more open and vulnerable, so when he gets hit he is much more hurt.

A woman's new task is to casually let him know what she needs before she begins to talk. By clearly giving him a job description in a language that he can understand, he can relax and not exert himself in trying to figure out what she wants. This is a new twist for a woman, but once learned it frees her to express her power as a woman in a new way.

Using Old Skills in a New Way

Although it has a new twist, "preparing" is really an ancient feminine skill at which women are very adept. Their instinctive nature demands that they prepare. While cavemen focused on the day's hunt, cavewomen prepared for the future.

There is an intuitive knowing in women that acknowledges that everything grows naturally in small steps when the right conditions are created and patiently nurtured. Her instinctive motto is: An ounce of prevention is worth a pound of cure.

Until now, a woman's traditional daily responsibilities reflected this tendency to prepare. Each day she would think ahead to plan and prepare meals for her family. To create a nurturing setting for herself and the family, she would prepare the home to make it as beautiful and uplifting as possible. To grow a garden, she would first prepare the ground before planting the seeds.

As mothers, women have always taken the time to prepare their children for the world, step by step. In guiding a child to play independently, a mother will first set up the appropriate toys or set the conditions. To prepare the child to read, *she* will read to the child. Through "preparing" a nurturing setting she knows that the child will automatically grow and flourish.

Traditionally, women put much more attention in how they dress and appear. When a women gets dressed, she instinctively takes more time to prepare so that her personal expression is appropriate to the event or setting. Preparing her face with the right makeup, preparing her skin because it is more sensitive, and wearing ornaments on her body to attract the appropriate attention are all expressions of this tendency to prepare.

Even biologically women require more preparation. To birth a baby, she prepares for nine months. To fully enjoy sex, her body requires much more time, stimulation, and preparation. Particularly before the convenient availability of sanitary napkins, a woman had to prepare in advance for her menstrual cycle.

Traditionally, a woman prepared herself for marriage by remaining a virgin. Before having sex and thus having a baby, she prepared herself by making sure that her partner was committed to her and could provide for her. Even life insurance is an ancient female ritual of preparation. In ancient days, she prepared herself for the possibility of her husband's death by maintaining a positive image in the community.

Women are always preparing. It is their nature, and they are good at it. One of their great hidden frustrations is that they do not know how to prepare a man to listen. Without a clear understanding of how men speak "Male" and not "Female," a woman cannot intuit the necessity of preparing to have a conversation. She naively assumes that if he loves her, he will instinctively understand her language.

Even so, women do prepare a man to listen but generally in instinctive ways that would work with other women but not with men. She mistakenly assumes that if she asks him lots of questions about his day, he will be prepared to listen to her. This kind of preparing doesn't work.

Preparing a man to listen is a new skill for women.

Just as men can extend their ancient warrior skills to duck and dodge, a woman can transform an ancient feminine art into a new relationship skill by learning to prepare a man to listen.

Times have changed so that even a well-meaning, intelligent man doesn't know what a woman really needs. While she talks, he will consistently offer a string of comments, corrections, and solutions. In response, she will say "You don't understand."

Misunderstanding is one of the most common complaints women have about men. It is so worn that when a man hears it, he immediately gets defensive, because in "Male," she is saying that he is stupid and thus incapable of helping her.

This phrase "You don't understand" is so automatic to a woman that she has no idea that she is preventing a man from giving her the support she needs. Not only does this phrase sound like criticism, but it doesn't make any sense to him.

He feels that what he is doing demonstrates that he does understand what she is saying, and to maintain his pride he is willing to fight to prove it. Although he started out to help, he ends up wanting to argue.

How to Get a Man to Listen

When a woman says "You don't understand," she really means "You don't understand that right now I *don't* need a solution."

He, however, hears that she doesn't appreciate his solution and then gets hooked into arguing about the validity of his approach and explaining himself at a time when she only needs to talk.

If a woman wants to get a man to understand what she really needs, she should avoid ever saying "You don't understand," even when she means it, because the phrase is so accusatory that it is hard for a man to hear her.

However, here's an alternative. First, pause and consider that he is doing his best to understand and then say "Let me try saying that in a different way."

When a man hears this phrase, it also conveys the message that the man has not fully understood her, but in a noncritical way. He is much more willing to listen and reconsider what she is saying. He does not feel criticized or blamed, and as a result is more eager to support her. Without understanding what makes men tick, it would be nearly impossible for a woman to figure out that a man would greatly prefer to hear "Let me try saying this in a different way" to "You don't understand." To a man, however, the difference is so obvious that he would never think to suggest it.

The Wisdom of Pausing and Preparing

When a man is offering solutions and a woman wants just to be heard, advanced relationship skills are available that do not offend him, through which she can assist him in giving her the support she wants. By learning how to "pause" and then "prepare" him to listen she can continue without getting interrupted by his solutions.

The sooner a woman makes it clear that she doesn't need a solution, the easier it will be for her mate to shift gears from the "fixing" mode to the "hearing" mode. For example, if a man has been listening and offering solutions for twenty minutes and the woman then pauses to let him know that she doesn't need his solutions, he will feel foolish, unappreciated, and defensive.

Sometimes, when my wife, Bonnie, is talking about her problems, I begin offering little solutions.

Even though I teach new relationship skills, I sometimes forget to duck and dodge.

Instead of expressing an immediate reaction like "You don't understand" or "You're not listening," she pauses and prepares me to support her. Instead of focusing on what I am doing wrong, she just reminds me of what I am supposed to be doing. This strategy is definitely a new relationship skill.

She says in a very casual matter-of-fact way, "Oh, you don't have to solve this, I just need to talk about it. I'm already starting to feel better. I think I just need to feel heard."

She does this in the same tone of voice as one might use with a dinner guest who after dinner starts washing the dishes. In that situation a gracious host would automatically say, "Oh, you don't have to bother cleaning up, I'll get to it later. It's no big deal. Let's just go in the living room."

When she gently reminds me in this way of my new job requirements, I am very happy to make the shift to support her more. When a woman uses this kind of casual tone when she reminds a man, she thereby minimizes his mistake and allows him to easily continue listening.

Helping a Man to Listen

Once, after listening to Bonnie for about ten minutes, I began to look pretty beat-up. When I first came home I felt wonderful, but after hearing her complain about her life for ten minutes, I felt like a complete failure. I also felt "bummed out" because I thought she was really unhappy and that there was little I could do to change it.

She eventually noticed how down I appeared and told me, "You look the way I felt."

This was a revelation for me, because I had no idea that she was feeling better.

"You mean you felt this way but you don't anymore?" I asked.

She said, "Yes, I feel much better now. I'm sorry you had to get bummed out, but I do feel much better."

I too suddenly felt much better. I told her, "Well, if you feel better, then I guess I do too. I thought we were destined to have a really awful evening."

I think that on an emotional level I was feeling we were destined to have an awful life. Bonnie's giving me a little positive feedback about how helpful my listening had been completely changed my mood.

Consequently, the next time we talked it was dramatically easier for me to listen without feeling defeated. Each time we talked *and* I experienced that she was happier as a result, it became easier the next time.

Helping Her to Pause with Reality Checks

I remember another time when Bonnie seemed really upset with me and said things like "I feel like you never spend time with me anymore. Your work is more important than me. We used to be so much happier. I feel like things are just getting worse." These were hard words to hear, but I just kept ducking and dodging. I remembered that she was not talking about me but was just exploring what was really upsetting her.

At a certain point, in order to avoid feeling hit

and getting even more upset, I helped her to pause by making a reality check. I said, "It's starting to sound like I do nothing right. Is there anything that has gotten better? Do I do anything right?"

In that moment she said, "Oh, yes, in the past I would never have been able to talk like this. I feel so much safer with you. I just need to get this out, and then I will feel so much better. I know this is hard for you, and I really appreciate it."

I said, "OK, tell me more." All I needed was to be reminded that her feelings were not directed at me as criticism.

One time she paused in the middle of a feeling conversation and said, "I know these feelings sound really unfair, I just need to express them and then I can easily let go of them. OK?"

Instantly I was able to relax and listen without feeling defensive. I said, "Thanks. Sounds good to me." It made a world of difference because she took a moment to pause and prepare me to listen.

Women in general are very unaware of how a few simple words can make a huge difference for men.

It Sounds Worse Than It Is

Another time in the middle of a difficult conversation she said, "I know this must be hard for you. I just need to talk about it. It sounds a lot worse than it is. It really isn't a big deal to me. I just want you to know what goes on inside me."

Those words, "It sounds a lot worse than it is" or "It really isn't a big deal," were like honey to a bee. Although a man should never say to a woman "It's not such a big deal," if a woman feels safe to share her feelings, and if she feels that he makes her feelings a big deal, then she can comfortably say "It's not such a big deal."

For many women, this saying of "It's not such a big deal" would be counterproductive, particularly if while growing up they repeatedly got the message that their feelings were not a big deal. However, as an adult, when she experiences her feelings being respected and considered, then it becomes easier to make the kind of comments that assist a man in listening.

As a woman begins to understand men she realizes that a man will make her feelings much more important if she doesn't demand it. By preparing a man by saying "It's not really a big deal. I just want you to consider how I feel," he will listen much more attentively than before.

At other times when a woman wants to initiate conversation, a good technique to use to prepare the man to listen is to say "I have a lot of feelings coming up, and I would like to talk about them. I just want you to know in advance that it sounds worse than it is. I just need to talk for a while and feel that you care. You don't have to say anything or do anything differently." This kind of approach will actually motivate him to think about how he might make changes to support you more.

What to Say When He Resists Listening

When a woman senses in advance that a man is going to resist what she is about to say, there are new ways to prepare him so that he can more easily duck and dodge. One woman told me that she just says to her husband, "Thanks for helping me here, I really appreciate your trying to duck and dodge what I'm saying. I know it must be hard to hear."

This is a great advanced relationship skills technique because many times, once a man is acknowledged for doing something difficult, he is happy to accept the job. A woman commonly takes for granted that a man should listen if he loves her. She doesn't instinctively understand how difficult it is for him to hear negative feedback from the person he cares most about. The expectation that he should easily hear and understand her because he loves her actually makes it harder for him to listen. When, however, she begins to acknowledge the difficulty, he is much more willing to do what it takes to listen.

At work, a man is happy to do a difficult job if he is paid accordingly. If, however, he is asked to take on a more difficult task and is not acknowledged or compensated for it, he begins to feel taken for granted, and as a result resists doing more. Likewise in a relationship, if a man is required to do something difficult, he wants his efforts to be appreciated; otherwise he may feel, Why bother? Let's look at a common example.

Pearl and Marty

Frustrated that her husband, Marty, "commonly missed exits," Pearl felt justified in giving him unsolicited

advice on how to drive. She had little idea of why this
so totally turned him off. She could see his resistance,
but she thought it was stupid and childish. So she
continued giving driving instructions, and he continued hating it.

After taking one of my seminars, Pearl realized
her mistakes. "I understand now that I should just let
him drive and learn from his own mistakes," she
shared. "I didn't realize before that this is a way I
could give him the love he needs. But what about
me? What if we are going to my daughter's wedding
and we are late because he takes the wrong turns?
Can't I ever tell him how to drive?"

The answer to her question is yes. Pearl can give
him advice, but extremely sparingly and only in situ-
ations that measure a ten on a scale of one to ten in
importance. If she has not been doing it all the time,
Marty should be able to take it without getting
annoyed.

> One way to prepare a man to hear
> advice at those really important times
> when you have to give it is to react in a
> very accepting way at those times when
> he makes little mistakes.

For example, if your partner misses exits, don't
give him driving instructions. Use the incident as an
opportunity to prepare him for more important feedback at another time. Try saying nothing, and act as
if it is perfectly normal for an extremely brilliant and
competent man to be so focused on thinking about
something that he forgets the exit. He will not only

be very grateful but he will be more open to your suggestions in the future.

In any situation, if a woman can be accepting of a man's little mistakes, when the big ones come along he will be much more willing to hear what she has to say.

Getting to the Church on Time

In response to Pearl's question, I explained that if she was worried on the way to the wedding, the best thing was to warn him in advance in a way that respects his sensitivities. She could say "I know you hate it when I give you directions in the car so I try not to do it, but today, would you mind if I helped navigate? I am so nervous about everything. It would make me feel much better."

When he says yes, she should thank him as if he is doing her a favor. Not only has he been willing to listen, but this kind of support prepares him to more easily hear her comments or advice in the future.

It is as though she is saying "I respect your need to do things on your own, and I don't have the right to invade your sensitivities. I do not expect more from you than you can offer. I appreciate your flexibility in supporting me today."

This kind of consideration gradually opens a man up to hearing a woman's concerns and advice in the future about other things as well. The bottom line is that the more a man feels appreciated and trusted as competent and capable, the more he can openly hear her requests for more.

In my relationship, when we are late or if I am not clear about the directions, I will take it upon myself to set up the situation. I know it will be hard for Bonnie to refrain from giving directions, and the truth is that I could use her help. At those particular times I will say, "It's OK today if you want to help navigate, I would appreciate the help."

Many times a woman senses that a man doesn't want to hear her but because she can't come up with a better way to say it, she mis-says it. To overcome his wall of resistance, she applies more force, and generally builds up her own sense of entitlement by remembering all the other times that he didn't listen. She forges ahead regardless of his resistance.

It is as if she has to say to herself, "I don't care if he doesn't want to listen. I have to tell him." This kind of aggressive assertiveness does not build bridges but usually turns him off and ensures his greater resistance in the future.

When a woman doesn't know how to say what she wants to say in a way that would be easy for a man to hear, the most effective technique is to let him know just that. He will appreciate her concern and try to help her. By having his support enlisted in this way, he will be much more accepting of any mistakes she makes and much more understanding of what she is really trying to say.

The most difficult female attitude for a man to cope with is the expectation that he should listen without getting bent out of shape by what he hears. If she senses that it will be hard for him to hear, she can start by immediately letting him know it. She could say, "There is something I'd like to talk about but I'm still in the process of working it out. I certainly don't want it to sound like criticism or blame, but I would also feel really supported if you knew what I was feeling. Would you take a few minutes to listen?"

By letting him know what he's in for, in advance, she says, in effect, that she knows it will be hard to hear and she doesn't mean it to be that way. Just this consideration makes it so much easier for him to hear her and try to explore what she is saying in "Female" rather than reacting to how it sounds in "Male."

You Don't Have to Change Your Mind

I remember once my stepdaughter Julie skillfully using a new communication technique when she was sixteen years old. I was very impressed. Bonnie and I had decided to take a three-day vacation while some work was being done on our house. For various reasons, Julie didn't want to go, but she also didn't want to stay in the middle of remodeling.

She said to me, "I have a lot of stay-home feelings about this and would like you just to listen. You don't have to change your mind, I just want you to consider my point of view." She then proceeded to tell me that she didn't like remodeling and wished we would do it in the future at a time when she could also be away from the house. As she shared her feelings, she became more emotional about it and then felt much better. I remember how much easier it was to hear her feelings because she had simply prepared me with the statement "You don't have to change your mind."

That one phrase set me free to listen. The result of that conversation was that in the future I was much more sensitive to her requests and made sure that we never left her at home with the remodeling again. It also made me more considerate in general.

This is the amazing thing about men. If they are approached in the wrong way, they get defensive and push away a woman's feelings and needs. Yet, in a positive sense, when a man is prepared in a way that helps him to be supportive, he is then much more considerate in general about everything.

It's Not Your Fault

The more a woman practices preparing a man, the less she will need to prepare him in the future. Each successful interaction assists a man in ducking and dodging more effectively the next time. As with the acquisition of any new skill, it is wise to begin with easy problems and then graduate to difficult ones. A woman's start-up assistance makes it easier for a man.

Just as men need assistance in learning to duck and dodge, so women sometimes forget to pause and prepare. At such times a woman must remember that it is never too late to correct things. If she notices that her man is having a hard time or is getting frustrated or angry, she can apply some pausing and preparing techniques.

She could say "It makes sense to me that you feel. . . ." These words are validating to him and will help him cool off. Another major reason men get upset when listening is that they feel blamed. To help him dodge, just a few words can make a world of difference. I remember many conversations with Bonnie when she just said a few words and it allowed me to relax and listen instead of defend and fight.

Right in the middle of a conversation, when she sensed that I was getting bruised by her words, she paused and said, "I know this is probably sounding like blame. I don't want to blame you. You don't deserve that. I just need to talk about these feelings. I know there is another side to this. Let me first work through my feelings and then I will be able to appreciate your side of it."

After a few minutes, she started saying things like "I can see that you really didn't mean. . . . I just misunderstood because I thought. . . . I really appreciate your not getting too upset about this."

When she finished, I really didn't need to say much in my own defense. I just said, "Well, I understand why you were upset, and I am glad we had this conversation." Even though at a gut level I hated having to listen to what sounded like blame, from a heart and head level of my being I knew that conversations like this were an important part of keeping the passion alive in a relationship.

You Don't Have to Say Anything

Probably the most potent and powerful phrase a woman can say to prepare a man to listen is: "You don't have to say anything." This message is important because it lets a man off the hook of needing to defend himself. In addition, it gently reminds him that he doesn't have to solve her problems.

A woman would generally not think of this because with other women it would be rude to say "You don't have to say anything." When one woman talks in "Female," tradition commands that it will next be the other person's turn to talk; the unspoken agreement is that if I listen to you talk for five minutes, you must listen to me for five minutes.

With a man it is different. If she says "You don't have to say anything," it is not rude—quite the contrary, he will be relieved. It is an easy job description.

"You're Not Listening"

Another common expression women use that is a complete turn-off for men is: "You're not listening." When a woman uses this phrase, it frustrates a man because he usually *is* listening in some way, or at least trying to. Even if he wasn't, it is hard for him to hear it because in childhood it was used repeatedly by his mother when she was upset with him.

Hearing it in adulthood, a man feels as if his mate is talking down to him and treating him like a child. He hears it as not only "degrading" but very "controlling." Just as a woman doesn't want to mother a man, a man does not want to be mothered. He feels she is blaming him when she is really just trying to be heard.

When a woman says "You're not listening," it is generally because a man is not giving her his full attention. He is hearing her with only part of his mind when she wants his full attention.

> To say "You're not listening" doesn't convey the correct message, which is "You are not giving me your full attention."

To a man, there is a world of difference between these two statements. He can't argue with the second message, but the first only pushes him farther away.

When a man is half-listening, distracted, or looking away while she is talking, women quite commonly communicate the message that he is not listening by raising their voices. Getting louder for a woman is another way of saying "You're not listening." The result, however, is the same; in the end he will listen less. Yelling at children also programs them to not listen.

Negative critical feedback just doesn't work. For most women, the only other option is to get upset and walk away. Although her options seem bleak, there is hope. By learning to pause and prepare a man, a woman can immediately begin getting the results she wants. Let's look at an example.

The Thirty-Second Attention Span

Many times, when a woman talks about her day, a man will focus on her for a moment, realize that she is going to talk for a while, and then pick up a magazine and begin reading it until she "gets to the point." If he is watching TV, he will listen for a few moments and then shift back to watching TV.

At the most, he will listen for about thirty seconds and then, when he experiences that she is not talking in a linear fashion, he automatically finds another focus for his masculine side. The news is great for focusing, since in the first paragraph of each article he gets the bottom line of who, what, where, when, how, and why.

In my seminars, I commonly ask how many women have experienced a man picking up a magazine to read soon after she begins to talk. Almost all the hands go up. I do this so that the women in the room can see that it is not just *their* husband who "doesn't listen."

Martha was one of those women. Her husband didn't take the course, but by learning at the seminar how to prepare a man to listen, she experienced an immediate and dramatic change. She was able to break through the thirty-second attention span and began getting his full attention.

Martha and Robert had been married for nine years. Quite commonly, when she talked he would briefly focus on her and then continue watching TV. Her reaction was to keep talking and then after a while get furious with him and complain that he didn't listen to her. Although this approach is certainly instinctive on her part, it doesn't work.

For years this pattern repeated itself. Even though Martha complained, Robert would still watch TV while she talked. If the TV wasn't on, he would pick up a magazine and read it while she was talking. Like many thousands of women, Martha was definitely not getting the support she most needed.

Robert didn't give her his full attention because he didn't feel the same need to talk about his day with someone giving him their full attention. It is not that he wasn't interested in *her*, it was that he wasn't interested in the details of her day.

To him, the details were unimportant unless they were directly related to some point. Men are used to organizing details in a logical manner to make a point or to figure out a solution. When a woman talks just to relax and connect with her partner, she commonly uses details that are not necessarily related to any point or solution. She is talking to share an experience, not fix it. When he recognized that she wasn't going to get to a point, he would then look back to the TV or pick up a magazine to find a point to focus on.

A man needs to have a goal or a focal point. At those times when a woman is sharing feelings, a man's mind begins to tense up while trying to find the point. When he realizes that it's going to be a while before she gets to her point, he relaxes his mind by focusing on a newspaper, magazine, or TV. He is generally not trying to be rude. Many times, he doesn't even know that he is doing it.

He Thinks He Is Listening

When a woman talks and a man looks away, he still believes he is listening. There is still a part of his mind following her words for when she gets to the point and his response is called for. In a sense, he is waiting for his turn to "do something." A small part of him is paying attention, scanning what she is saying for any problems that may require his full attention to solve. When she says he is not listening, it doesn't make sense to him because he knows that it's not completely true.

As long as she complains that he is not listening, he will never hear her actual message. What she is really saying is, "When you watch TV, I don't feel that I have your full attention. If you give it to me and turn off the TV, it will help me get this out much faster and it will feel very good." This is a message that a man can hear and understand. It also gives him a focus or reason to listen.

Men don't realize how important and soothing their attention is to a woman.

When a woman doesn't understand the way a man thinks and talks, she mistakenly assumes that he doesn't care about her. Martha was ready to end her marriage because she had become convinced that TV was more important to Robert than she was. When he picked up a magazine as she talked, she thought he hated her.

Quite commonly, they would argue about whether he was really listening or not.

She said, "You're not listening."

He said, "I am listening."

She said, "You can't listen and watch the TV at the same time."

He said, "How do you know what I can do?"

She said, "Well, I know I can't talk to you."

He said, "Look, I'm watching TV now, and I am hearing everything you are saying. I can repeat back everything you have said."

She said, "I knew it, I can't talk with you."

Various versions of this same argument went on for years until Martha tried a different approach.

The next time Robert picked up a magazine, instead of complaining or storming off in frustration Martha practiced a new skill. She paused from talking and looked *with* him at his magazine. After thirty seconds, he noticed that she had stopped talking. By pausing, she got his attention, and he remembered that she was talking.

Then she said, "Thanks, I really appreciate it when you give me your full attention. This will only take about three more minutes. Is that OK for you?"

After talking for about three minutes, she then thanked him for giving her his full attention. Instead of fighting about who was wrong, Martha got what she wanted. Robert started giving her his full attention when she spoke. Whenever he'd forget, she knew just what to do to get it back.

By gradually experiencing how much Martha appreciated and thrived on his full attention, Robert was instinctively motivated to give her his full attention when she talked.

When a woman wants a man to listen, it is important to make sure that he feels there will be closure. He needs to know what is required of him, how long it will take, and what he will get in return.

In this case, Martha let him know in positive and clear terms that she needed his full attention (not just for him to listen). She let him know it would only take three minutes, and when she was done, she let him know how much she appreciated it.

Three minutes is a good starting-out time for a man to practice building up his emotional support muscles. As he can do that, then she can begin to go on for longer and longer periods of time. Gradually, Martha would increase the time of her sharing.

When she noticed him starting to get frustrated, she would again pause and prepare him to listen by saying, "It will only be another three minutes and I'll be done." This kind of support for him ensured that he gradually learned how to support her. If she had more to say, then she used another new skill. She "postponed" sharing her feelings for another time.

A Woman's Lifeline

Good communication is a modern woman's lifeline. Without it, she loses touch with her ability to feel the love in her heart and receive the loving support of others; she loses her ability to feel warm, tender, and sweet feelings. By learning to support a man in a particular way, she can ensure getting back the support she needs to nurture her female side.

To achieve this end, it is important for her to realize that men have never been required to be good listeners of a woman's feelings and that they don't know how. By clearly understanding this fact, it gives her the patience and the awareness to appreciate each step he makes toward her fulfillment.

Women generally feel that if a man loves them, he will want to listen to their feelings. A man doesn't feel this way because sharing feelings is not as important to him and, traditionally, women didn't want to share their feelings with men.

When a man loves a woman, it doesn't mean that he will be motivated to initiate conversations, nor will it be any easier for him to listen.

It actually works the other way around. The more a man cares, if he hasn't learned how to duck and dodge it hurts more when he gets hit. When she is unhappy, it is much harder for him to listen without feeling blamed. It is harder because the more he loves her, the more he feels like a failure when she is not feeling loved and supported.

By understanding that a man really needs her support to support her successfully, a woman can then be motivated to help him without feeling as if she is begging for love. This insight that a man could deeply care but also resist her when she starts sharing feelings helps her to take responsibility for communicating in ways that are supportive for her and also for him.

The Importance of Timing

I've already mentioned how vital timing is to good communication. When a man is recuperating from the demands of his workday, it is counterproductive to make more demands on him. Until he becomes proficient in the art of listening, trying to converse when he first comes home feels to him like more work, which he will tend to resist. Even if he is eager, his mind will wander to something less demanding like the TV or a magazine. To fight this innate tendency is useless, but by working with it a woman can get what she needs.

In my book, *Men Are from Mars, Women Are from Venus,* I explored in great detail this tendency men have to temporarily pull away from a relationship to recharge and described it as cave time. I first heard this concept from a Native American woman who said that in her tribe, when a woman was married the mother gave her this wise warning: "When a man loves you, at times he will pull away and go to his cave. A woman should never try to follow him or else she will be burned by the dragon. After some time, he will be back and everything will be fine."

Cave time for a man is solitary time when he can

most effectively recuperate from the day, forget his problems by staring off into the fire, and gradually connect with his loving feelings and remember what is most important to him. Once he feels better, he automatically comes out of the cave and is available for a relationship.

To ensure mutually supportive conversations, a woman needs to postpone her immediate needs to share her feelings until her male partner is out of the cave. It is disastrous to initiate a conversation before a man is actually capable of listening and sharing. Through "pausing" in this way and waiting for the right time to share her feelings, a woman can get the support she most needs.

One woman in my seminar shared that she was a cave buster. She would use dynamite to get in his cave, only to find that her husband would dig deeper and deeper tunnels. Without an understanding that her husband needed solitary time, trying to get closer only pushed him farther away.

When a man can't take the time he needs for himself, it is extremely difficult for him to find the loving feelings that originally attracted him to his partner. In a similar way, when a woman doesn't get the chance to share her feelings and connect with her female side, she, as well, loses touch with her deep, loving feelings.

Understanding the Cave

Most women do not understand the cave, nor do they recognize when a man is out. A woman is easily frustrated because she feels the need to talk but doesn't know how long it will take before he comes out. She wants him to come out, but she doesn't know what she can do to help. This uncertainty makes her need to talk even more urgent.

Men in relationships experience a similar frustration when women talk about problems. A man doesn't know how long she will talk before she feels better. He is afraid she will never be happy. It is hard for a man to figure out when she wants his advice or when she just wants to talk.

In a similar way, it is hard for a woman to understand if he is watching TV because there is nothing else to do or if he is in his cave and is not open to having a conversation. To solve these common problems, we not only need to understand our differences but must learn new skills for getting what we need.

The Need for Clear Signals

A woman needs clear communication signals to know when a man is open and when he is closed in the same way that a man needs to know when she is open to solutions and when she just needs to be heard.

Just as it is hard for a man to trust that a woman will feel better again after sharing negative feelings, it is equally difficult for a woman to trust that a man loves her when he pulls away and ignores her.

To pause before talking or making requests of a man, a woman needs to first know if he is in the cave. If he is not available, she needs to postpone getting her needs met by him. If she can support him in this way, not only will he spend less time in the cave, he will be much more loving when he is out of the cave.

Through persisting in this process of not trying to change him but instead trying to assist him in being successful in supporting her, a woman can dramatically improve her relationship.

When a man is in his cave, it is the time for a woman to be less demanding of him. This nondemanding and trusting attitude is very attractive to a man, and will definitely shorten cave time.

When Is a Man Out of His Cave?

Even when a woman begins to understand a man's need to be in the cave, it is still difficult to tell when he is out. Women persistently ask me, "How do I know when it is a good time to talk? How do I know when he is in the cave?"

My favorite example to answer this question has to do with my daughter Lauren. One evening when she was seven years old she had attended one of my lectures on the differences between men and women. Although much of the time she was playing in the back, she had actually taken in a lot.

In that lecture I talked about not going into a man's cave. I hadn't thought Lauren was listening, but on the way home she said, "Daddy, you said if you go into a man's cave you get burned by the dragon. Is that why sometimes you get angry at me? Is that just your dragon? Do you still love me?"

I said, "That's right. Sometimes I am in my cave and just need to be alone for a while and then I come out again. Even if sometimes I feel frustrated or angry with you, I still love you very much."

She said, "Thank you, Daddy, I'm sure glad I know about the cave."

The next day she came up to me while I was reading the newspaper and said, "Daddy, are you in your cave? I don't want to bother you if you are 'cause I don't want to be burned by the dragon." I told her that I was in the cave, but soon I would be out.

She then said, "Would you let me know when you are out, because I want to tell you about my day."

When I finished reading the paper, I then easily remembered to find my daughter and ask her about her day.

Sometimes the answer to the most complex problems can be right before our eyes. Volumes of books have been written trying to answer the question of how to get a man to open up and yet, given the right understanding, a little child could find the answer.

The way to tell if a man is in his cave is simply to ask. Although it sounds simple, it does take a lot of practice not to feel rejected if he doesn't want to talk. It is hard for a woman to ask because instinctively it is a shock to her when a man doesn't want to talk.

**The way to tell if a man is in his cave
is simply to ask.**

This is because when she loves a man and feels safe to share her feelings, then after a long day she looks forward to sharing and talking with him. When she wants to talk and he doesn't, it is embarrassing. It feels as though she loves him more than he loves her.

Initiating Sex Versus Initiating Conversation

A way for a man to understand a woman's sensitivity to this issue is to compare it to a man's sensitivity on the issue of sex. If he is turned on to her and she is not even interested in having sex, it can be very embarrassing to him.

When a man deeply loves a woman, one of the most potent ways he can feel her love is during sex. During arousal he is most sensitive to receiving and giving love. To be rejected when he is aroused is generally the most difficult challenge for him to handle in a relationship.

Every man who has passionately loved a woman knows how painful it is to love her and want to make love to her and then feel rejected sexually. If he then continues to initiate sex and his partner is repeatedly not in the mood, he then automatically stops feeling his desire for sex with her.

Why Men Lose Interest in Sex

He may not even know why he is not so interested in sex anymore. The thought of sex may just make him tired. This fatigue sets in because he is suppressing his sexual drive. It takes up a lot of energy to suppress one's sexual feelings. When a man is repeatedly rejected, it happens automatically.

In a similar way, when a woman feels rejected because a man doesn't want to talk, she loses touch with the tender part of her femininity that wants to talk and share. The opportunity to talk may sometimes just make her feel more exhausted or more overwhelmed. The energy it takes to suppress her female side wears her out.

With this understanding, a man is much more motivated to make it safe for her to talk. Without this awareness, a man can't be sensitive to the ways in which he may be hurting her.

Although a woman needs to understand and accept a man's need for the cave, he can, however, be sensitive to her feelings about it. By making it clear to her when he is in and when he is out, it makes it much easier for her to handle.

In a similar way, to keep the passion alive in her man, a woman needs to give him clear signals about when she is in the mood for sex and when she is not.

Signals That He Is Out of the Cave

The way a man can help a woman know when he is out of the cave is to give her clear signals in a language that she will understand. Touching a woman in a nonsexual but affectionate way is probably the most effective and simple way.

When I am out of the cave and available for conversation, I search out my wife and touch her in some affectionate way or offer to give her a hug. This clear signal tells her that I am approachable.

This certainty regarding when I am available and when I am not makes a world of difference for her. She does not have to worry or try to figure out my moods.

When a man is out of the cave, it is even more helpful for her to recognize it if he initiates a conversation. This does not mean that he has to talk much. It means that he briefly communicates the message that he is out and is open to hearing her. This is best done by simply asking her a question about her day.

Initiating a conversation is particularly helpful because women today are many times so much in their male sides that they don't even know they need to talk until they are asked. Particularly if she has been burned in the past while sharing her feelings she will not consciously feel the need to talk.

> With a clear signal from her mate
> initiating the conversation, she does not
> have to fear his lack of interest in
> what she has to share.

Pausing to Postpone Sharing Feelings

A woman has to work hard at not reacting in a way that says to a man that he is a bad boy and that he is not making "Mommy" happy. To support him, she is required to nurture him with an accepting love and not be a mother trying to teach him how to be "good."

Even if these messages are her true feelings, when he is on his way to the cave it is not the time to share those feelings. To accomplish this feat she needs to practice "postponing" her feelings until she has a more receptive listener.

These kinds of feelings are a negative influence on him and are best shared with a woman friend. Through putting off giving a negative message she ensures that he will come back sooner. It is much easier for her to give him this support when she clearly knows when he is in the cave and that he will come out of his own accord.

If I am in a bad mood and needing cave time, quite commonly I will go for a drive. All I need to say is, "I need to go for a drive," and my wife understands that I am in my cave. My car is actually black with a black interior. To me, it feels like a moving cave. If I am watching TV and I am in my cave, I will scan the channels with my remote control at the commercial breaks. If I am open and receptive to her, then at the commercials I put the TV on mute and talk with her.

Generally speaking, when a man does something that a woman thinks is a waste of time or is unproductive, he is in his cave. It could be fiddling with his computer or fiddling with an old car in the garage. For some men, their cave is the workshop in the garage, a walk over the hill, a jog around the neighborhood, a workout at the gym, or going to a movie.

How to Ask a Man to Talk

Unless a man understands the importance of making clear signals that he is in the cave, a woman must depend on herself to figure it out. Even if a man knows the importance of giving signals, he will inevitably forget at times to use them. This being the case, it is essential for women to be skilled in checking out when he is in the cave and when he is not.

Just as a man can test to see how upset a woman is by gently touching her and asking her if she needs to talk, a woman can test a man by asking him a few simple questions.

When a woman wants to talk, instead of assuming that a man is immediately available she needs to first "pause" and then approach him to see if it is the right time for him. She can "check it out" in a variety of ways.

By asking a man questions about his day she can quickly tell if he is in the mood to talk. If she says "How was your day?," when he gives a short answer like OK or fine, it's a clear signal that he is in his cave or that he is open to having a conversation but would prefer that she talk more.

She can then say "Is this a good time to talk, or would you like to do it later?"

If he is not deep in his cave, he will generally say "This is a good time." Although he may still feel some resistance, it is not because he is in his cave or because he doesn't care, but because he doesn't have much to say. Don't be disappointed if he doesn't say "Oh, thanks for asking, I would love to talk."

If he is hesitant but clearly says "Not right now," then she can say "OK, I'll check back later. How about twenty minutes?"

Generally speaking, that should be enough time. If he needs more time, it is important to be prepared to accept what he needs. The more gracious and nondemanding she is, the more he will think about taking the time to talk.

This situation is similar to when a man reaches out and gently touches his wife; he cannot expect that she should always receive his touch with a warm, loving response. If she pulls back and he doesn't react with anger but dodges and remains open to her, then she is much more willing to open up to him.

In a like manner, the more space or acceptance a woman can give a man while letting him know that she is looking forward to talking, the more open and willing he will be to make the time to talk.

The Unspoken Rules for Communicating

If a woman wants to talk with someone, she generally waits for her turn. It is her way of being polite. She either listens for a while and then begins to talk, or waits until the other person asks her about her day.

These unspoken rules are foreign to most men. If a woman waits for her mate to talk first, she may never get the chance to talk because he doesn't automatically have a lot to say.

A man's unspoken rules are that if you have something to say, say it. He doesn't feel the need to wait to be asked. If he wants to talk, he talks. When he asks questions, he rarely has the expectation that she is supposed to ask questions back.

When a woman asks him questions and he does talk, he thinks he is pleasing her by answering her questions.

Men don't have a clue that after talking for a while they are supposed to take turns and ask women questions.

Even if a man has learned that a woman wants him to ask her questions about her day, he will tend to forget. When she is asking him questions, he is so busy thinking of what to say that it is hard for him to remember to ask her about her day.

If a man gives short answers, a woman does not need to wait until he has had his turn. He doesn't mind if she begins talking about her day. It would not be rude to him if she began talking about her own day without first listening to him.

Men Who Talk Too Much

A single woman at one of my relationship seminars asked this question. She said, "You say men don't want to talk. My experience is with men who talk too much and don't listen to what I have to say. How do I get them to listen?"

I asked her if she herself was a good listener. She very proudly said yes. I then asked if *she* asked lots of questions. She again proudly said yes.

She then said, "I do all the right things, but they still don't listen to me."

I said, "You are doing all the right things to get a woman to listen, but not a man. If you want a man to stop talking and listen more, then you have to stop asking him questions."

The more a man has to think about answering questions, the less he will think about her or pause to let her talk.

To get a man's full attention, this woman first needed to stop asking more questions. Then, when he paused, she should say something like this: "That makes sense to me because . . ."

With this kind of lead-in phrase, a woman can get any man's attention. Men love to be acknowledged for making sense. These three simple words, "That makes sense," are so soothing to a man that he will immediately stop talking and listen to what she has to say.

The most effective way to get a man's full attention is to "prepare" him for the conversation by letting him off the hook of needing to talk more. By letting him know in advance that he doesn't have to talk, he can relax and listen instead of figuring out what to say. After all, she is the one who wants to talk.

This is a very important awareness. A man can be out of the cave and be open to conversation but not have anything to say. Instinctively, he doesn't feel the need to initiate conversation. When a woman senses that he doesn't have anything to say, she feels awkward talking more or asking him to listen as I have suggested.

It feels rude to her to say something like "Well, even if you don't feel like talking, I have a lot to say. Would you listen to me? You don't have to say anything." She doesn't know that to him this is not rudeness. It is directness, and it is not demanding. Men love this kind of support.

By being prepared in this way, a man doesn't need to resist the listening process because it is clearly stated that he doesn't have to say anything.

Why Women Don't Initiate Conversations

There are actually many times when a man is out of the cave and available to have a conversation but is waiting for a woman to initiate the conversation. She may not know this because at other times when he was in the cave, she tried conversations only to find that getting him to talk was like pulling teeth.

After a few futile stabs at conversations, many women give up without even knowing it. They actually believe that they have nothing to say and don't want to talk. When they get home, they go to their caves as well.

These women do not realize that they are missing out on the thing that can bring them the greatest happiness. Life has taught them that it is foolish to try and share feelings with a man. But with new relationship skills and a new job description, they can get the support and respect that they require in order to risk sharing their feminine feelings.

Still other women know that they are missing out, but blame the men for not wanting to talk. Their mothers did not teach them about the cave. The worst thing a woman can do is to blame a man for not wanting to talk. It would be like a man blaming a woman for talking too much. Neither approach is valid or productive.

A woman needs to understand her needs and persist in creating opportunities to get the attention and understanding she needs from her partner.

New Communication Skills

To ensure the best communication in a relationship, both men and women can begin applying new skills. An easy way for women to remember what is required of them is to remember the four Ps: pausing, preparing, postponing, and persisting. In a similar way, men can remember the four Ds: ducking, dodging, disarming, and delivering. A relationship will be easiest when both are doing their best. Without these insights, relationships are much more difficult than they need to be.

Even when a woman's husband or boyfriend has not read this book, by applying these skills she will begin to get so much more. She will learn to talk in ways that are natural for her but that will also motivate him to listen and support more. This summary of the four Ps can be helpful for a woman to remember what the basics are for getting the support she needs.

1. Pause
   A. Check it out. Ask him if this is a good time.
   B. Don't interrupt him if you know he is in the cave.

2. Prepare
   A. Set a time limit. Tell him how long it will take. When a man doesn't know where the conversation is going, he begins to panic. When he knows there is a time limit, then he can relax.
   B. Give him a clear job description. Tell him that he doesn't have to say anything or make other supportive comments.
   C. Encourage him. Occasionally remind him that he is not being blamed or that you understand it is hard to listen.
   D. Appreciate him. Each time when you are finished talking, let him know that you really appreciate his listening and that you feel much better because of his support.

3. Postpone
   A. When he is in his cave, postpone sharing your

needs for another time when he is more available and able to give.

B. Put off expecting him to do more until he has
become proficient in listening more to feelings,
then begin to ask for more physical help in
small increments.

C. When you are feeling blame or criticism, talk
to someone else first to become more loving
and centered and then talk to your partner.

4. Persist

A. Continue giving him the support he needs to
support you. Don't expect him to always
remember.

B. When he resists conversation, persist in asking
him to listen even if he has little or nothing to
say.

C. Overcome the tendency to give in and not
communicate with him. Patiently persist in
practicing these skills.

One of the biggest obstacles to practicing the
four skills for women and the four skills for men is
not understanding that men and women essentially
speak different languages. A man could be growing
in his skills slowly but surely, but when he fails to listen or respect her feelings, she feels it is hopeless. In a
similar way, a woman will be progressing in supporting her male partner, and then when she forgets to
pause and prepare and he feels blamed, he may automatically assume that nothing is working.

Through understanding the different languages
we speak it is much easier to recognize that our partners do love us and that they, in their own way, are
doing their best.

CHAPTER 7

Men Speak "Male" and Women Speak "Female"

IT IS OBVIOUS TO A WOMAN when another woman is upset and needs to talk in order to feel better. It is also obvious when her talking has been successful in releasing stress. To men, none of the above is obvious at all. It is as if men and women secretly speak different languages with a whole series of complex and different verbal, physical, and emotional signals. Here's a graphic example:

Bob and Marge: Before

Bob and Marge have been married for six years. They love each other very much but just don't understand this basic difference between men and women. When Marge comes home from work feeling overwhelmed, Bob can tell she's upset.

"Marge, what's wrong?" he asks, trying to be friendly and supportive.

Sighing deeply, she answers, "Everybody wants something from me; I feel like I have to do everything!"

Bob immediately feels frustrated. He is trying to help, but he hears her blaming him for how she feels and begins to get defensive. "What do you mean you do everything? That means I don't do anything?"

"No, I am not saying you do nothing. I am saying I feel like I do everything. That doesn't mean you do nothing. It's just how I feel. Can't I express my feelings without you taking it personally?"

Bob reacts, saying, "Listen, if you say you do everything, then that means I do nothing. If you say everyone wants something from you it means that I want too much from you."

"But I didn't say you wanted too much from me," Marge countered. "I said I felt like everybody wants something from me. I wasn't singling you out. I was just expressing the feeling that I can't be everything to everyone."

Bob, getting angrier, says, "Sure, sure. You do it all. And I do nothing. You know what I think? I think it doesn't even matter what I do. It's never enough. No one could make you happy."

"Why can't I just express my feelings without everything being about you?" Marge demands. "I'm not saying it's your fault. I just want you to let me talk."

"Right," replies Bob sarcastically.

"I knew I couldn't talk to you." Inwardly, Marge is deciding to never again discuss her feelings with Bob.

"You *can* talk to me," Bob calls after her as she storms out of the room. "Just don't be so negative!"

Why We Argue

At this point, Bob feels blamed and unappreciated, while Marge feels even more overwhelmed. As in most arguments between men and women, Bob doesn't understand that Marge just needs to talk about her feelings in order to feel better. Like most men, he makes the mistake of taking her literally and trying to correct her. He has not yet learned the new skill of listening without feeling blamed.

Like most women, Marge expects Bob to understand that she wasn't blaming him, and doesn't even realize that there are new relationship skills she could apply to prevent him from feeling blamed or unappreciated.

When a man is unskilled in correctly translating what a woman means, it becomes increasingly difficult for him to be a sympathetic listener.

A man cannot tune in when he feels his efforts are unacknowledged and unappreciated. Although her overwhelming feelings may have little to do with him, he takes them personally.

Instead of understanding what is happening and using a new relationship skill to remedy the situation, Marge feels like giving up. Bob's natural resistance to listening to her feelings signals to her that she is not loved and will never get the support she needs. This only compounds the problem and increases her feelings of being overwhelmed and isolated.

Bob and Marge: After

After retraining in new relationship skills, Bob has learned to dodge Marge's emotionally charged words and not feel blamed. Marge, in turn, has learned to prepare him for her feelings and thus make it easier for him to dodge the bullets. Now, after much practice, their conversation sounds like this:

"Marge, what's the matter?" Bob asks.

Marge pauses to think about how to prepare him so that he won't feel criticized, then says, "Thanks for asking. (pause) I had a terrible day. (another pause) I just need to talk about it, and then I'm sure I'll feel better, OK?"

"Sure." Bob is now prepared. He knows he really doesn't have to do anything to make her feel better. This allows him to relax and listen without having to think about solving her problems.

"Everyone wants something from me," Marge tells him. "I feel like I do everything." Once Marge has set the stage and prepared Bob, she doesn't need to edit her feelings and can freely express them. Free expression is essential if she is going to let go of her frustrations.

This time Bob is not frustrated because he understands she just needs to talk. He easily dodges the bullets of frustration and simply listens. When she pauses, he invites her to say more with a warm, sympathetic "Hmmm."

"Today," Marge tells him, "I was supposed to finish the books when Richard called. He still hasn't paid his bills, so I had to go to the bank and make a wire transfer."

"Humph!" Bob responds with empathetic annoyance.

"And," Marge goes on, "there was so much traffic. It didn't used to be that way. Everything's happening too fast. There's too much to do for too many people and no time. Everybody's rushing. It's crazy out there!"

Bob shakes his head in agreement.

"And," she tells him, "when I finally got back to work, there were fifteen—fifteen!—messages on my voice mail. I just don't have the time to run around doing errands for everyone."

"Hummph!" Bob validates her irritation.

"I mean, I handled them but . . . it's just all too much."

"It's awful," Bob exclaims, moving closer to her. "Marge, you give so much of yourself. Let me give you a hug."

After the hug, Marge takes a deep breath as if she just let go of a heavy weight and exhales slowly. "I really needed that! I am so glad to be home. Thanks for listening." Marge is careful to acknowledge his help.

Throughout their conversation, Bob remembers not to minimize or argue with her overwhelmed feelings. Instead, he skillfully supports her by focusing on her female side and not keeping her in her workday male mode by trying to help her resolve her problems. To the best of his ability, he is trying to talk her language.

The Benefits of Improving Communication

Through updating and improving their communication skills, Bob and Marge not only avoided arguments but were able to solve the real problems: Marge feeling overwhelmed and overworked, and Bob feeling defeated and unappreciated. With a basic grasp of "Female," Bob was able to nurture Marge's female side, while Marge was able to appreciate Bob more.

Marge was able to release her overwhelming feelings by being able to talk about them in an uninhibited manner, in "Female." Bob was able to feel appreciated because he had provided Marge with the emotional safety and support that she needed in order to feel better.

Although Bob was not his family's sole provider, he could still feel needed and appreciated in his new role as a skilled listener. Although Marge was not happy and fulfilled when she got home, she was happy to see Bob, and soon after their conversation she was much happier and very appreciative of him. Without focusing on solutions to her problems at work and at home, Marge was able to release her feeling of panic and begin to return to her female side.

Most couples today are not fluent in each other's language. When they talk, they experience increasing frustration instead of fulfillment.

> Quite commonly the relationship
> becomes another of the woman's
> burdens rather than a way to find
> release from them. For the man, the
> relationship increasingly signals
> his defeat rather than giving
> meaning to his life.

When we consider these new stresses on relationships and family life, and the absence of traditional support systems, it is no wonder that it's so hard to stay together and it explains why millions choose to be single. Neither sex is being nurtured and supported in the ways that matter most because they are speaking different languages.

Breaking the Language Barrier

As we've discussed, it no longer has to be that way. For instance, male frustration could be helped if at the end of an emotional talk, women could say any combination of the following:

"Thanks so much for listening."

"I just needed to get that out."

"I'm sorry it was difficult for you to hear."

"You can forget everything I just said."

"It doesn't matter as much now."

"I feel much better."

"Thanks for helping me sort this out and letting me talk."

"This conversation has been really helpful for me to get a better perspective on things."

"I feel so much better now, thanks for listening."

"Wow, I sure had a lot to say. I feel so much better."

"I feel so much better. Sometimes I just need to talk about things and then my mood changes."

"I appreciate your patience in helping me to sort things out through talking."

Any of these comments would be heaven to a man and would make him feel warmly appreciated. This is because in "Male," his native language, they have a special and positive significance.

When a woman says in a friendly tone, "It's OK,"

or "It's no big deal," or "It's all right," or even "Forget it," to a man, it makes it easier in the future for him to listen. It also makes him remember what he did to upset her and try in the future to make things better.

When a man begins to see how willing a woman is to forget the things that upset her, his tendency is to remember more and be more considerate in the future.

When a woman says, "Thanks for listening. I know it was difficult to sit through," a man tells himself in "Male," "It was tough, but I can handle it!" The next time she is upset, he will be much more willing to listen because he's confident he can cope, and he knows he will be appreciated.

When, after sharing her feelings, a woman dispenses with her feelings by saying, "Now that it's out, it doesn't matter as much," his "Male" reaction is, "That's sweet of her to say, but I know how much it mattered to her. Next time, I'll try to be more sensitive."

When Women Can't Talk "Female"

For a woman to restrict herself by only talking the way a man does goes against her instincts. It eventually prevents her from coping successfully with stress and disconnects her from the warm, open, loving, and feminine feelings that allow her to trust, accept, and appreciate life.

It is very helpful for men to remember that women are instinctually suited to communicate as a means of sorting out their thoughts, clarifying their priorities, and exploring their feelings. As we have discussed, this is because early on in history women learned to cope with life's problems through talking all day and into the evening with other women. A woman's security was assured through talking and forming alliances and friendships. Just the act itself of talking brings up an instinctual feeling of security.

With this increased security, she begins to think more clearly and can sort things out much more effectively and in a loving way. In a very real sense, talking for women is like a pump that generates greater clarity. Through helping her to speak "female," he gives a precious gift.

Without the opportunity to share freely, something very important to women is lost.

Why Men Don't Talk

For a man, it is the opposite. Silently achieving a goal generates an instinctual feeling of security. While doing seemingly meaningless tasks, like waxing the car or driving a golf ball, a man can silently sort out his thoughts and concerns; he can clarify his values and priorities as well as develop a plan of action.

He can forget the stresses of his day and begin to relax back into the joys of his relationship and the comforts of his home. This silent inner process gives him a sense of security.

A hunter's survival and security were ensured by moving quietly, and then successfully achieving his goal. Hunters spoke "Male," a language of few words. Silence is a man's birthright.

When a woman feels free to talk, she feels greater security. Sharing about her problems and feelings is an automatic and natural expression of the way her brain processes information, and the way her nurturer/ancestors survived. Nurturers spoke "Female," a language with an infinite vocabulary. Talking is a woman's birthright.

Through understanding this crucial difference, men and women can more lovingly and effectively support each other.

How Men React to Feelings

When a woman says she needs to talk, most men feel that they are being told they are doing something wrong. When she talks about problems, a man mistakenly assumes that he has failed her and that she will never be happy. When she wants to talk about the relationship, he does not know that she is just trying to find her female self again. He thinks she is only trying to criticize or change him.

That is because he is hearing her remarks in "Male," while she is speaking "Female." Their lines of communication have completely broken down.

A man who misunderstands "Female" reacts in one of three basic ways:

1. He offers a solution. A woman may just want her partner to listen and be sympathetic, but if he can't be, he should at least listen and not interrupt. Even making a sound like "hmmm" will signal that he is considering what she is saying and is trying to understand her.

2. He minimizes her problems. He thinks this will make her feel better. What he doesn't know is that she is more concerned with discovering her feelings than with the accuracy of her description. He says things like:

"It's not such a big deal."
"We don't need to talk about this."
"So what's the point?"
"Well, there's nothing we can do about it now."
"Just forget it. I'll handle it."

3. He invalidates her feelings. He mistakenly thinks he is helping her to analyze and correct her thinking but ends up invalidating her feelings. He does not realize that she sorts things out as she talks. He says things like:

"You shouldn't get so upset."
"Don't worry about it."
"I think you are overreacting."
"We have already talked about this."

Non-Goal-Oriented Talking

When allowed to talk in a nonlinear, non-goal-oriented manner (pure "Female"), a woman can reconnect with her female side and can most effectively cope with the stress of working in a traditionally male role all day. If a man offers advice or tries to help her solve her problems, he is actually holding her in her masculine side, which wants to solve problems. He is demanding that she continue speaking "Male." By allowing a woman to talk about problems without the urgency to solve them, he assists her in moving back toward speaking "Female." By simply responding with empathy, sympathy, and understanding, he nurtures her female side. With this kind of support, she is able to throw off her burdens and release her overwhelming feelings. Gradually, her energy returns, and her heart is full of appreciation and love.

If a woman is able to release her negative feelings in this way and not secretly cling to them, it will also assist a man in being more present in the relationship. When a man initiates a conversation it sometimes is particularly helpful because women today are so much in their male sides that they don't even know they need to talk until they are asked. Particularly if she has been burned in the past while sharing her feelings, she will not consciously feel the need to talk. With the clear signal of a man initiating the conversation, she does not have to fear his lack of interest in what she has to share.

Even when she does feel the need to talk, she sometimes doesn't know where to start.

Questions to Help Her Open Up When He Is Ready to Listen

A man can assist a woman in opening up and letting her know he is ready to listen by asking any of these questions or making any of these comments:

1. "Did you have a bad day?"
2. "How was your day?"
3. "I'm so glad to see you. Let me give you a hug."
4. "Is there anything I can do for you?"

5. "Tell me about your day."
6. "You look good, did you have a nice day?"
7. "You look like you had a great day."
8. "You look tired . . ."
9. "Are you upset today?"
10. "How are you feeling?"

Each statement conveys the nondemanding message that she is invited to talk briefly or at length. If she fires off a quick answer, he should assist her in saying more by responding with any or all of the following four questions:

1. "What happened?"
2. "Tell me more."
3. "Then what happened?"
4. "How did that feel?" or "How does that feel?"

However, if a woman asks a man any of the ten questions above and he gives a curt reply, she should grant him space. If she needs to talk, she should ask if this is a good time.

Signals That He Can't Listen Right Now

If a man is still too stressed by the pressures of the day to hear her, he must give his female partner clear signals. A way he can communicate that he is not yet ready to hear her is by simply saying any of the following phrases:

1. "I need to spend some time alone and then I'll be back."

2. "I need to spend some time doing XYZ and then I'll be back."

3. "I'm in my cave right now. I need to XYZ and then I'll be back."

4. "I'm in my cave right now. When I'm out we can talk."

It is important that a man feel free to make these statements. Any negative message can make it harder for him to come out. Some common messages a woman mistakenly gives verbally or with a look are as follows:

1. "But why now?"
2. "But we haven't spent any time together."
3. "Why can't you be there for me when I need you?"
4. "All you think about is yourself!"
5. "Did I do something wrong?"
6. "How could you leave me now?"
7. "You are spending too much time away."
8. "You don't love me!"
9. "I can't handle this. I feel so abandoned and rejected."
10. "I knew it. You don't really care about me."
11. "But you have already been to the cave this week."

Avoiding any of the above messages can give a man the freedom and support to pull away when he needs to so that he can come back sooner. Many times, after a man has pulled away he wants to come back, but he remembers her negative comment or message and is not sure that he will be welcomed back. Then he has to deal with the problem of whether he has to apologize for pulling away when this is something he needs to do. Having to cope with the fear of her rejection when he comes back definitely prevents him from coming out until it becomes very clear that all is forgotten and forgiven.

Helping a Man Duck and Dodge

During a difficult conversation, there are many little comments or "softeners" that a woman can make to help a man duck and dodge so he can hear her feelings without becoming argumentative. Here are a few examples:

Don't Say:	Do Say:
1. "I strongly feel that . . ."	1. "I am not completely sure about this but I feel like . . ."
2. "I am sure that . . ."	2. "I don't really know if this is true for you, but for me it feels like . . ."
3. "I don't think that's right. I feel like . . ."	3. "It's not that I have this all thought out. It's just a feeling. I feel like . . ."
4. "No, that's not what I mean. I feel like . . ."	4. "I haven't really thought about this, but for this moment I feel like . . ."

Don't Say:	**Do Say:**
5. "I disagree because . . ."	5. "I have another way of looking at it. I feel . . ."
6. "I don't agree at all. I feel . . ."	6. "I don't know what's right, but I feel like . . ."
7. "That's not true! I feel like . . ."	7. "Based on my experience, I feel . . ."

Statements like these assure a man that his mate's words and feelings aren't written in stone. They remind him that the action of sharing feelings is a work in progress. Thus a man can most effectively dodge criticism and avoid taking his partner's momentary emotions as facts.

Each of the above examples is equally useful for a man to apply as well. Many times a man will speak his ideas with such certainty that a woman feels he is not open to hearing her point of view. When a man uses softeners, it helps a woman feel free to share her perspective.

When a Man Withdraws into His Cave

Commonly, when men pull away into their private caves, women mistakenly think that something is wrong and try to pull their mates out. Misreading her mate's needs, the woman thinks he is wasting time and begins to criticize him.

A man is able to emerge from the cave only when

he has substantially forgotten the problems of his day. When his wife is waiting at the door with more problems, he just won't come out. And it is her resistance to his being in the cave that actually keeps him there.

**The more women try to get their men
to come out of the cave,
the longer they will remain in it.**

To gradually draw a man back to the family is a crucial element of a woman's new job description. Here are the three basic steps they should take:

Step 1. Give him lots of alone time and let him see that you don't mind. Encourage him to spend time with his male friends by not getting upset or feeling hurt when he expresses the desire to do so.

Try to avoid crowding him or being critical. Remember that giving unsolicited advice is generally taken as criticism in the "Male" language. Whenever possible, tell him how much you appreciate his efforts to succeed at work.

If possible, act as if his going into his cave is no big deal. When he returns and begins to be affectionate, be sure to let him know how good it feels.

Step 2. Ask him to do specific little things for you, and express your gratitude when he carries them out. For example, don't complain that he doesn't spend enough time with you. That's an accusation and will put him on the defensive. Instead, ask him to take you to a specific restaurant or movie on a specific day. Don't leave it to him to figure out where and when to go. Make it as easy for him as possible.

Let him repeatedly experience success in fulfilling you. That way, he will gradually associate pleasing you with releasing stress. Eventually, when he wants to de-stress he will begin thinking of little things he can do for you.

Step 3. This third technique is the most important and requires the most skill and practice: at chosen times, ask him to listen to your feelings. At such times be careful not to offend him or give him the impression that he is not doing enough. By preparing him to not feel blamed and appreciating him afterward for listening, you allow him to learn slowly to bring his awareness back to the relationship.

Talk about problems and feelings. If he begins to be frustrated, remind him that you are not asking him to solve your problems and only want him to listen. Without feeling the pressure of problem solving, he will relax and become an increasingly better listener.

Even if a man knows that you are using new relationship skills with him, he will still be grateful. Keep in mind that men want to be in relationships. These three steps are just common sense when a woman understands how her partner's needs are different. Just as she needs his support to listen to her feelings so that she can forget her problems, he needs her support to remember what is really important to him.

What to Do When a Man Is Upset

While women directly process their feelings through talking, men need to do something while silently thinking about their feelings. Only after first thinking about his feelings will it benefit him to talk about his feelings.

Generally speaking, a man will feel the need to talk mainly when he thinks it will help convey information to solve a problem. If someone has offended or hurt him, he may feel the urge to talk to convey that what this person did was wrong and that they should change.

> **When a man talks while angry, he is generally heavily invested in being right.**

A man greatly misunderstands when a woman who is upset wants to talk because he mistakenly believes that she is saying he is wrong and should change. Why? Because when an emotional man feels the same need, he *is* blaming and accusing. Men must learn that when a woman shares feelings, no matter how angry and accusing she sounds, she is really asking for empathy.

With this new understanding, a woman can appreciate the wisdom of *not* persisting in trying to draw a man out when he doesn't want to talk. Not only should she not question him, she should take special pains to postpone conversation gracefully even if he *is* willing to talk while emotionally upset.

The old advice that warns couples never to go to bed upset or angry can make a lot of trouble today. When a man is angry, I strongly recommend that a woman give him lots of space and let him sleep on it. Wait till he has cooled off a bit before talking together about what is bothering him.

However, if a woman is upset and a man is centered enough to listen without getting upset, then it is advisable for him to initiate a conversation, ask questions, and draw her out by making it safe for her to talk. The old adage about not going to bed angry was mainly for men to understand about women. A woman didn't need to apply it because when her husband was upset he usually went off to deal with his feelings alone.

Men today are more in touch with their female tendencies, and when they are upset or angry they sometimes want to talk. It is important for women to understand the wisdom of postponing these kinds of conversations, particularly if you have previously had negative and painful arguments. This skill of postponing is another skill your mother could not teach you.

What Do You Say When a Man Is Upset?

If a man is upset and wants to talk, a woman tends to assume that he will calm down through talking. This is true only if she agrees with what he says. Remember, men want to be right when they talk and are upset at the same time. If she is not prepared to agree with what he has to say or at least appreciate his points, then it is important for her to postpone the conversation.

Most women would not consider postponing a man from sharing his feelings because they would not want him to postpone them if he could listen. If a woman postpones another woman, it is rude. If a man can possibly listen and postpones a woman, it is rude. But if a woman feels that she can't agree with or at least appreciate his points when he is angry, then although it may feel rude to him, it is very important that she postpone him.

How she handles the postponement is very important. She should not be accusatory because it will only inflame him. What she should do is briefly validate his feelings and then postpone discussion. Then, without saying anything else, she should walk away as if what she is doing is perfectly normal and everything is fine. This is a new relationship skill which allows him to save face and cool off.

What a Woman Shouldn't Say:	**What a Woman Should Say:**
1. "I can't talk to you when you're angry."	1. "You have a right to be upset. I need some time before I can talk."
2. "You don't care about me. Why should I talk to you?"	2. "I want to hear your feelings, but I need some time to sort out my own."
3. "You just want to be right! You don't hear what I say."	3. "Let me take some time to appreciate what you said, and then I can talk about it."
4. "You don't understand!"	4. "I need some time to think about what you are saying."
5. "I can't believe the way you are speaking to me!"	5. "I understand that you are upset, and I need some time before I can talk about this."

> **Women should remember that, unlike themselves, men feel better by taking time to cool off and think things through. Asking a man questions when he is upset and angry will tend just to make him angrier.**

The best time to talk with a man is after he's had a chance to think about a problem, has released any negative feelings, and has reconnected with more positive ones. If, after spending time by himself, he still seems upset, a woman should definitely not press for a discussion. Wait till the next day to ask him casually if something is going on that he wants to talk about. If he says "It's nothing," but isn't being warm and loving, the chances are that he needs a little more time to feel accepted and appreciated for what he does for her before beginning to come back.

Just as a cold may no longer be contagious but still produces symptoms, a man may have already resolved his feelings and solved his problems but needs to be loved and appreciated before his warm feelings reemerge.

Reassuring Sounds

In learning to speak "Female," one of the most supportive things a man can do is to be an alert listener prepared to offer simple gestures of support and reassurance. These can be as basic as a hug, eye contact, an occasional nod of the head, or sounds from him that translate into calm and soothing coos of understanding in "Female."

When a woman talks, these are some of the sounds that make her feel heard by a man. Each sound is accompanied by a short translation.

He Says:	She Hears:
1. "Hmmm"	1. "I am thinking about that."
2. "Oh"	2. "I am amazed by that. Now I can understand."
3. "Ahhuh" or "Umhuh"	3. "I am following you, I am right here with you, keep going."
4. "Huh"	4. "I think I am getting it, tell me more."
5. "Mmmm"	5. "I am so sorry that happened, I feel really bad about that."
6. "Hunnh"	6. "I can't believe that happened. You don't deserve to be treated that way."
7. "Ooo" (as in *soon*)	7. "I am shocked. That must have really hurt."
8. "Ouch"	8. "I empathize with your pain."

He Says:	She Hears:
9. "Wow"	9. "Really, that actually happened?"
10. "Auool"	10. "That's too bad, I feel so sorry."
11. "Hmmph"	11. "What they did is wrong; you don't have to put up with it."
12. "Wooo"	12. "That's exciting, how interesting!"

These various sounds should be expressed primarily when she pauses. Practicing them can help a man duck and dodge. Instead of offering solutions when she pauses, he can focus on making a reassuring sound.

If a man is not used to making these kinds of sounds, it may feel very contrived at first. Once he sees that it works, it will, however, gradually become more automatic and natural.

When a Woman Has Strong Feelings

Sometimes when a woman has strong feelings, she talks to discover what her feelings are. If her partner is a good listener and practices ducking and dodging and not interrupting, she can get it all out. By noticing when she is feeling upset, tired, or overwhelmed and then initiating a conversation by asking questions, it can help her a lot.

Here are questions a man can ask to initiate a conversation. They are:

1. "Looks like you've had a long day."
2. "What's the matter?"
3. "What's going on?"
4. "Do we need to talk about something?"
5. "How was your day?"
6. "Are you upset with me?"
7. "Did I do something to bother you?"
8. "Is there something we should talk about?"

In most cases, she will say something like "Oh, it's not you. There is just so much going on," and then continue to talk about it. Even if she was a little upset with him, she will quickly tend to dismiss those feelings because he has initiated the conversation. When she feels supported, she can be very generous with her love. If a woman agrees to talk but is overwhelmed, having trouble getting to her feelings, or directing her negative emotions at him, here are five basic "disarming" questions a man can use to draw her out and deflect her verbal bullets:

1. "How do you feel when . . . ?"
2. "How else do you feel when . . . ?"
3. "Tell me more."
4. "What would feel good to you?"
5. "What do you need to feel supported by me?"

Requests like these impress a woman as supportive. When she doesn't feel the responsibility for initiating conversation, she can much more efficiently move through her feelings.

A Woman's Need for Downtime

After a woman has expressed her feelings, she may not even know exactly what she has said until some minutes later. That's because she is working things through as she is talking. She is in a process. Once she has finished, she then has a chance to look back at what she has shared.

Generally speaking, if a woman is upset and shares her feelings, it takes her about fifteen minutes to reflect on what she said. After such consideration, she begins to appreciate a man's strong support.

However, if a man says something in "Male" (which is bound to be provocative) during that fifteen minutes, it can undo all the good he did. It will be as though he gave a gift and then took it back. And to a woman that is worse than not giving it in the first place.

That fifteen minutes is a very vulnerable time for a woman. It is a time for her to reflect on what she has said. If a man is trying to tell her that she is wrong, or if she feels she has to defend herself, then it is very hard for her to see her mistakes and release any negative feelings she is holding on to.

How Men Learn from Their Mistakes

In a similar way, when a man makes a mistake and a woman is on his case to remind him, he is not free to reflect on his error and plan to learn from it. When a woman corrects a man's behavior, he instinctively moves to defend it by returning to his cave where only "Male" is spoken.

Women generally feel a strong urge to correct a

man's behavior. Instinctively, they will offer advice or criticize his decisions or behavior, not knowing that they are preventing him from making the inner adjustments he needs to make.

How We Influence Each Other

When men and women begin to understand their differences in a new and positive light, learn each other's languages, and practice new relationship skills, they are able to draw out of their partners the best they have to offer. As a result, both men and women are more fulfilled. A man is greatly fulfilled because he feels successful in supporting his partner, and she feels fulfilled because she has created a relationship in which to grow and thrive. They may still speak different languages, but harmony grows as they begin learning how to correctly translate and convey important messages.

As we have discussed, when a woman can understand a man's behavior and is able to express a greater acceptance of him, over time he begins to change and become more attentive. Her nondemanding attitude draws him out into the relationship like a magnet.

When a man begins to duck and dodge by correctly interpreting his partner's feelings, he is able to listen to her with greater empathy and comprehension. At the most basic level of her being, she feels seen, heard, understood, and supported. Her feminine spirit soars. As a result, she is able to be more loving and accepting of her man. As he increasingly understands her, he quite naturally begins to share more with her.

While these skills may seem unnatural in the beginning, in time they will become very automatic. They are merely the extensions of social and language skills we have already been using for centuries. In the next chapter, you'll understand why men forget things and women remember every detail of men's mistakes.

CHAPTER 8

Men Are Still from Mars, Women Are Still from Venus

IN MY RELATIONSHIP SEMINARS, I explain that the differences between men and women make it seem as if we are from different planets. I explore these differences in much greater detail in my book, *Men Are from Mars, Women Are from Venus*.

While thousands of people nod their heads in agreement when I give my examples, there are some who don't fully relate. In fact, it is not at all uncommon for many women to say that they more fully relate to my examples of being a man. They feel that they are from Mars and not Venus. I assure them that nothing is wrong, and that even though society has to a great extent influenced them to become more masculine, they are still from Venus.

There are many factors that influence a woman having a more developed masculine side or a man having a more developed feminine side. Quite commonly, if a girl bonds more closely with her father or if she was raised in a very male-dominated household, she will tend to more fully develop her masculine side. Likewise, if a boy bonds more closely with his mother or if he is raised in a very female-dominated household, he will tend to more fully develop his female side.

Generally speaking, though, a woman becomes more masculine when she has not witnessed a woman being feminine and also being respected. Likewise, a man becomes more feminine when he has not witnessed a man being loving and also being strong and powerful.

Cultural backgrounds and certain ethnic groups also have characteristics that are more "masculine" or "feminine." For example, Germans and Swedes tend to frown upon open displays of emotion or talking just for the sake of talking instead of trying to make a point, whereas Italian families are much more emotionally expressive.

Sometimes the different feminine tendencies don't show up in a woman because when she is single and rather isolated, she has become the Martian and takes care of herself. Once she is in a relationship, many traditional female tendencies begin to emerge.

In other cases, a woman will become more masculine or Martian because in her relationship over time she experiences that it is not safe to be feminine.

For example, the feminine need to talk more may cause too much frustration or make her look weak. Rather than appear too needy or cause conflict, she automatically begins to suppress her feminine side.

Men sometimes also feel that they are from Venus. Creative men in particular experience both their male and female sides. These men generally are attracted to women who are more on their male side. Again, the formula holds true: differences attract.

In some cases, these men didn't have positive role models for expressing masculine power. They do not know how to assert themselves and set limits, but also be loving and caring. To fulfill the woman, they are willing to sacrifice their needs. Not only are they personally weakened, but when they become more feminine, women lose their attraction to them and leave. By using new relationship skills, these men can automatically begin to develop their masculine sides while also respecting their feminine sides.

Emotional Role Reversal

When a man is more on his female side or a woman is more on her male side, he or she is experiencing an emotional role reversal. As we discussed earlier, this term does not in any way imply psychological neurosis. It is merely an imbalance.

To improve relationships, balance must be reestablished. To create ideal relationships, both the male and female sides of each partner must be nurtured.

When couples are not skilled in supporting each other, a woman will automatically begin to close down to her female side, and a man will withhold his instinctive desire to support from his male side. She feels "I will not give of myself anymore because I am not supported," and he feels "Why should I be giving of myself when it doesn't make a difference?"

When a Man Is on His Female Side

When a man is operating too much from his female side, the antidote is for him to do things that will immediately allow his mate to nurture his male side.

He should look to her for appreciation and acknowledgment. When she supports him in this way, and he can more quickly reestablish balance, she benefits as well.

If a man is on his female side, applying new relationship skills may not at first feel natural. His female side will say "Why do I have to duck and dodge and make it safe for her? I want her to make it safe for me! I want to talk too."

By overcoming this resistance and learning to listen first and "contain" before expressing his own feelings, a man exercises and strengthens his male side. When his male side has successfully supported her female side, it is then productive and healthy for him to allow her to be there for his female side. After he has nurtured her female side and she has nurtured his masculine side by appreciating his support, then it is fine for him to look freely to her to nurture his female side.

If a man has a more developed female side, he will feel a pull to be nurtured by his mate's masculine side. He will feel a greater need for her to be there for him. He will get upset when she doesn't want to talk or work on the relationship. He will complain that she is not there for him in the relationship. He will ask lots of questions to get her to talk more. He will want her to listen and understand his feelings and offer sympathy and help him in various ways.

A man's female side has legitimate needs, but to allow them full access in a relationship will tend to push a woman to her masculine side. Such a man can better support the needs of his feminine side by going to a men's support group, spending more time with his male friends, doing personal growth work, or looking to God for this kind of support.

Requiring his partner to support his female side puts an enormous strain on the relationship.

A woman is already needing more support to connect with her female side; she can't find her female side and also be the man for his female side.

When a man looks to a woman primarily for this kind of support, not only does he push her to her masculine side but it may even weaken him. Unable to talk with other males about their problems, many men complain to their wives. This creates even greater imbalance.

After a while, as he talks more and more she will talk less and less. A man needs to be careful not to "whine" too much with his wife or she will begin mothering and her desire for him will flicker and dim. As a general suggestion, a man should not express more sensitivities than his mate. If he is more sensitive, he will need to toughen up a bit by nurturing his male side more.

When a woman says she wants a sensitive man, she really means that she wants a man who is strong but is sensitive to her needs. Quite commonly, women are turned off when a man becomes more sensitive than she is. Briefly, in the beginning, it may seem very attractive, particularly if she is on her male side, but very quickly, if it persists for too long, she becomes increasingly annoyed.

A man needs to be careful not to look to a woman to fulfill his feminine needs. Ideally, a man should look to a woman primarily to nurture his

male side and not his female side. His male side is
nurtured every time he feels appreciated, accepted,
and trusted. The more nurtured he feels, the stronger
and tougher he will be, but at the same time he will
grow more sensitive to her needs. This strength and
sensitivity to her needs is what women really appreciate, and it makes him feel both strong and loving.

If he happens to be more sensitive than she is, it
may take a few years to balance out and find his masculine strength in the relationship. In the meantime,
he should not burden her with his sensitivities. For
example, if his feelings are hurt or if he feels more
emotionally needy, he should then talk with men
friends and not look to her primarily to support his
need to talk and share feelings.

A man achieves balance in a relationship primarily through successfully supporting the female. When
a man succeeds in supporting her, then to a great
extent his own female side is automatically nurtured.
When she is happy, he feels happy because indirectly
his own female side is automatically supported.
When a man loves a woman and feels a deep connection with her, it is then as though her female side
becomes his. Through fulfilling her female side not
only is his male side appreciated but his female side is
also nurtured.

When a Woman Is on Her Male Side

When a woman feels responsible to nurture a man's
female side, it actually puts her out of balance. For
example, when he expects her to listen more to his
feelings, it has the effect of turning her off not only to
him but to her own female side. Automatically, she

begins to become more masculine. New relationship skills are required to assist women in returning to their female side.

A woman feels most nurtured when her female side is directly supported. A woman achieves balance through successfully supporting her male partner in supporting her. If she can create a climate in which to receive the support she needs in order to be happy, her male side is also simultaneously developed.

In this way a woman is able to assert her male side to solve the problems while safeguarding her female side through being directly nurtured by her partner. On the other hand, when she directly supports her male partner's female side, she overlooks her own, until one day she wakes up angry and resentful that their caring and understanding are no longer reciprocal.

When a woman is too much on her male side, the antidote is creating relationships in which her female side blossoms. If she works in a traditionally male role all day, she will have to make deliberate efforts to overcome much inner resistance in order to do this.

When a woman on her masculine side gets home, she may want to go to her cave. She is definitely not in a communicative mood. She feels a much greater need for space than her man does. She needs to solve problems and can't waste time talking about them.

Since her male side wants to be appreciated, accepted, and trusted, she resents it when her partner gives her advice or doesn't recognize all that she does. In most cases, she would rather do things herself. She definitely feels that her partner isn't giving her the appreciation she deserves as a provider.

To support her male side she needs to spend time

with other women who can nurture her male side's need to be appreciated.

Ideally, a woman should look to the man in her life for caring, understanding, and respect. These qualities of love nurture her female side. As she gets those needs fulfilled and her appreciation for her partner increases, then she can expect that he will overflow and appreciate all that she does as well.

It is definitely not healthy for a woman and a man to compete for appreciation in a relationship.

While it is important for women to be appreciated, they should look to their male partners to support their female sides. Women today need a man's support more than ever to be able to return to their feminine sides at the end of the day.

Emotional Role Reversal and Attraction

With so many women in the workforce, it is becoming more common for them to begin a relationship in emotional role reversal. By pursuing him more actively, a woman causes a man to move more to his female side. Rather than feel a responsibility to initiate a relationship, he waits and lets her do the pursuing.

When a woman is on her male side, she tends to be attracted to a man on his female side and vice versa. Many men sense this automatically and move to their female side. This is a trap. Unless men consciously work to find balance, they will eventually lose their appeal.

When a woman is more masculine, a man tends to become more feminine. Likewise, if a man becomes more feminine, a woman becomes more masculine. If she doesn't learn skills to assist him in nurturing her female side, she will become even more masculine. The more masculine she becomes, the more feminine he becomes.

If a very masculine man becomes more feminine, he is moving toward balance. But if he is already too much on his female side, pushing him farther into it creates greater imbalance.

If he is very feminine and she is very masculine, maintaining attraction requires his slowly but surely developing his masculine side as she develops her feminine side. By developing the male and female sides in tandem, new relationship skills promote greater balance and attraction.

Conventional Relationships

In more conventional relationships, the man is more masculine and the woman is more feminine. The attraction lessens over time if the woman repeatedly experiences that she cannot be supported on her female side. Rather than risk the pain of repeated invalidation or rejection, she closes up and becomes in certain ways more masculine.

The same is true for men. Rather than continuing to do masculine things like make decisions, initiate sex, and solve problems for her, when he doesn't feel appreciated he suppresses his male side. In various ways he will automatically become more feminine.

Without the sexual polarity, the attraction between partners dissipates.

Although couples may start out very masculine and feminine, over time they begin to reverse roles emotionally. When a man doesn't feel his masculine side being supported, he then automatically begins to go out of balance. Likewise, when a woman doesn't get the support she needs at the office and at home to be feminine, then she also goes out of balance.

Balancing the Masculine and the Feminine

Ironically, men go out of balance because they are not getting the support from women that they used to get in the old days, while women go out of balance because they are not getting a new kind of support from men.

To solve our modern problems, women need to find within themselves the feminine love they used to share, but without giving up the new power they are expressing. A modern man's challenge is to draw upon his ancient courage and risk failure by trying out new formulas for success in order to support the woman he loves in new ways.

When men and women are unaware of the necessary techniques needed to create balance, emotional role reversal automatically kicks in. For both sexes, it commonly happens in distinct stages.

Emotional Role Reversal and Doing It All

When a woman returns home from work, her tendency is to stay in her masculine side, particularly if there is more work to be done. Instead of relaxing and talking about her problems, she feels that she faces a new list of problems *that need to be solved*. She either talks about them to get her partner's help to solve them or she doesn't want to talk at all. She feels she has to do it all. To cope with her frustration, she too may begin to withdraw from the relationship and feel a need to go to her cave.

Her experience changes when she is on her female side. When a woman is connected to her feminine side, she is capable of enjoying and appreciating the small details of living. She may be aware of problems, but she does not have to solve them immediately in order to feel good.

When she is too much on her male side, she then suddenly feels an urgency to solve all of life's little and big problems. She feels too responsible for doing "everything" and taking care of everyone. She feels overwhelmed. Instead of feeling loving, peaceful, warm, and happy to be home, she feels, to various degrees, frustrated, overworked, unappreciated, and unsupported. It is then extremely difficult for her to take time out for herself and appreciate life's simple pleasures.

When a woman feels overwhelmed at the end of the day, she is generally enough in touch with her female side to remember all her problems, but her male side demands that she find solutions and do something. In this state, it is hard for her to relax or even know what would nurture her female side.

When women are feeling overwhelmed, they are so focused on getting things done that they literally can't feel the inner needs and wants of their feminine sides. Each time they finish a task, rather than feel relieved, they begin to feel the inner emptiness and longing of their female sides.

Three Ways a Woman Goes Out of Balance

When a woman feels heavily overwhelmed, she doesn't feel safe talking in a non-goal-oriented manner because she has moved out of balance to her problem-solving male side and can't get back. This tends to manifest itself in three distinct ways.

Stage One: Feeling Overwhelmed and Overeating

A woman's most common reaction to undernourishment of her female side is to eat. Eating is an easy replacement for love. Through feeding herself, she can temporarily suppress the painful feelings of insecurity that are emerging from her female side. By numbing feelings, her potential for passion is stilled.

Women overeat to quench the deeper thirst for nurturing and secure relationships. This tendency is technically called a "need replacement." If she can't get what she really needs, the real need is replaced by another need that appears more attainable.

In this case, her need for love is replaced by her need for food. Until the craving for love is satisfied, she will always be hungry. Through eating more she is able to temporarily repress the persistent longings of her female side and find relief. In some cases, she may even fool herself temporarily into believing that she is quite happy and that she doesn't need to talk or share in a nurturing relationship.

Why Women Gain Weight

Quite commonly, soon after a woman gets married she frequently begins to put on weight in excess of the natural gain mandated by aging and childbirth.

This shift takes place not because the relationship has problems, but because marriage itself makes a woman relax and feel more secure. As her female side begins to blossom, it says "Now that I am loved, I can finally come out and be nurtured, supported, and heard." She begins involuntarily to experience emotions and urges that women have felt for centuries but which have been suppressed by modern independent living.

You see, as a woman connects more deeply with her female side, her natural tendency to talk about feelings and problems abruptly emerges. It is as if she is possessed by the spirits of her female ancestors. These alien feelings from her ancient past make her modern self feel that she is overly needy, emotional, illogical, petty, even weak. Many women are embarrassed by these feelings.

In a state of emotional confusion, the last thing a woman wants is to share the origins of that confusion with her spouse. In most cases, she doesn't even feel comfortable sharing these new feelings with other women. She doesn't know what to do because she never saw her mother successfully sharing feelings or problems with her father that resulted in her getting his respect and support. To avoid creating unnecessary conflict or frustrating her mate, she chooses to suppress the need to share these feelings coming from her female side and, as a result, feels a new need to eat more.

The more she eats, the more she is able to keep at

bay these strange new feelings and tendencies, but only temporarily. Until she finds a way to fulfill and directly nurture her female side on a regular basis, she will continue to use food as a painkiller.

When a woman tries to solve the problem of overeating through dieting, she goes even farther out of balance by moving toward her male side. During a diet, the body feels the panic of famine and craves food even more. The female side is nurtured by feeling secure and supported. The imposition of strict discipline requiring control nurtures and strengthens the male side, not the female side.

Ease, comfort, effortlessness, security, fun, recreation, pleasure, and beauty all nurture the female side. Dieting does not. Recent diet programs that encourage women to *eat more* low-fat foods and exercise at a slow, easy pace instead of depriving themselves are definitely a better approach to losing weight. However, the most effective solution to female weight problems is more nurturing relationships and a less pressured, more relaxed lifestyle.

Stage Two: Women Who Do Too Much

When women are deprived of the support their female side requires to avoid feeling the pain of rejection, they move to their male side and begin exhibiting traditional masculine tendencies. They become increasingly goal oriented, competitive, assertive, independent, and efficient. They take great pride in being logical and rational. In most cases, life experiences or certain messages in childhood have conditioned them to reject feminine feelings as weak, undesirable, and unlovable.

It is hard for these women to see themselves as being lovable to men if they were to be soft and feminine. They work hard to hide their feminine sensitivities and needs. Incorrectly assuming that "femininity" is undesirable, they have no idea why a man would be attracted to "that."

These women deal with their inner female side by becoming hard instead of soft, tough instead of sensitive, and independent instead of dependent. Self-sufficiency is their primary method of coping. They tend to pull away from intimate conversation. In some cases, they even scorn the male support that could eventually bring them fulfillment and prevent them from shifting into the mode of doing more.

For some women, the tendency to "do more" means more domestic perfectionism. Everything has to be in its place, organized, and clean. For others, it simply implies that there is never enough time to relax. If women cannot relax because their male side demands solutions to their problems, passion quickly loses its magic and disappears, and sex becomes mechanical.

Other women do too much by taking on excessive responsibility. They have a hard time saying no when they feel needed. They may even feel compelled to do things that they are not even asked to do. They pride themselves on anticipating the needs of others and "being there" for them.

What a Man Can Do for Her

To support a woman, a man must understand that, deep inside, she longs to relax, let go, and surrender to someone she trusts to care for and support her. This is the true inner need of the female side.

However, because she judges her need for help as unacceptable, it is unconsciously replaced by a false need. The replacement need emerges as an urgent calling to fulfill others. She feels as if her happiness is based on providing fulfillment for others instead of getting her own needs satisfied. In a sense, she becomes the responsible and caring man she wishes could fulfill her.

This insight is valuable for both women and men. When a woman is becoming overly responsible, instead of chastising her for doing too much, a man can realize that she needs help in getting back to her feminine side. Without a supportive partner, women on their male side tend to become increasingly self-sufficient and thus decrease the possibilities of having a man support them.

Women who feel overwhelmed rarely get the support they need. They do not know how to be vulnerable or to ask for it. Since they are seen as self-sufficient, help is rarely offered. If it is, it's rejected. No one is allowed to see the vulnerable part of her. Everyone is encouraged to regard with admiration the strong and giving side.

Such women have trouble even contacting their needs and giving to themselves for a change. There is little a man can do for them unless he understands that the stronger these women appear, the more needy they are deep within.

Men without a deeper understanding are easily frustrated by women who do too much. The busier she is, the less time and appreciation she has for him. He does not feel that he can help her and then fulfill her.

No matter what he does for her, she is always driven to do more. On a feeling level, he feels cut off from her. If he cannot do for her, then he cannot receive her love. He doesn't feel that he can make a difference in her life. In a very real sense, her independence and sense of autonomy push him away.

These women do not understand that men love to make a difference; to be fulfilled a man needs to feel successful in providing for her fulfillment. This is how men experience greater intimacy with women.

How to Attract Mr. Right

Because it's more difficult for women who do too much to start relationships, they commonly ask me how to attract a man.

My response is to ask them why they *need* a man. The question invariably takes them by surprise. They give answers like:

"Well, I don't know if I really *need* a man" or "I'm not so sure that I *need* a man."

Others are more deliberate, clearly stating, "I don't really *need* a man, but I want one."

If these women are to secure a lasting relationship, they must first begin to open up to their feminine side, which feels no shame in saying "I need a man."

If women are to secure a lasting relationship, they must first begin to open up to their feminine side, which feels no shame in saying "I need a man."

When a woman is in a hurry or desperate for a relationship, she is definitely feeling from her female side, but it's not sufficiently nurtured to attract the right man. Through nurturing her female side something magical begins to happen. She feels her need for a man and trusts that at the right time and in the right place she will find him. This openness can be cultivated by finding fulfillment in her female friendships without depending on a man, yet remaining open to receiving a man's support.

How Men Experience Intimacy

We must always keep in mind that a man bonds emotionally by successfully doing for a woman. A man experiences greater intimacy each time he succeeds in providing his partner with fulfillment. We must also remember that women experience greater intimacy primarily by receiving love and support. This is a very important distinction. If a woman *cannot* slow down and allow a man to nurture her female side, she will have trouble creating a bond in the first place.

A simple example of the new relationship skill of slowing down can be seen simply and graphically: a man and a woman approach a door. Women who do too much will speed up, politely open the door, and wait for the man to walk through. They give to others what they need themselves, which only reinforces the tendency to give and not receive. To nurture her female side, a woman should practice slowing down to make sure he gets to the door first, waiting for him to open it, walking through, and thanking him. When she lets him open the door for her, she gives him an opportunity to support her successfully.

Rituals for Finding Balance

Through this dynamic, a man is placed in the masculine role of providing, and a woman moves to her feminine role of graciously receiving. It also clarifies her real need, which is to be cared for. She doesn't physically need him to open the door, but when he does, it supports and nurtures her female side. Her femininity needs and thrives on this kind of support in order to find balance.

When a man opens the door for a woman, it is as if he is saying "You are special to me, I care about you, I honor you, I am here for you, I understand you do so much for everyone so I am happy to help make things easier for you whenever I can."

This loving message is given each time a man goes a little out of his way to show consideration for making his partner's life easier and more comfortable. Actions speak much louder than words.

Stage Three: Women Who Want Men to Talk More

The third most common reaction women have when they experience the imbalance of emotional role reversal is to long for their men to talk more and share themselves in traditionally feminine ways.

A woman in this third stage longs for a man to open up and share his feelings the way she would if she were in balance. It is as though she wants him to be feminine before she can feel safe in being feminine.

These women fully believe that they would be fulfilled if their partners would only open up and be more sensitive and vulnerable.

> **This longing for men to be softer and
> more sensitive is really a replacement
> need. It covers the women's real
> longing to be more sensitive
> and soft themselves.**

Just as the overweight woman replaces her need for love with the need for food, or the woman who "does too much" replaces her need to be supported with the need to support others, this woman replaces her need to be feminine with the need for her partner to be feminine.

These replacement needs are not deliberate choices but are reflexive reactions that occur when women are required to function like men without the support they need to be feminine.

When a Woman Doesn't Feel Safe

A woman in a loving relationship may feel unsafe because she feels unlovable or because her partner hasn't yet learned how to make her feel secure. Regardless of why she doesn't feel safe, when she can't express her female side, she will automatically move to her male side and exhibit more masculine traits. To find balance, she will begin to crave a more "feminine" partner.

Generally, the man she chooses is already more sensitive and open. In some cases, though, he is originally a less sensitive man, but over time she tries to make him more feminine by demanding that he open up and share more or become more domestic. This reaction occurs because the woman doesn't have a clear picture of how to get the nurturing support she needs for her own female side. She feels driven to support his female side.

Instinctively she feels "If I can listen sympathetically to his problems and feelings, he'll listen to mine. If I can fulfill his feminine needs, he'll fulfill mine." While this formula works with other women, it does not work with men.

When a Woman Wants to Talk

I can tell when my wife really has something to tell me because she inevitably asks me lots of questions. For example, when I return from teaching my weekend seminars, she will sometimes be particularly interested in seeing me and asking lots of questions. This is a signal that she has a lot to share. I now understand that after answering a few questions, I am supposed to ask her questions about her weekend.

By cracking the secret feminine code, I have learned to give Bonnie what she's asking for. Before I understood how we were different, the same situation would turn into a major argument.

She would ask me questions about my weekend when she wanted to talk instead of simply telling me what she wanted to share. What I really wanted to do was relax quietly. But I could tell she wanted me to talk, so I would try. When I look back at those times, I can see that it was like pulling teeth. The more she wanted me to talk, the less I wanted to.

After a few minutes of answering her questions as briefly as possible, I felt as if I'd answered her questions (as a gift to her) and then would go relax and watch TV (as a gift for me). Little did I know that this was not what was expected. Now she was even more upset. Not only had I resisted her questions, I wasn't asking her questions in return.

The process only became positive when I could read the signals and begin applying new relationship skills. Now when Bonnie asks me lots of questions, I talk a little and then ask her lots of questions. If she is still not talking, I gently persist. Once she gets going, I let her do most of the talking because it is her need more than mine.

Never talking more than a woman as a general guideline counteracts the tendency to go into emotional role reversal. Certainly, on some occasions I will talk more, but when I begin to notice it is happening a lot, I pull back and focus on assisting her in opening up.

The startling truth that I have discovered only in the past ten years is that the more a woman is dependent on her partner to talk and open up, the farther she gets from her female side.

With this insight I eventually came to realize that the greatest gift I could give my clients was to help the men be successful in listening to the women. I would also help the women "prepare" them so that listening was not insurmountably difficult. Once a man eventually learned this skill, he didn't get so upset with his female partner's feelings. Suddenly, women were feeling much safer and freer about expressing their feelings. Using this approach, couples quite quickly felt more successful in their relationships.

How Women Begin to Feel
When Men Open Up

Let's explore some of the diverse comments made by different women whose partners were more expressive of feelings than they themselves were. While not every woman will relate to each of these, they are very common, particularly to women who have lived with men who are more sensitive.

He Does:	She Feels:
1. He shares how upset he feels when she talks about her feelings.	1. "I didn't realize he was so sensitive. Now I have to be careful all the time. I don't feel safe saying anything to him."
2. He becomes angry and shares his gut reactions to her feelings before taking time to cool off.	2. "No matter what I say, it's upsetting to him. I am afraid to open up with him."
3. He shares openly about all his problems in response to her talking about hers.	3. "He has enough problems. I don't want to burden him with mine. He is just too needy. I don't want another child."
4. He complains too much and always wants things to be better.	4. "I really appreciate that he's opened up, but now that I know him, I'm not really that

He Does:	She Feels:
	attracted to him. I feel bad about it, but I really don't want to be with him anymore."
5. He shares his deep feelings of insecurity and his need to be loved.	5. "I care about his emotions, but I feel like I can't be me around him."
6. He talks too much about his feelings whenever he gets ticked off.	6. "I feel like I have to walk on eggshells when I am around him. I don't feel heard or understood."
7. He shares his hurt feelings and cries more than she does.	7. "I am embarrassed to say this, but when he cries all the time I can respect his feelings, but I lose all my romantic feelings for him."
8. He gets angry a lot and feels that he has to get it out rather than silently contain his feelings in order to cool off.	8. "When he gets angry, I feel like he is a child throwing a tantrum. Automatically I begin to feel like I have to always please and mother him."

He Does:	She Feels:
9. He talks about his problems more, or the problems with the relationship, than she does.	9. "I am really glad we are in therapy. He really needs it. I didn't realize he had so many problems. It's not that I'm perfect, I just feel like he needs someone else. I want to leave because I don't know what to do for him."
10. He whines and complains about things more than she does.	10. "I resent that he whines about everything. I want to be with a more masculine man. I don't want to be married to another woman."
11. He talks about his needs for more in the relationship and looks to his partner to fulfill his female side.	11. "He is always very attentive to me, but I feel that he is always needing more. When I don't talk, he gets upset, and when he talks, I just want to get out of the room. I listen, but I really don't want to."

None of these women could have predicted that they would feel this way. Like many women, they thought that if their male partner would just open up they would be in marital bliss.

How Women React to a Man's Sensitivities

The way a woman reacts to her partner's vulnerabilities is practically the opposite of how a man will respond to hers. If he hears her feelings *and doesn't feel blamed,* then he cares and connects with his own female side. By listening to a woman share, a man can feel sensitive to her feelings and yet strong and determined to help.

When a woman listens to a man's feelings, she also becomes stronger but resents having to care more for him when she needs him to care for her.

This shift in women can be extremely gradual and hard to detect. As a man opens up, she is initially very impressed and finds his behavior endearing. Unfortunately, she eventually tires of it and turns off to him. Even when she wants to leave him, she will feel that it is "not him but her." In many cases, however, it is because he opened up more than she did and she was simply turned off.

The bottom line here is that women are more fulfilled if their male partners reveal less but help them to reveal more.

When a woman longs for a man to open up and be sensitive, she is really longing to open up and become more sensitive and vulnerable herself.

Three Ways a Man Goes Out of Balance

When a man doesn't feel appreciated in his relationship with a woman or at his job, he begins to shift out of balance in any of three ways.

Each of these reactions is counterproductive. They may bring immediate short-term relief from feeling the pain of not being supported on his male side, but in the long run they only weaken him more. They are addictive behaviors that assist him in avoiding his pain but do little to directly solve the real problem.

Stage One: Overworking

A man's most common impulse when he doesn't feel supported at home is to work harder at the office. As we have already discussed, a man reacts instinctively to a woman's dissatisfaction by trying to provide more money, so he becomes increasingly driven to achieve more and succeed more. No matter how successful he is, it is never enough. He silently criticizes himself for not being better, for making mistakes and not being good enough.

Through repeatedly focusing on his need for success (or his failure to achieve that success), he is temporarily freed from feeling his unfulfilled need to be appreciated by others. He avoids feeling unappreciated in his relationship by asserting his independence and competence at work.

He will convince himself that he doesn't need to be appreciated. This is only because he has not tasted the fulfillment of being appreciated for his every effort and action regardless of the result. Forgiveness, acceptance, and appreciation have not been his experience growing up or while in relationships with women.

In most cases, when a man begins drifting from a relationship focus to a work focus, he doesn't even know that he's missing the appreciation he used to get from his spouse. He may agree with her when she says, "Why should I appreciate him for emptying the trash, it's his trash too." Unaware that he needs to be appreciated for the little things, he seeks to do big things for her that should reap the reward of her favor. But they don't.

Without the daily experience of appreciation at home, a man begins to measure himself solely by the results of his work. Because his hunger for success is really a replacement for his true need to be appreciated, he is never satisfied with his success.

He is in a self-defeating pattern and is spiraling down. The more he focuses on work, the less he does directly for his wife. If he is not doing things directly for his wife, her appreciation will not touch him. Even if she does appreciate him, he can barely feel it. The less appreciated he feels, the more self-critical and dissatisfied he becomes.

This first stage inevitably leads him to the second stage of imbalance. When he comes home, he is unable to shift from the work mode to the relationship mode.

Stage Two: He Doesn't Come Out of His Cave

When a man comes home feeling unsuccessful at work, he immediately pulls away from his partner to relax and forget the problems of his day. As we have already discussed, temporarily pulling away is quite normal. However, since he is recovering from the added stress of feeling unsuccessful, it will take him much longer before he is ready to emerge.

But in stage two, he simply cannot forget the pressure. If a man feels bad about his work, it is much harder to feel good, even while pursuing a hobby or watching his favorite team. When the pressure to succeed predominates, the power of his cave time activities to release him from the grip of work diminishes proportionally.

When a man's male side is not sufficiently nurtured by his mate, he has little energy when he gets home. It is as if he is storing it up until he can confront his problems the next day. The masculine energy he used to bring to the relationship is greatly suppressed.

Men experience difficulties in forgetting work-related problems and pressures because their female side keeps reminding them of the problems, while their male side feels incapable of solving them. As a result, they become addicted to cave time activities in an attempt to forget the problems and pressures of work. Such men tend to be disinterested in what is going on around them.

It is hard for a man like this to connect with his partner because not only is he so preoccupied, he doesn't even have the motivation he once did. He has low energy because deep inside he feels like a failure.

Failure is deadly for a man.

A Man's Replacement Needs

In stage one, a man's replacement need is to succeed; in stage two, it is to rest and relax—even though his real need is to be loved and appreciated. He feels as though he wants to be ignored so that he can rest, nap, relax, or zone out by watching TV. While his "vegging out" is a legitimate need, his mate believes that he is just being lazy. That only makes it more difficult for him to hear or be responsive to her requests and needs.

Instead of being assertive, he becomes passive; instead of being interested, he is distracted; instead of wanting to connect, he wants to be left alone. Although resting will bring temporary relief, it does not satisfy his need to be energized by appreciation.

Without an understanding of what their mates require, women unknowingly make the situation worse. They complain that he is not there for them. They do not instinctively focus on appreciating what he does do for them. Even if a man does very little, a woman can still focus on what he *does* do instead of what he doesn't do. In this way, he will be assisted in eventually doing more and getting the appreciation he needs.

Once he gets going, it is like a snowball rolling down a hill, building up speed and growing bigger and bigger. As a man is appreciated for what he does, he will do a little more. When a man is appreciated, he will summon up the energy and motivation to do still more. With a woman's love, he can build up his strength to come out of the cave.

**When a man is appreciated, he will
summon up the energy and motivation
to do still more.**

A woman can also help a man by helping herself. Her being happier will even help him to come out. When he sees that she isn't unhappy and blaming him for not coming out, he feels he must be doing something right.

When a woman is happy, a man tends to take the credit and feel good about himself. For example, if he supports her financially, if she goes shopping and returns thanking him for what she bought, he'll feel much better.

The downside of a man's taking the credit for a woman's feelings is that when she is not happy, he feels that he's more of a failure and retreats even deeper into his cave.

When men are in this stage, women tend to criticize them for being lazy and unsupportive. By understanding this second stage, it will be much more possible for her to be compassionate and supportive instead of nagging and complaining.

Comparing Men and Women

By comparing a man's second stage to her own, a woman can increase her understanding. Just as it is difficult for a woman to move out of stage two, it is equally difficult for a man.

A woman in the second stage feels compelled to do more. For her to relax and slow down, she needs a lot of support. When she is married or has children, she is even more driven. Almost every woman knows how hard it is to relax and have a good time when feeling overwhelmed and needed by others.

In a similar but opposite way, a second-stage man feels driven to do less. He can easily relax but

cannot feel motivated to do more. He is energized by
the thought of some recreational activity but becomes
suddenly exhausted by the thought of being domesti-
cally responsible. He feels a strong need to rest, and
do less, while she feels a strong need to do more. Just
as she can't do something fun and for herself, that is
all he has the energy to do.

Without understanding this dynamic, a relationship can just make it worse for the man. The more he
is needed, the more disappointed others who depend
on him will be. As a result, he becomes even more
immobilized.

With this knowledge, a woman can begin to
imagine what her man is going through. In a similar
way, men can fathom why women in stage-two
imbalance can't just "relax and take it easy."

Moving the Couch Potato

Understanding stage two of emotional role reversal
has helped me immensely. At times when I am not
feeling good about my work, I tend to stay in my
cave for extended periods of time. Even though I
would like to come out, I feel trapped.

To get myself out, I remember that what I really
need is appreciation. My body is telling me that I
need to rest and relax, but my mind now knows better.

So I force myself up off the couch even though
every cell in my body is saying rest, relax, don't get
up. I imagine I am lifting weights to build up my
muscles. When I am out of shape, lifting weights is
always a strain and I don't want to do it. But once I
do, I feel much better and stronger.

In a similar way, when I am feeling like a couch potato and I am glued to the couch, I lift myself up and do something physically that I know my wife will appreciate. It can be as basic as getting up to empty the trash. Once I start moving, she can give me some appreciation. Soon my engines start pumping again.

This technique works especially well because Bonnie takes pains to appreciate my effort. When I do something at home, instead of reacting like "So what, I've been busy since I got home," she will take a moment to articulate her gratitude.

If she doesn't notice what I do, instead of missing an opportunity to be appreciated I can say, "Did you notice that I emptied the trash?"

In response, she will always take a moment to say, "Oh, thanks."

Even if she is resenting me and her guts are saying "Big deal," she makes a point of saying something brief but nice.

Knowing that I can easily be appreciated in my relationship helps me tremendously in coming out of my cave. The repeated experience of appreciation allows me to feel my need for it and then come out and get it. The certain anticipation of her warm responses always helps motivate me to get out of my cave.

If Bonnie takes the time to appreciate me when she is in stage two, it helps her as well. By appreciating me, she is taking a moment to become aware that she really isn't alone and that she does have my support. So she begins to relax. For example, when I come out of my cave to empty the trash, she is not just appreciating me for emptying the trash, she is appreciating me for being her companion, friend, and partner in life.

Her support frees me from getting trapped in my cave. This does not mean that I don't take cave time. When a man is stressed, it is healthy and natural for him to go to his cave. It only becomes unhealthy when he can't come out again.

Twelve-Step Programs

Generally speaking, it is in stage two that a man turns to drinking excessively or other forms of addiction. These elements, of course, only lock him into the cave even more. When a man knows he can spend time with a friend or friends who appreciate him and don't expect anything much from him, it is much easier to leave the cave. This is one of the reasons the twelve-step sharing programs and other sharing programs which validate his adequacy have been so helpful.

When a man is stuck in his cave, one of the ways to bury the pain of not being appreciated is to begin drinking. In a twelve-step program, for example, if he can do one important thing, he will win the appreciation of many others. By abstaining from drinking and showing up, he immediately wins their approval. By continuing to not drink and come to meetings, even if he feels inadequate at work or in his relationships, he feels good about himself because he is not drinking. This is a tremendous help.

Generally speaking, alcoholics in AA are very proud of how many days, weeks, months, or years they have been sober. They wear it like a merit badge, and as the years pass gain seniority. They suddenly have a right to feel better about themselves, and a lot of other people admire and appreciate them as well. They have all been there and understand and appreciate the strength it takes to stop an addiction. This admiration strengthens the male side and counteracts emotional role reversal.

Women also turn to addictions as a result of emotional role reversal. Twelve-step and other sharing programs are again particularly helpful, but for a different reason. The sharing gives women the nurturing that their female side primarily needs.

I do not want to imply that men do not benefit as well by the sharing of feelings. They also have a female side, but before they can come out of their caves they first need to feel that they can do something they will be appreciated for.

One of the many great values of AA for people is that it is a place where they share what they have done or overcome to become sober again. Men get the appreciation they primarily need, while women get the empathy they primarily need.

Relationships and the Cave

When a man is single, there is nothing preventing him from coming out of his cave whenever he feels like it. When he is in a relationship, however, it is nearly impossible for him to come out if his mate resents his pulling away, and sits waiting at the door. Too many women unknowingly make this mistake and actually end up working against their own desires.

When a man is in the cave, a woman wants more from him but can sense that if she asks he will resist like a grumbling bear. It doesn't occur to her that like a bear he is hungry for the honey of her love. She believes that if he talks about his feelings, he'll feel better. Needless to say, the more she tries to get him out by suggesting he do things or by asking him questions, the more he resists.

How to Get a Bear Out of His Cave

With this new awareness, she can use the new relationship skills that her mother never knew to get him out. She can do it by pretending that he literally is a bear.

No one in their right mind would enter a bear's cave while he was sleeping, nor would they try to pull him out.

Instead, you would indirectly draw him out by leaving little pieces of bread outside his door. If the bread doesn't work, you put honey on it. When he smells it, his instincts will tell him to follow the scent. He appears.

Now you begin to sense that he will go wherever you want him to if you leave a trail of bread and honey behind you. If the "bear" is a human male, the bread is the opportunity to do something, and the honey is the appreciation he will get by doing it. Men, like bears, are looking for honey. When they clearly smell acceptance and appreciation, they are motivated to leave the cave.

Stage Three: He Wants More Support from Her

When a man's male side is not supported and he feels stuck in the cave, a third reaction occurs. His male side stays in the cave, but his female side comes out.

Suddenly, he wants his partner to take care of him, but because he is still a man, he demands it in an aggressive way.

We know that when a man is in his cave, a woman should not try to go in after him. In third-stage imbalance, he comes out all right—but with all guns blazing. He is easily hurt, offended, and provoked.

Like a woman, he feels he is "doing everything" and not getting nearly enough back. He has moved way over on his female side and is generally very verbally expressive.

Whenever a man cannot fully come out of his cave, his female side tends to emerge and take control of the relationship. He will tend to overreact to his mate's mistakes, feel a much greater need to talk about his feelings, become much more defensive of his actions, and will demand apologies when she has upset him.

The Need to Be Respected

In this stage of emotional role reversal, a man's real need is still to be appreciated, but because he is not getting the kind of support he really requires, a replacement need takes over. The true need to be appreciated is replaced by the need to be respected.

This tendency is most clearly exhibited in a more extreme manner by an abusive alcoholic father. Quite often he will tend to demand respect by remarks such as "This is my house, and as long as you live here, you will do things my way. . . ."

Even if he is not an alcoholic, a man in this third stage will from time to time present these kinds of demands. When he does, the most effective steps he can take to stop himself are to cease talking to his partner about his feelings and set about containing them. Talking only makes him more rigid, righteous, demanding, and punishing. These are examples of remarks that indicate that a man must get a grip on himself.

What Happens:	**His Gut Reactions in Stage Three:**
1. She expresses feelings of frustration or disappointment.	1. "If you can't be happy, then we should just end this relationship."
2. She expresses unsolicited advice.	2. "You know I don't like it when you talk to me that way. Don't do it."
3. She expresses disapproval about something he did or forgot to do.	3. "No one can treat me this way. If you do not change, then I will leave you."
4. She is in a bad mood and unable to be appreciative.	4. "I do everything for you and this is what I get in return."
5. She complains about something he hasn't done.	5. "How dare you treat me this way. I will not stand for it. You are so ungrateful."

What Happens:	His Gut Reactions in Stage Three:
6. She disapproves of something he did and gives advice.	6. "I will not put up with this anymore. I do everything right, and you are wrong."
7. They get into a heated argument over something petty.	7. "I just can't stand this anymore. I don't deserve to be treated like this. You will never learn. That's it, I'm finished."
8. She does something to annoy him.	8. "I don't want to be mean, but you make me this way. I have to teach you a lesson."

While the above expressions may accurately reflect what he's feeling, it is lethal to express them to his mate. They are entirely negative, selfish, arrogant, shaming, and controlling and can do nothing to create a climate of trust and openness. If he is at all interested in getting the love and support he truly needs, then he must practice containing these kinds of feelings. Yes, they are his gut reactions but not the reactions of his heart and mind. Before he talks, he should first be centered in his heart and mind, not his guts.

A man in emotional role reversal has gone respect crazy. When he gets through making others feel guilty or intimidated, he is only temporarily satisfied. His hunger for respect will grow because his soul is really asking for appreciation. Whenever there is a problem, he has to be right and he is quick to blame and reject others.

In the third stage, a man may want more communication. He demands to know his woman's feelings, yet when she tells him, he argues and wants to share more of his own. Although he is acting like a woman in needing to share, he is still a man and generally wants to be right and is very willing to argue.

These spirited arguments feel good to him but bring only temporary relief. He will continue to feel a strong need to be heard and obeyed. No matter what a woman does for him, it will never be enough.

When Men Get Angry

The difference between men in this stage and a woman who needs to be heard is that when a man feels the strong need to share his feelings he will also want to be right. When a woman needs to share feelings, generally speaking she only requires that she feel heard and validated. She does not require a man to agree with her.

This third stage is greatly encouraged by popular culture. In the last twenty years, men are repeatedly encouraged to get in touch with feelings and to express them. In many cases, they are shamed for not being more expressive of their feelings.

As we have already noted, when a man expresses too many sensitivities, a woman tires of him. Particularly when a man expresses anger, a woman begins to close up. Because she doesn't feel safe in sharing with him, she refuses to talk. Suddenly *she* is in her cave and *he* is trying to get in.

When a Woman Won't Talk

At my seminar, men in the third stage generally share similar complaints. Let's explore a common example.

Tim was very angry when he stood up to share his story. He complained that he was much more willing to work on the relationship than his wife.

"You say women want to talk," he grumbled. "I want to talk more, but my wife won't talk to me."

The righteous tone in his voice tipped me off to what was wrong. "Has your wife ever said to you that you don't listen and that she can't talk to you?" I asked him.

"Sure. That's all she'll say," he answered. "But it's not true. I will listen. I am the one who wants to talk more. I do all the things you say a man should do. I cook, clean, make dates, and do all the things women are supposed to want, and then she spends all her time in the cave. I have had it."

"Well, that's the reason she won't talk to you. You don't listen," I told him flatly.

He then proceeded to prove my point by arguing with me: "No, you don't understand. I do listen, I am supportive, I listen to her feelings, but I also expect her to listen to mine."

"The way you are talking to me is probably just the way you talk to her," I persisted. "By arguing, you are ensuring that she will not want to talk with you. Even if she was warming up to the idea of sharing with you, your approach would stop her dead in her tracks."

A woman simply cannot feel protected or respected when a man speaks to her in such a righteous and demanding tone, particularly when it comes to talking about her feelings.

When a man is too emotionally demanding or overly sensitive and easily hurt, a woman feels as if she can't trust him to hear her feelings correctly.

She will not feel safe opening up with him when he feels he needs to talk more than she does. The only recourse left open to her is going to her cave.

This means moving more to her male side, because to protect herself from her partner's emotionally charged attacks and demands, she has to become like a man. After a while she will feel so comfortable in her cave that her female side will *want* to stay there.

Why a Man Gets So Upset

When a man is on his female side, it will sound very unfair to him when his partner won't talk to him or apologize for upsetting him. He feels powerless to get what he needs unless she agrees with him and expresses a willingness to change. He does not know how naturally women change when they feel loved.

When a woman feels loved, she slowly begins to open up and is willing to change unsupportive behaviors. When her mate is demanding, she will inevitably resist him, which of course only makes him feel angrier and more demanding.

When a stage-three man is upset, he is basically feeling deprived of the support he wants and deserves. To feel better, he needs an effective game plan for getting what he wants.

When a man comes up with a workable solution that makes sense to him, he begins to move back to his masculine side, which wants to solve the problem.

When a woman doesn't want to talk and a man does for healthy reasons, this is what he can do:

He should say: "I can tell something is bothering you. What's wrong?"

He should not say: "I am upset and I need to talk with you."

She says: "I can't talk to you."

He should say: "Hmmm," and then just pause and consider how he probably gives the message that it's not safe for her to talk.

He should not say: "Of course you can talk to me. I am the one who is trying to get you to talk. I am the one who is trying to make this relationship work."

If she says: "You will just argue with me. I don't want to even get started."

He should say: "You're probably right."

What is most important is that he should remain calm and accepting. This is the only way to win his partner over. He needs to prove to her that he can duck and dodge her provocations without getting mad. With this kind of safety insurance, she will begin to open up.

He should not say: "I will not argue, I just want to talk!" That would be arguing.

To argue with a woman when she doesn't want to talk just confirms that she can't open up and talk to him. To make it safe for a woman to open up and be feminine in a relationship, he must practice containment. He should contain his feelings so that she can first feel heard.

This does not mean that he should never feel or express his feelings. It means that he shouldn't overwhelm her with more negative feelings than she can handle. Instead of spilling his guts, he should go to his cave and think. After he has calmed down, he should focus on the solution, not the problem. He should come up with a workable strategy for doing something that will get him the appreciation he really craves.

When Men Make Lists

I can tell I'm in stage three of emotional role reversal when my female side comes out and starts making lists of all the things my partner is doing wrong. When I start making lists, unlike a woman who primarily just needs to talk about her lists, I want Bonnie to agree with me and promise to correct her behavior.

When I used to express myself in this way, Bonnie felt that she was living with a domineering tyrant. It was the "me" I become when I am not able to be my true loving self. The domineering tyrant is my shadow self.

If we are not feeling loved, we become the opposite of who we are when we are wonderful and loving. People who are very generous become very tight when their gifts are not appreciated. People who are very trusting and open become completely closed when they feel disappointed. When people who are very patient and flexible finally reach their limit, they become impatient and rigid. This is how love turns to hate. As a man or a woman moves into emotional role reversal, their shadow selves make more and more appearances.

If we are not feeling loved, we become the opposite of who we are when we are wonderful and loving.

To create and preserve a loving relationship, we need lots of ways in which to help us keep our balance, particularly when strong winds blow and the earth shakes beneath our feet.

For example, I still sometimes feel like a tyrant, but I do my best to keep these feelings to myself. I recognize at these moments that my male and female sides are imbalanced and do something to recover my equilibrium. Instead of acting out, I go to my cave. From inside my cave, I wait till I want to feel better. Then, to come out, I do something that will ensure my getting the appreciation from Bonnie that I really need in order to feel better. Instead of complaining that I am not appreciated, I do things that will garner her appreciation.

Through the application of new relationship skills the pitfalls and dangers of emotional role reversal can be gradually overcome. In the next chapter, we will explore more ways in which men and women can find balance. We will also explore how to sustain the passion in a marriage through maintaining balance and being monogamous. We will explore the secrets of lasting passion to create a lifetime of love.

CHAPTER 9

A Lifetime of Love and Passion

THE HIGH RATE OF DIVORCE is not a sign that people today are less interested in marriage. On the contrary, it indicates that we want more from our relationships than ever before. Men and women alike are dissatisfied because their marital expectations are much greater than in the past. We want a lifetime of love; we want lasting passion with one special person.

Even with the high level of divorce, there is also a high rate of remarriage. If the flame of passion goes out, both men and women would rather risk the pain of divorce than the loss of feelings. We intuitively know that through continuing to nurture a special relationship something much greater can be experienced. Deep inside, we sense that passionate monogamy is possible, but we do not have the skills to fully experience it.

The enormous market for women's romance novels, TV soap operas, and male pornography is not the cause of this dissatisfaction but is actually the symptom of an unfulfilled desire for passion in our relationships.

> Generally speaking, when a man's
> emotional and passionate needs for
> love are not satisfied, he becomes
> entranced with sex, while a woman
> tends to become captivated
> with romance.

These strong tendencies are not necessarily symptoms of dysfunction but are the natural expressions of a frustrated deeper need for emotional support in their relationships.

In Our Parents' Generation

In our parents' generation it was expected that the passion would lessen over time. Lasting passion and emotional fulfillment were not the goal of relationships. Relationships were formed primarily to fulfill our survival needs, not our romantic emotional needs. That's why my mother admired my father for staying with the family although he was having an affair with another woman and had long since stopped considering her romantic emotional needs.

To a great extent, it was just accepted by most that passion would burn out once the honeymoon ended and the children arrived.

I remember vividly that to the teenagers of my generation, the loss of passion after marriage was an accepted fact. Before marriage you couldn't have sex, all you ever thought about was sex, and if you were having sex you did it every chance you had. There were definitely not enough chances. But once you got married and you could have sex whenever you wanted, for some mysterious reason you stopped wanting it as much.

When I was in college, it was quite common for young men to be told this story by the coach or some other authority figure.

"When you men get married, you can expect to have lots of romance and sex. When you get married, get a bottle, and every time you have sex, put a bean in that bottle. After one year, every time you have sex, take a bean out of that bottle. If you can empty that bottle, then you will be real lucky."

This was his way of letting us know not to expect the passion to last in a relationship. In most world cultures, men and women have coped with the loss of passion by having extramarital affairs. The survival of the family was much more important than whether one got laid or with whom.

When Men Have Affairs

In the past, if a man was reasonably discreet about his affairs, a woman would quietly accept them. As I've described, my mother did.

My father and mother continued to love each other, but my father also kept his mistress. Somehow my mother found a way to continue loving and sharing her life with him—even though the romance in their relationship had faded away.

Since contemporary women increasingly can provide for themselves, they want more from a partner than helping to take care of the family. Women today want the emotional support and romance that only monogamy can provide. If her husband needs another woman to be passionate, a woman today would rather start over with another man who wants her passionately.

In reaction to the lack of passion in their relationships, some women have also taken the traditionally male escape route of having affairs. It is only natural, because working outside the home side by side with men creates more opportunities.

For men or women, having an affair is ultimately an attempt to fulfill our need for love. While it may temporarily satiate this need, an affair leads us farther and farther away from being able to have a truly fulfilling relationship with our mates. When either a man or a woman is having an affair, the opportunity to grow together in loving passion is greatly restricted.

A Relationship Is an Investment

A relationship is like an investment. We give to our partner and hope over time to get more and more in return. Initially, getting the emotional support we are looking for may be difficult, but through the years, it becomes easier and easier.

Having an affair is like taking all your savings and blowing them in Las Vegas. You spend it all and you are quickly back to where you started.

Whether the partner finds out or not, the effect is there. On an intuitive level, the other partner loses the feeling that they are special. Without this feeling, love and passion cannot grow. It will then take years to recapture that "special" feeling.

This does not mean that an affair necessarily ends a marriage. I have helped many couples revitalize their relationships over time as they healed together. Forgiveness is very powerful and can solidify a loving bond forever.

In these cases, the affair was a turning point because it allowed both partners to see clearly and talk decisively about problems that had been developing for years. Through forgiving and effectively communicating about the hurt and being motivated to make necessary changes, some couples are able to start completely over in love and experience greater passion and intimacy than ever before.

Sometimes it takes the threat of permanent loss to make people appreciate what they have; sometimes the imminent death of a relationship must stare us in the face before we can feel our deep love and longing to live together. Just as a near-death experience will often motivate or inspire a person to greater heights, so also can an affair exert an inspirational influence on the relationship.

This does not imply that we should risk making our mates feel betrayed and rejected in order to bring feeling back into the relationship. There are other ways. Through practicing new relationship skills, we can revive the passion even if it has been declared dead.

The Seven Secrets of Lasting Passion

To sustain passion in a relationship, there are seven important secrets. To apply new skills in each of these areas, we will discuss each one in greater depth.

1. Differences Attract

The most important aspect of attraction is that we are different. Just as the positive and negative poles of a magnet always attract each other, when a man remains in touch with his masculinity and a woman feels her femininity, the attraction can be maintained in a relationship.

Having to give up who we are to please our partners ultimately kills the passion. By seeking to resolve our differences without having to deny our true selves, we ensure lasting attraction.

Without a doubt, a man feels most turned on and attracted to his partner when she makes him feel like a man. Likewise, a woman is most attracted to a man when he makes her feel totally feminine. By taking the time to make sure that we avoid emotional role reversal, we can maintain the attraction we feel to each other.

This attraction is not just physical. When passion is sustained, our curiosity and interest in our partners also grow over time. We find to our surprise that we are still interested in what our partners think, feel, and do.

Working with our differences is a requirement for keeping the passion alive. If we consistently have to give up or change who we are to please our partners, passion dies.

Using new relationship skills, we can make small changes that stretch us but do not reshape us. Through stretching, we actually connect to more of who we potentially are.

The most important differences that need to be nurtured are our gender differences. For a woman to stay attracted to a man, he must be in touch with and express his male side. It is fine for him to express his female side, but if he suppresses his male side to be in a relationship with her, she will eventually lose her attraction for him.

In a similar way, for a man to stay attracted to a woman she must continue to express her female side. She can also express the qualities of her male side, but if her female side is not available to him, he will turn off.

How a Woman Can Nurture Her Female Side

Besides using new relationship skills and assisting a man in supporting her, a woman—single or married—must take pains to nurture her female side. Here is a list of the many things she can do:

1. Taking more time each day to share in a non-goal-oriented way about the problems of her day. This is best done on a walk or by having lunch with someone she does not look to for solutions to her problems.

2. Getting a massage or some kind of nurturing body work every week is extremely valuable. Being physically touched in a nonsexual way is very important to relax her and bring her back to a pleasant awareness of her body.

3. Talking on the phone and/or staying in touch with friends and relatives. It is vitally important that she not let the pressures of work and keeping a family and home together prevent her from taking time to talk with friends.

4. Making regular time for prayer, meditation, yoga, exercise, writing in a journal, or working in the garden should be observed with great commitment. Ideally, she should create twenty to thirty minutes twice a day when she can just *be* without having to *do* anything for anyone.

5. Creating a working style that supports her feminine side. Practice enlisting the support of others rather than being too independent and autonomous. Never miss an opportunity to let a man carry a box for you or open the door. Have pictures of your family and friends around you while you work. When at all possible, surround yourself with beauty and flowers.

6. Getting at least four hugs a day from friends and family members.

7. Taking the time to write thank-you notes for the support you receive from others.

8. Varying routes home from work. Try to avoid the tendency to most efficiently get home each day by following the same route every time.

9. Becoming a tourist in your own town and regularly taking a mini vacation. Also try to get away from the home and enjoy new settings and vacations.

10. Joining a support group or visiting a therapist to make sure you can share your feelings freely without being concerned about your professional reputation.

11. Setting aside one evening a week for yourself. Go out and enjoy a movie or the theater, or stay home and take a long, warm bath. Play beautiful music, light candles, and either read a wonderful book or turn down the lights and fantasize. Take the time to do what you would most enjoy doing.

12. Listing everything that needs to be done and

then putting in big letters at the top, "Things that don't have to be done immediately." Take at least one day a month to rest and not solve *any* problems. If you are a mother, take the day off, and get away from your home and children.

To suddenly try to do everything on the above list would, in itself, be overwhelming. Post a customized version somewhere, and slowly but surely begin incorporating these suggestions. Without taking deliberate steps to nurture her female side, a woman today will tend to automatically stay in her masculine side and unknowingly sabotage not only her relationships but her relationship with herself as well.

Ways a Man Can Nurture His Masculine Side

In my seminars, men commonly ask how they can develop their masculine side—particularly if they are not in relationships and don't have a woman to appreciate their actions when they need support.

Whether a man is single or married, there are many things he can do to stay strong. He should pick and choose which suggestions are appropriate for him. Here is a list of twelve:

1. Spend time with other men competing on a team or individually. By channeling your competitive tendencies in a playful way, you are released from feeling so driven by your work. You are automatically released from measuring yourself only by your work. Watching your favorite sports on TV or going to a game has a similar cathartic effect.

2. Go to action movies. It is healthy for adult males to experience violence on the big screen, particularly if it is expressed skillfully and ultimately to protect others. Watching movies like *Rocky*, *The Terminator*, and *Universal Soldier* is a way for you to feel and redirect your own violent tendencies. When children, however, experience violence on TV or in the movies, it has the opposite effect: it creates more violence in them.

3. Take cave time in your relationships. You should not feel guilty saying no to others when you need to be alone to recharge. You should not feel obligated to talk when you don't feel like it. This does not mean that you should never talk but that you should carefully pick the times.

If you tend to rarely take cave time, then you should do it even though it is lonely and painful. In ancient times, a boy became a man by fasting alone for a week in the wilderness. His aloneness forced him away from his mother, or female side, and he found the man within.

In a similar way, a man doesn't continue to experience his male power unless he takes the risk to put himself in a situation where he needs his strength. Courage grows through doing courageous actions.

4. If you do not have a sexual partner and you want to be more in touch with your male side, then practice self-control and don't masturbate. This suggestion is not moral advice. Masturbation is innocent, but it does nurture the female side, not the male side. Excess masturbation moves a man to his female side.

Practice abstinence from casual or recreational sex if you are not presently in a loving relationship because abstaining from sex is one of the most powerful ways to find male strength if one is too much on the female side. To restrain oneself sexually in this manner dramatically assists a man in connecting with his male side.

If a sexual release is needed, it will naturally occur during sleep. Regular cold showers, exercise, and some form of spiritual discipline like prayer, meditation, or yoga can help transmute sexual needs until you have a loving relationship with a sexual partner. Also, when a man waits in this way, he is much more motivated to find a sexual partner.

Frequenting adult bookstores or theaters, watching videos, or reading magazines that overstimulate you sexually is not advisable if you are practicing abstinence. A moderate amount of stimulation is, of course, fine. Just enough to keep you remembering what you are missing is just enough to keep you motivated.

5. Make sure you exert your muscles every week. Lift weights, jog, ride a bike, climb a mountain, swim, et cetera. Make sure that at least once weekly you push your muscles to the point of strain or exhaustion. Press your limits.

6. Make sure your life doesn't get too comfortable and cushy. Do something each week that requires you to overcome your inner resistance to exerting your different strengths. That could mean getting up earlier than usual to finish a project or staying later to make sure that you did the best you could do. Apply discipline in order to build your male strength.

7. Try each week to do random acts of kindness—for others you care about or complete strangers. When an older person needs a seat, offer yours. While driving, when someone needs to cut in,

graciously slow down. Be magnanimous in your generosity.

When someone needs you and you feel like resting, make the effort to help them anyway. I am not saying that you should do this every time, but just occasionally.

8. When you are upset or angry, don't punish others. Instead, focus on your breathing. Count to five on the in breath and then count to five on the out breath. Count ten cycles of this process, and then start over until you are not upset.

9. Make a list of all the things you most enjoy doing. Make sure that you are creating time each week for your favorite hobby or hobbies. Do things that make you feel accomplished and in charge.

10. When something needs to be done that won't take a lot of time or energy, do it immediately. Repeatedly affirm inside, "Do it now!"

11. When you feel afraid to do something that would really be good to do, feel the fear and do it anyway. Take reasonable risks. It is better to have tried and failed than never to have tried.

12. Practice containing your anger. You can redirect it either through some physically constructive activity, or privately expressing your feelings in a journal. Look for other feelings underneath the anger. When you do express anger, ideally it should be without having to raise your voice, but in a firm, confident but centered, and nonintimidating manner.

Talk about feelings with male friends, or create a male support group. Don't rely primarily on women to heal or hear your feelings. It is very helpful for some men to experience gatherings of the "men's movement," reading poetry, telling and listening to the ancient myths, dancing, singing, or drumming.

Through these techniques, a man in a relationship can ensure that he doesn't swing too much to his female side. A single man can help strengthen his male side and attract a woman who will support his being both powerful and sensitive.

2. Change and Growth

Living with the same person can, over time, eventually become very boring if they are not regularly changing. Staying fresh is crucial for both partners in a marriage. Just as listening to a favorite song a hundred times in a row makes it grow stale, so also may our partners become boring if they do not grow and change.

Just as physical growth is so obvious in our children, we must always continue to grow emotionally, mentally, and spiritually. We must be careful not to sacrifice or deny ourselves too much. When a relationship does not allow us to grow, the passion between two people begins to fade.

Change is automatic if a relationship is to nurture us in being true to ourselves.

Loving your partner does not mean spending all your time together. Too much time together can also make a relationship commonplace and devoid of mystery. Enjoying other friends and activities means that you can always bring back something new to the relationship. This applies to doing things separately from your partner and doing things with your partner and others. Having dinner with another couple on a regular basis is a good idea.

Good Communication

If a woman doesn't feel safe in talking about her feelings, she will eventually have nothing to say. Creating the safety for her to talk freely without her having to fear rejection, interruption, or ridicule allows a woman to thrive in a relationship. Over time, she can continue to trust and love her partner more if he is a good listener.

Men quite commonly grow bored when women tell them the details of their days. They are more interested in the bottom line. As a man begins to understand how to listen in an active way that his mate can appreciate, listening and sharing stops being a chore and becomes an important nurturing ritual. With open lines of communication, a woman will continue to grow.

Lots of Appreciation

When a man does not feel appreciated in a relationship, he also stops growing. He may not know why, but when he returns home he feels increasingly passive and disengaged from his partner. He stops initiating things to do. His routine becomes rigid and fixed.

What makes my relationship with my wife so uplifting is that she never expects me to do anything in the home. Almost every domestic responsibility I have doesn't feel like a chore that gets taken for granted, but is a gift that she appreciates as if I didn't have to do it. This makes me want to do it rather than feeling that I have to do it.

Creating Change

It is important to schedule special occasions. A man needs to remember that women tend to feel the weight of domestic responsibility and find it hard to take time off for themselves. If a man creates special times when she can get out of the routine, she is free to feel nurtured.

Celebrations, parties, presents, and cards also affirm the passage of time. They are particularly important for women. A woman greatly appreciates a man's special attention to her at these times. His remembering birthdays, anniversaries, Valentine's Day, and other holidays means a lot to a woman. Doing something special on those days for her frees her from feeling overwhelmed by life's repetitive responsibilities and assures her that she is loved.

One of the chief passion assassins is routine. Even if you are comfortable in your rut, it is helpful to break out of it from time to time. Even doing silly things can help make a moment special and memorable. For example, on our last vacation, instead of just taking a picture of my family in front of the Washington Monument, I lay down on the sidewalk and shot a picture from a lying-down position. Everyone laughed, and as a result, that moment will be remembered. All of our little efforts to occasionally break the routine make a difference.

Ultimately, what keeps passion alive in a relationship is growing in love. When, as a result of living, laughing, crying, and learning together two people are able to love and trust each other more, the passion will continue.

3. Feelings, Needs, and Vulnerabilities

To continue feeling our love, we need to feel. When it is not safe to have feelings or sensitivities, we quickly lose touch with our passion. While women need to talk more about their feelings and be heard if they are to feel vibrant in a relationship, men need to be appreciated for their actions if they are to feel like doing things for their partners.

When a man stops feeling a tender desire to please his partner, his tender feelings are automatically repressed. When a woman stops feeling the safety to share her feelings, she also begins to close up by repressing emotions.

Over time, when a woman or man continues to repress feelings, they begin to build walls around their hearts. Each time a woman feels ignored, minimized, and unsupported, another brick is placed in her wall. Each time a man attempts to be there for her and he ends up feeling ignored, criticized, corrected, or taken for granted, another brick is placed in his wall.

In the beginning, we can continue to feel love because the wall of repressed feelings is not fully blocking our hearts. But once it does, it cuts us off from our loving emotions.

To bring back the passion, this wall has to be dismantled brick by brick. Every time we remove one by applying advanced relationship skills, a little light begins to shine through. We then suddenly become aware of the rest of the wall and again feel that we are shut off. Slowly but surely, by continuing to successfully communicate and appreciate each other, that wall can come down and feelings can be fully experienced again.

Feeling Pain

When we are not getting the love we need, but remain vulnerable to our partners, we feel pain. Many couples deal with this by numbing themselves. They might say to themselves "It doesn't matter, I don't care." They may begin to close up, saying "I can't really trust him to be there for me, so I won't rely on him."

The most painful and lonely feeling is lying next to someone you don't feel you can reach out and touch with love. At this point, you may turn to an addiction to avoid feeling the pain of not being loved. Such dependencies free us from the pain but kill the passion. Only by learning to reach out for love and ask for what we want in skillful ways can we really heal our pain.

By turning off our feelings, we lose touch with our inner passion. We may not even know what we actually need more of because we have stopped feeling.

Without having the skills to get the
love we need, we may automatically
begin to stop feeling our needs.
When this happens, passion
begins to disappear.

Working on Trust and Caring

The challenge women face in their relationships is to keep opening up when feeling disappointed or unloved. It is of paramount importance that they work on trusting their partners more and more and continue to be receptive. Otherwise, they will lose touch with their vulnerability and needs.

The secret to growing in trust is not to expect your partner to be perfect but to believe that you are growing in the skills that help you help him give you what you want. Through understanding how men are different, a woman enables herself to trust that he loves her even when he doesn't instinctively do the things *she* would do to demonstrate caring.

Over time, she can begin to see the ways in which he thinks he is loving her. Most important, she can apply advanced relationship skills to help him be more successful in supporting her.

To take down the wall around his heart, a man must work on caring. To bring back the passion, he needs to remember that it will require hard work and effort. At times, it will be like lifting a heavy weight.

If there is no wall around his heart, doing things is easy. Once he is taken for granted, the wall begins to rise again. Each time he feels his efforts are not appreciated, another brick is added to the wall.

But as he consciously begins doing little things that she can appreciate, if only for brief moments, the wall building stops. When his determination frays, and the wall suddenly looks higher, he becomes weary and resistant once more. He craves only to spend a lot of time in his cave.

A man can eventually come out and overcome the inertia of not caring if he is aware of the effort required to open his heart again. As he does, he will see that he is truly becoming a stronger person. With this strength, his road ahead will be less rocky. Eventually, he will be energized as never before by pleasing his partner.

Healthy Dependence

As we grow together in love and trust, open up and feel our mutual needs more strongly, our vulnerability increases too. Passion is most powerfully experienced when we know how much we need someone.

In the beginning of our marriage, securing Bonnie's appreciation was relatively unimportant to me. Over the years, I have grown to love receiving it. It brightens my day, and when we are having sex allows me to feel how deeply I need her in my life.

After years of my consistently trying to be there for her, she can freely feel her needs for my love as well. The more she can depend on my support, the more passion she can feel. Bonnie is also realistic. She knows that I am not perfect and that I cannot always be there for her.

Bonnie's dependence on me is healthy because it is based on what I can really give her. This allows her to be more vulnerable, which in turn allows me to feel like I make a difference.

**Need and dependence become a
turn-on when we are needing what
our partner can give us.**

It is unwise as well as naive to expect our partners always to give us the love we need. Sometimes they have none to share and yet we demand more (in a sense, it is as though we are saying to a person in a wheelchair, "If you love me, then you will stand up and walk"). Sometimes they just can't be there for us in the ways we mistakenly think they can or should. But once we begin to need our partners in ways that they can't or don't support us, we will not only turn them off but will disappoint ourselves as well. When we need our partners too much, we will eventually pull away our trust and caring.

The more successful we are in fulfilling each other, the more we can rely on that support. With this kind of trust, even when our partners let us down, we will know that they did the best they could and we can be much more forgiving.

4. Personal Responsibility and Self-Healing

As we continue to open up and have our emotional needs met in a relationship, our unresolved past feelings ultimately begin to surface. When they rise up, they don't say "Hi, I'm your anger with your dad"; instead, they are directed at our partners.

It is an irony that when we feel most loved, the unresolved feelings from past experiences of not being loved begin to affect our moods. One minute we are feeling passion, the next we are considering divorce. Such radical shifts we always justify by our partners' behavior, although it really isn't primarily about them.

For example, I come home in a great mood and my wife greets me at the door by saying, "You forgot to call and tell me you were late. I didn't know what had happened." Certainly, I don't like being greeted with such a negative mothering statement, but if I suddenly get really upset and go to my cave and even consider divorce over that one statement, I have to take responsibility for my strong reaction.

Blaming your partner is looking in the wrong direction and aggravates the wound.

Whenever you feel you were fine until your partner did one thing that ruined your day, it is generally something deep inside you that needs to be healed.

When past feelings begin to surface, they generally make us feel uncharacteristically negative. We may feel a lot of blame, criticism, doubt, resentment, confusion, ambivalence, judgment, and rejection. For a moment, we regress back to feeling and reacting the way we did as children when we didn't feel safe to freely react. When such feelings surface, it is vital for us to work on taking responsibility for being more loving and forgiving.

We should not expect our partners to be our loving parents. That, as we know, is a surefire passion killer. At those times, we need to parent ourselves, or work with a surrogate parent in a psychotherapeutic setting. It is up to us to re-parent ourselves, not our partners.

When we start blaming our partners for our unhappiness, it is a clear signal that our own "old stuff" is coming up. Although we feel especially entitled to demand more from our mates, we should demand nothing. It is a time for self-healing. It is a time for us to give ourselves the comfort and understanding that our parents may have failed to give us.

Remember, to expect our partners to make us feel better is to put them in the role of parents. The more dependent we become on them to change before *we* can change, the more stuck we will be. By parenting ourselves, we are free to release them from being the targets of our blame.

Feeling Powerless

Another signal that we are dealing with the past is powerlessness.

Whenever we feel out of control and therefore seek to control another, our childhood is generally affecting us.

We *were* controlled as children. We were genuinely powerless to get what we wanted and needed. As adults we have many more choices and opportunities.

Even with new relationship skills you will at times feel like nothing is working and that you'll never get what you want. When this feeling emerges, we need to embrace it and sympathize with ourselves, but must also keep in mind that we are not really powerless. It is rather that our present assessment of the situation is definitely being clouded by old feelings seeking release. By applying self-healing techniques, a clearer vision of your abilities and opportunities will begin to come back into focus within minutes.

Impatience

When our hearts are open, we are patient toward our partners' limitations and our own. When strong feelings of impatience appear, they are another signal that childhood feelings are clouding our vision.

As adults we have learned how to wait patiently for desire to become reality. Patience is a skill and a part of maturity. When we suddenly begin to feel impatient, we lose our realistic perspective and immediately demand more than is possible.

Instead of feeling good that progress is being achieved, we feel frustrated that not enough is happening fast enough. With each setback, we negate our progress.

Quite commonly, after taking my seminar or reading my books, men will begin to make changes. Then, after a while, they stop. At that point, a woman may begin to feel "I knew it, he didn't care. He's just going back to the way he always was." Her negativity prevents her from assisting him to continue supporting her.

If he offers to do something, she withers him with "Well, I'll wait to see if you really do it before I get excited." There is no better way for him to lose his motivation.

When a woman becomes impatient, she will demand that her partner make his changes permanently instead of realizing that he is engaged in an ongoing process to give her the support she needs. Instead of giving up or demanding more, a woman needs to focus less on changing her partner and more on changing her own attitude.

How We Stop Loving

When we feel blame toward our partner, it is difficult to accept, understand, and forgive their limitations and imperfections. Only through learning to love them in stormy times can we grow together. Anybody can love somebody who's perfect.

The test of love is caring for a person even though we know them to be less than perfect and have experienced their daily limitations. We claim that we want to be loved for who we are. But can we really love our partners for who *they* are? When our hearts are open, love is automatic.

When our hearts are closed, we are responsible for opening up. We are no longer children. To have an adult relationship, we must shoulder responsibility.

The reemergence of our childhood feelings threatens that sense of responsibility. We always feel that it is the other person's fault. Although we feel blame, by committing ourselves to finding forgiveness, we can bring ourselves back to being adults and release ourselves from immature feelings. These are the six ways in which we stop loving our partners when we are in the grip of past feelings that cause our hearts to close up:

1. Loss of Trust. It is suddenly hard to trust that your mate is doing his or her best or that they care. Suddenly, you may begin to doubt their best intentions. This is the person who would risk death to save your life, yet you begin to judge them as if they do not care about you.

Women generally have to work harder than men

to overcome this tendency. To re-parent herself at those times, a woman needs to open up again slowly by first being caring to herself. She needs temporarily to stop depending on her partner to nurture her female side. By taking responsibility for re-parenting herself even if she still blames her partner, she will release herself from the spell of past feelings and will remember that she is cared for by a partner who is doing his best. Each time this process happens, her ability to trust increases.

2. Loss of Caring. Suddenly, you feel as if you don't care at all about your partner's needs and feelings. Your justification is the mistreatment that you have suffered at their hands. Here is the person we would risk our life to save, and suddenly we don't care about them.

A man generally has to work harder to overcome this tendency. To re-parent himself at those times, he needs to slowly open up by trusting in himself to be successful in the future. He needs to stop depending on his partner's trust in him to feel successful.

At this time, a man should do something to nurture his male side. By taking responsibility to re-parent himself even if he is still blaming his mate, he is automatically released from the grip of negative feelings and will soon remember how much he cares for her. Each time this process happens, his ability to care increases.

3. Loss of Appreciation. In an instant, you begin to feel that this relationship gives you nothing, whereas at other times you were so very happy and grateful. You feel as if you're doing more, while they do zilch. With this sudden memory lapse, you suddenly begin to feel deprived and totally without appreciation for your partner.

A woman generally has to work harder to overcome this tendency. To re-parent herself at those times, she needs to slowly open up again by respecting and supporting herself and nurturing her female side.

Even if she is still blaming her partner, she will begin to remember the ways in which he respects and supports her. Each time this process happens, her ability to appreciate him increases.

4. Loss of Respect. Suddenly, you begin to feel like withholding love and punishing your partner when just a few minutes before you wanted only to love and support her. You genuinely feel that you want to make your partner happy, and then abruptly care only about yourself.

A man will work eight hours a day to earn the money to buy a present for his mate, then turn around and resent doing something small, like picking up his socks, to please her.

Men generally have to work harder to overcome this tendency. To re-parent himself at those times, he needs to slowly open up by appreciating himself for all he does, even when his partner doesn't. For the moment, he needs to stop depending on his partner's acknowledgment and appreciation of him.

Now he should nurture his male side. By taking responsibility for re-parenting himself even if he is still blaming her, he will begin to remember how much he respects her and wants to please her.

It is important that he not feel he has to surrender his sense of self in order to please her. Otherwise he would be weakened. Each time he is able to come back and be supportive of her after doing something for himself, he gradually learns that he can please her without giving up who he is. Making a small shift in our behavior does not mean that we can't be true to ourselves. This awareness gives a man the flexibility to create win/win solutions in a relationship so that everyone gets what they want.

5. **Loss of Acceptance.** Suddenly, you begin to notice all the things your partner does wrong or needs to change. This is the person that you have felt was perfect, and out of the blue comes the compulsion to change, improve, or even rehabilitate them.

One minute you love and accept them, the next they're in the doghouse for making a mistake. Under these circumstances, a woman begins to feel that a man should know better. She forgets that he is from Mars and doesn't readily understand her needs.

Women generally have to work harder to overcome this tendency. To re-parent herself at those times, she needs to slowly open up again by taking the time to understand and experience what she is feeling and validate her own needs. She must release her need to change him before she can feel better.

By taking responsibility for re-parenting herself even if she is still blaming her partner or demanding that he change, a woman will begin to remember the things her partner does right as well as his openness and willingness to respond to her needs when he can remember or when he is approached in a positive way. Each time this process happens, her ability to accept her partner's imperfection, along with her own, increases.

6. **Loss of Understanding.** Our partners may say something that makes us critical or judgmental of their feelings and reactions. We tend to minimize their pain as if it doesn't matter, and yet, if they were physically wounded, we would risk our lives to save them. We quickly become impatient or disinterested

even when this is the person we care most about in our life. We easily become defensive and feel we are being attacked when they are just sharing their feelings.

Men generally have to work harder to overcome this tendency. To re-parent himself at those times, a man needs to slowly open up by appreciating himself for all that he does, even if his partner doesn't.

At such times, a man should graciously excuse himself, go into his cave, and do something that will nurture his male side. By taking responsibility for re-parenting himself even if he is still feeling defensive, he will be released from negativity and will eventually begin to think about what she was really saying or wanted to say. He will begin to understand her needs and consider how he can best support her.

It is important that he take the time to consider what her feelings are without feeling pressured to immediately respond or say something. One of the best things a woman can say to a man when he is having difficulty listening to her is to remind him that he doesn't have to say anything. A powerful phrase is: "I would just like you to consider what I am saying. You don't have to do or say anything."

Opening Our Hearts

If we feel we are not getting the love we need and are blaming our partners, it is a clear sign that we need something our partners simply cannot presently give us. Taking responsibility for supporting ourselves when our hearts are closed frees us from dwelling on our partners as the problem and allows us to examine the situation on a much more fundamental level.

We are able to nurture ourselves and then come back to the relationship with more to give, not more to demand.

Instead of drowning in negativity and reacting in unloving ways when our hearts are closed, we can use this "downtime" for self-healing. Instead of looking to our partners to change when we are blaming them, we should focus on changing ourselves. When we are feeling open and forgiving, we can refocus and look for ways in which to solve or correct the problem that originally upset us.

The Feeling Letter Technique

A method I use to help release my negative feelings is called the feeling letter technique. By taking a few minutes to do this technique I can free myself from the grip of negative feelings and then feel more forgiving and agreeable.

For over twelve years I have used different versions of this technique and it still works dramatically for me at those times when I am not feeling very loving. It is a very powerful tool for both men and women.

Writing a feeling letter not only strengthens a man's ability to contain his feelings but is also helpful when he is on his female side and needs to be heard. Instead of dumping his negative feelings on his partner, he can write them out and achieve his goal more effectively than he could by talking.

A man can use this technique particularly when he needs to share his feelings but knows that this is not the time. As we have discussed, when a man displays more feeling or emotional vulnerability than a

woman, it may push her to her male side. Rather
than risk that, he should enact the following three
steps.

This exercise is equally useful for a woman if she
needs to share her feelings when her partner is in his
cave and can't hear her. If she is feeling in the mood
to blame or change her partner, it is also a good idea
for her to practice this technique and get more centered before he returns.

We will briefly explore each stage. For more
information on this technique, refer to my book,
What You Feel You Can Heal.

Step One

Begin by writing out whatever you would have liked
to say to your partner. It is perfectly OK to blame or
sound critical.

Set down what makes you angry, sad, afraid, and
sorry. Take a couple of minutes to dwell on each of
these emotions. Even if you don't actually feel some
of them, ask yourself what you would be experiencing if you did. For example, if you are not angry,
write: "If I was the angry type, I would say . . ."
Spend about two minutes on each of the emotions.

After taking a total of eight minutes to express
your different emotions, take two more minutes to
focus on writing out your wants, wishes, needs, or
hopes, and then sign your name. In just ten minutes,
you're done. Try not to spend more time than this
unless, of course, you enjoy it and find an immediate
release by writing out your feelings. With practice,
this will automatically begin to happen.

Step Two

In step two, write a letter from your partner to you saying the things that you would want to hear him or her say. Pretend that you have shared your letter with your partner and that they have really heard you. Write out the words that would make you feel heard.

Have them first thank you for sharing your feelings. Then have them express an understanding of your feelings. Finally, have them apologize for their mistakes and make promises to support you better in the future. Even if your partner would not respond in such a positive way, use your imagination.

Take about three minutes to write this response letter. If it takes longer than that, it is certainly OK. Simply writing out the words you would want to hear will make you feel better. Even though your partner is not really saying these things, you will benefit by hearing them.

Step Three

In step three, take two minutes to respond back the way you probably would if your partner really did hear you and apologized for their mistakes. In this short forgiveness letter, be as specific as possible. Use the phrase "I forgive you for . . ."

If it is still hard to forgive, remember that you are not saying that what they did is OK. When you forgive, you are clearly pointing out their mistakes but at the same time are releasing your tendency to continue withholding your love, compassion, and understanding.

Forgiveness doesn't mean the problem went away. It means that you are not closing yourself up to dealing with it in a loving manner. By practicing this feeling letter exercise at those times when you are resentful or your partner won't talk, you will suddenly feel relieved. Then you can patiently wait for the right opportunity to share your feelings, thoughts, and desires in a way that works for you, your partner, and the relationship.

5. Love, Romance, and Monogamy

Through taking responsibility for our reactions and actions in a relationship, we can truly begin to give and receive love successfully. Without an awareness of how our partners specifically need love, we may be missing priceless opportunities.

Women primarily feel loved when they are receiving from their men the emotional and physical support they need. It does not matter as much what he provides but that he does it in a continuous way. A women feels loved when she feels that a man's love is consistent.

When a man doesn't understand a woman, he tends to focus on the big ways to fulfill her all at once but will then ignore her for weeks. While good communication provides a healthy basis for a loving relationship, romance is the dessert. The way to a woman's heart is through doing lots of little things for her on a consistent basis. Here is my "short list" of twenty "kitchen-tested" things a man can do to create romance.

1. Buy her cards or write her a note.
2. Bring her flowers.
3. Buy her chocolates.
4. Bring home little surprises that say you were thinking of her while you were away.
5. Give her random hugs.
6. Be affectionate at times when you are not wanting sex.

7. Light a candle at dinner or in the bedroom.
8. Put on her favorite music.
9. Notice what she is wearing and pay her a compliment.
10. Take notice of the foods and restaurants she likes.
11. Plan dates ahead of time.
12. Put the remote control on mute at the commercials and talk with her instead of scanning through the channels.
13. Look at her when she talks.
14. Don't interrupt her or finish her sentences.
15. Notice when she is upset and offer her a hug.
16. Help her when she is tired.
17. Help her with her domestic chores.
18. Call her when you are running late.
19. Call her just to say "I love you."
20. Plan little celebrations and do something different.

What Romance Says

When a man does little things that say, "I care, I understand what you feel, I know what you like, I am happy to do things for you, and you are not alone," he is directly fulfilling a woman's need for romance. When a man does things without a woman having to ask, she feels deeply loved. If he forgets to do them, though, a wise woman graciously persists in reminding him by asking in a nondemanding manner.

A man, however, receives love differently from a woman. He chiefly feels loved when she lets him know again and again that he is doing a good job of fulfilling her. Her good mood makes him feel loved. Even when

she enjoys the weather, a part of him takes the credit.
A man is happiest when a woman is fulfilled.

While a woman feels romanced by the flowers,
chocolates, et cetera, a man's sense of romance is
fueled by a woman's appreciation of him. When he
does little things for her and she appreciates it a lot,
then he feels more romantic.

Women generally do not realize that the kind of
love a man needs most is her loving message that he
has fulfilled her.

> **The basis of almost all romantic rituals
> is a male giving and a female receiving.**

When she is happy about the things he provides
for her, he feels loved. When he can do something for
her, he lets in her love. The most important skill for
loving a man is to catch him when he is doing something right and notice and appreciate him for it. The
most significant mistake is taking him for granted.

A man feels loved when he gets the message that
he has made a difference, that he has been helpful in
some way, and that his partner benefits from his
presence. The other way to love a man is whenever
possible to minimize his mistakes with statements
like "It's no big deal" or "It's OK." Downplaying
disappointments makes him much more open to
future requests and needs.

When a man does things for a woman and she is
fulfilled, they both win. When I bring in the logs and
build a fire, Bonnie feels special and cared for. Her
romantic feelings begin to ignite. Knowing that, I am
also quite pleased and confident.

However, when I sit on the couch and watch her bring in the logs and build a fire, although I feel relaxed and grateful, our romantic feelings aren't being charged. It is a very different dynamic that occurs when a woman takes care of a man.

Passionate Monogamy

Although women need romance to feel loved, for passion to grow over time their most important intimacy requirement is monogamy. A man can make the romantic gestures, but if he is not monogamous, her passion cannot grow. Romance tells a woman that she is special. And there is nothing that makes a woman feel more special than a man in touch with his passions and wanting only her.

As a woman ages, her ability to feel and express passion increases if she feels she can fully trust her partner to be there for her. If she feels she is being compared to another woman or that she has to compete, she cannot continue to open up.

If she senses that he is having an affair or could have an affair, she shuts down. Like a delicate rose she needs the clear and clean water of monogamy to gradually unfold, one petal at a time.

> **By clearly committing himself and assuring a woman that they are going to grow old together, her mate gives her the special support she needs to discover the fires of sexual passion deep within her soul.**

Not only does she benefit from monogamy but he does too! When a man is trusted by his wife and family, others sense something they can trust about him. Sexual monogamy strengthens a man and makes him worthy of the highest trust.

In the famous best-seller, *Think and Grow Rich*, Napoleon Hill interviewed five hundred of the most successful men in America about the qualities that created success. Remarkably, all of the men were sexually active in a passionate, monogamous relationship of over thirty years' duration.

These powerful, successful men had somehow learned to maintain passion with one woman for decades. Their sexual fire had not burned out, nor did they require the stimulation of an affair to be turned on. As they grew in passion through sharing their love in a sexual way with their wives, they grew in personal power and made a difference to the world.

Greater drive and success are waiting for those men who realize this simple secret of love. Through creating and sustaining a passionate monogamous relationship, not only can a woman grow in sexual passion but a man can be more powerful and effective in his work.

This study of only men was conducted many years ago. I am sure without a doubt that as women learn to master having careers in tandem with an ongoing passionate relationship, they too will be even more effective and influential in their work.

Knowing and sensing my ever-increasing sexual fulfillment with her and my clear commitment to our monogamous relationship, Bonnie is more satisfied, more centered. Even though she is not with me when I am away, she continues to feel the special sexual connection that only we share. I may share my mind and spirit with many, but only Bonnie gets my sexual energy.

Mental Monogamy

Not only are men not taught why monogamy is important, they are not taught how to be monogamous. The technique is very simple. When a man notices another woman and automatically starts getting turned on, he should just begin thinking about having sex with his wife, or he can just begin remembering a particularly exciting memory of having sex with his wife. This way, each time he gets automatically turned on, his sexual energy is consciously directed to his partner. After five to eight years of this practice, he will become even more attracted to his wife. He will also have learned to master his sexual energy. Not only will his wife grow in passion with him, but he will have more power and success in his life.

Romance for Women, Sex for Men

Just as romance is important to a woman, sexual gratification is important to a man. He needs constant reassurance that his partner likes sex with him. Sexual rejection is traumatic to a man's sense of self.

I'm not saying that a woman should feel obliged to have sex whenever her partner wants it. I am saying that she needs to work hard to be hypersensitive when sex is the subject under discussion. If he initiates sex and she's not into it, she shouldn't just say no. Instead, say "A part of me wants to have sex, but I think I would enjoy it more later." By considering his feelings, she frees him to continue initiating sex without feeling rejected.

Or she may say, "I'm not really in the mood for sex, but we could have a quickie." I explore this subject in much greater detail in my book *Mars and Venus in the Bedroom.*

Just as communication and romance are the primary means for a woman to experience love, sex is the primary way for a man to connect with love and passion on an ongoing basis.

6. Friendship, Autonomy, and Fun

Friendship is a breeze if we suppress our feelings. If one partner is willing to sacrifice who he or she is to the relationship, they will always get along—but the passion will die.

Make no mistake, although women quite commonly will "lose themselves" to accommodate their partners, men also surrender a major part of themselves. To avoid conflict, a man will also hold himself back. Without good communication skills, quite commonly a couple with a lot of love will choose to maintain the friendship and sacrifice their feelings. They do not realize that by suppressing negative feelings they are also suppressing their ability to feel in general.

When a woman cares for a man but doesn't help him in supporting her, she is actually hurting, not helping, the relationship. A man can only thrive in a relationship when he truly fulfills her needs. If she pretends to be fulfilled he will "think" he is fulfilled, but he doesn't even know what he is missing.

To be really good friends in a relationship requires a balance of autonomy and dependence. As we have explored, needing our partners is the basis of passion. However, if we are not also autonomous, at those times when our partners have little to give to us, we will feel powerless to get what we need.

Through practicing personal responsibility and self-healing we can nurture ourselves at those times when our partners can't be our nurturers. The real test of love is when we can be our partner's friend, and give without any expectation of return. This becomes easier when we are not too dependent on them and when at other times we have repeatedly experienced that they can be there for us. When we are confident that we can get what we need at other times, then we are not so demanding at those times when our partners have little to give.

Lightness and Fun

A man is almost always annoyed when a woman wants to "work on the relationship." He doesn't want to work on it. He would rather just live in it.

A man needs to feel that sometimes he is on vacation in the relationship and, in a sense, can do no wrong. He wants to feel that he is fine the way he is and that he is not required to change. When a woman says "It's no big deal" or "It's OK," he tends to lighten up. When a woman can be lighthearted about her problems, a man feels like a success.

On the other hand, for a woman to feel friendship for a man it means that he can be relaxed about her getting upset. If he can just give her a little sympathy without taking the issue so personally, she can shift her feelings without making a scene.

Friendship for a woman means that her mate will, from time to time, go out of his way to support her or offer his help. Friendship for a man means that a woman will go out of her way not to be demanding or expect too much.

Being our partner's friend means never trying to change their mood or taking it personally when they are not feeling the way we want them to. Learning this lesson of detachment can totally transform a relationship.

In the next chapter, we will discuss the seventh secret of lasting passion: partnership and service to a higher purpose. Together we will explore dance steps for lasting intimacy through creating a win/win partnership which contributes not only to a more passionate relationship, but to a better and more loving world.

CHAPTER 10

Dance Steps for Lasting Intimacy

I ALWAYS ENJOY WATCHING older couples dance. They seem so happy together. They know just what to do, he has all the moves down, and she trusts him to lead her exactly where she wants to go. She melts into his arms and he holds her charmingly and confidently. This trust and confidence can only come with years of practice.

When couples start out in love, they are always willing to do whatever it takes to make the relationship work. The problem, as we have discussed, is that the dance steps that worked for past generations don't work today. The music has changed, and new steps are required. Without an awareness of these new advanced skills, it is inevitable that the special light of love we feel in the beginning will grow dimmer.

When a man is skilled in loving a woman, there is no question that his love can sweep her off her feet. In a similar way, a woman's love can help plant a man's feet firmly on the ground. By learning new skills to express her love, she can be a mirror to help him see and feel his greatness. She can be a motivating force that helps him succeed in expressing his most competent and loving self.

The Well-Earned Gift of Love

The support I have experienced through my wife's gentle and sometimes fierce love for me has dramatically influenced my ability to relax and feel good about myself. It has allowed the real and loving person to come out of me.

For example, instead of being critical when I would forget things, she was accepting and patient. This was the gentle love. But instead of giving up and doing things for herself without my help, she persisted in a nondemanding way. This was her fierce love. She didn't give up like so many women do. She kept on practicing the dance steps.

Although Bonnie's love is a gift that I have earned, it is also given freely. Through her willingness to "pause and postpone" her immediate needs, "prepare me" to listen and respond to her requests, and "persist" in asking for my support in a nondemanding way, I gradually discovered how important love was and how to get it.

The growth we have experienced together has been the result of hard work. Now it is much easier. Life always has its difficult challenges, but with new skills for relating we are able to grow closer instead of farther apart in our journey together. We are able to support each other in our ongoing process of living, growing, and sharing ourselves in the world.

As I have focused on developing my masculine side to improve communication by learning to duck, dodge, disarm, and deliver, she has focused on developing her female side to assist me in being successful in fulfilling her. Through her learning to pause, prepare, postpone, and persist, it has made a world of difference.

Although neither of us is perfect in these skills, each day we get better. They are no longer difficult to practice because we know they work, and we know how painful it is when we don't use them. Sometimes she is the more supportive, while at other times she has little to give. Even when both of us are empty, just knowing how to start giving again to get the support we need is a tremendous source of strength.

When I am in my cave and Bonnie is not getting what she needs, instead of panicking or feeling responsible, she knows how to pause and give me space. She practices preparing me to do more by asking for support in easy ways and then appreciating me.

Instead of trying to change me or improve the relationship, she focuses on using her feminine skills to give me space and gradually draw me out of the cave with her patient love.

Two Steps Forward and Then Back Again

Just like dance partners, when a woman takes two steps back, the man can take two steps forward. When he takes two steps back, she can take two steps forward. This give-and-take is the basic rhythm of relationships.

At other times, they both pull back and then come back together. Every relationship has those times when both partners have little to give and so they pull back to recharge.

While dancing, a woman gracefully swings into the man's arms, then spins away. In a successful relationship, this same pattern is expressed. A woman is happy to see her partner, she moves into his arms, and then after pausing and preparing him, she spins out of his arms and shares her feelings in a circular manner.

At other times, he will hold her in his arms as she swings back and dips. In a similar way, as a woman shares her feelings she may dip. With his sympathetic support she is able to go almost all the way down to the dance floor and then experience the joy of coming back up.

In dance, a woman naturally spins around while the man stays steady. In a similar manner, when a woman can share her feelings without a man reacting with his, she can feel heard. Certainly, there are also times when they both spin, but as in dance they need to pull away to do the movement before again making contact.

While dancing, a man gets to feel his sense of independence and autonomy by leading, and a woman gets to feel her need for cooperation and relationship through supporting him as he supports her in the moves she wants to make.

The Care and Feeding of Partnerships

In our journey we must remember to nurture and respect our differences. Differences create passion. We start relationships because we are drawn to another person who is different but complements us.

In the beginning, Bonnie and I had no idea how different we were. We were so focused on the ways in which we were similar. We were both very spiritual, we both enjoyed sex, we both liked to go for walks, we both liked tennis, we both liked movies, we had many friends in common, we were both easygoing, we were both interested in psychology. The list of commonalities was delightfully long.

Once we were married, we began to notice the differences. I was detached, she was emotional. I was goal oriented, she was relationship oriented. She liked discussing problems, I wanted to solve or postpone them. Besides these and other standard gender differences that create the inherent attraction between the sexes, there were many other differences as well that are not necessarily gender based.

She liked the bedroom temperature cool, and I liked it warm. She liked antiques, and I liked high tech and modern. She liked to balance her checkbook to the last penny, and I would round it off and get a vague running total in my mind. She liked to get up early, and I liked to stay up late. She liked eating at home, and I liked going out. She drove the speed limit, and I liked to drive fast. She liked to save money, and I liked to spend it. She made decisions slowly, and I liked to make them fast. She held on to old relationships, and I quickly moved on. I have big ambitions, and she is quite content with her life the way it is. I like electric gadgets, and she likes the garden and other "real" things of the earth. She likes to visit museums, and I like elegant hotels. I like new, modern homes, and she likes older, more charming homes. I like views with a vista, and she likes being in the woods.

Although each of these differences creates a possible conflict, they also create the opportunity to grow together as well. In relationships, we are generally attracted to a person with certain qualities that, in a sense, are either dormant within or yet to come out of us. When we are one way and our partner is another way, we are instinctively attracted to them to help us find balance with ourselves. Finding this balance creates passion and attraction.

After about a year of being married, I confronted my first big challenge relating to our differences. I wanted to buy a larger-screen TV. I love new technology and gadgets. Bonnie wasn't in favor of the idea. She said that she didn't like the idea of having to see it looming in the living room every day.

This was a very difficult moment for me. I began to feel that to make her happy, I had to give up something that would make me happy. At that point I was just beginning to understand how we could resolve our differences by working out a win/win solution.

Internally, I was furious. All kinds of buttons were being pushed, but I contained myself by remaining focused on finding a solution. As long as I kept thinking that we could both somehow get what we wanted, the frustration did not turn to anger at her.

"I want to respect your wishes," I finally told her. "And I really want to get a bigger TV. I've waited a long time to be able to afford one. I also really want you to have a beautiful home. What do you think we can do?"

Bonnie answered, "I wouldn't mind a big TV if it was in a cabinet that closed in the front. Then when you weren't watching it, I could close it and not always have to see it."

I immediately said great, and we went together to buy a cabinet. I thought it was going to be an easy solution. We soon found that we had completely different tastes in furniture.

The Win / Win Solution

The cabinet I picked out was high tech and would hold all my stereo equipment. The cabinet she wanted had glass-backed shelves with lights for displaying china and crystals, but it didn't have a big enough space for the TV that I wanted.

For weeks we looked for something that would accommodate our differing needs. During this process, I felt like I wanted to explode, but I did everything I could to contain my frustration. It was a very difficult time. I thought that she was so stubborn and resistant, and I became very judgmental of her. In my darkest moments I thought, I'm getting a divorce!

Hindsight helps us to see how we tend to blow things out of proportion. Although I thought she was being stubborn, I was being just as stubborn. I wanted my big-screen TV, and she wanted it covered. I wanted a cabinet to hold my stereo, and she wanted something to hold her crystal and beautiful things.

We teetered on the brink of hating each other, and then came the day when we finally found a cabinet we both agreed on. It was a miracle. Except that we had to wait another three months for it to be shipped to us. The whole ordeal couldn't have been more frustrating, but once the cabinet arrived, we were both very satisfied with it.

Building Relationship Muscles

What we ended up getting together was much better than what I would have gotten if I'd gone shopping on my own. By stretching myself to include and respect Bonnie's tastes and wishes, I had achieved an end result far greater than anything I alone could have created. Through exercising our patience and flexibility we were both able to strengthen our relationship.

This experience became a strong metaphor for all our future conflicts. I realized that even when it seemed that I could not get what I wanted, with persistence and a willingness to fulfill both our wishes, we would always end up with more. Although I didn't initially care much for the display shelves, I love and greatly appreciate them now. And Bonnie greatly enjoys the thirty-six-inch TV.

Once we had worked through this problem successfully, I realized that we were much closer than we had been before. Our trust level had gone up. The strength, patience, faith, and flexibility it took to find a win/win solution made other challenges much easier.

Partnership and Service to a Higher Purpose

Partnership is the seventh secret to creating a lasting and passionate relationship. To create a mutually fulfilling partnership, it is helpful to understand how men and women experience partnership differently.

A woman feels partnership when she and her partner are doing things together in a cooperative manner toward the same goal. There is no hierarchy or boss. They make all decisions together, sharing their input equally.

A man experiences partnership very differently. He likes to have his department, where he is in control, and he is happy for her to have her department, where she is in control. He doesn't want her telling him what to do, nor does he feel he has to be involved with what she is doing. Together, doing different jobs with different responsibilities, they are a partnership teaming up to get the job done.

With an awareness of this difference, both men and women can create the partnership they want. Using sexual intercourse as a metaphor, we can easily see the solution. In sex, a man leaves his world and enters hers. This brings them both great pleasure. Then, quite naturally, he pulls back into his world (or department), leaving her alone in her world (or department). Then again, back and forth, he moves in and out of her world. In a similar way, to create a win/win partnership, a couple can have more or less clear departments, and the man can occasionally move into hers and help her as an equal.

As he gets better and better at working and cooperating with her in her departments, then slowly but surely he will begin to invite her into his departments. Using this as a general guideline can be very helpful, particularly when couples work together.

For a partnership to thrive and not be self-serving, it must have a purpose beyond itself. For the passion to grow, partners must share a common interest and work toward that end.

We all come into this world with gifts to share and purposes to fulfill beyond our personal happiness. They may not be earth-shattering, but they are there. For a relationship to grow in love and passion, the love we share with another needs to be directed in some loftier way.

Having children is a natural fulfillment of this need. As a team, parents give to each other so that they can more successfully give to the children.

Once children grow up and leave home, couples

need to find a new goal or purpose. When as a partnership we are serving the highest good of the family, community, or world, our love can continue to grow without limit.

The Power of Forgiveness

To fully open our hearts to each other and enjoy a lifetime of love, the most important skill of all is forgiveness. Forgiving your partner for their mistakes not only frees you to love again but allows you to forgive yourself for not being perfect.

When we don't forgive in one relationship, our love is, to various degrees, restricted in all our life relationships. We can still love others, but not as much. When a heart is blocked in one relationship, it beats more weakly in them all. Forgiving means letting go of hurt.

Forgiveness allows us to give our love again and helps us to open up both to give and also to receive love. When we are closed, we lose on two counts.

The more you love someone, the more *you* suffer when you don't forgive them. Many people are driven to suicide by the agonizing pain of not forgiving a loved one. The greatest pain we can ever feel is the pain of not loving someone we love.

This agony drives people mad and is responsible for all the violence and craziness in our world and in our relationships. It is this pain of holding back our love that moves many people to addictive behaviors, substance abuse, and random violence.

We stubbornly hold on to bitterness and resentment not because we are not loving, but because we do not know how to forgive. If we were not loving, then ceasing to love someone would not be painful at all. The more loving we are, the more painful it is to not forgive.

How We Learn to Forgive

If when we were children our parents had asked for our forgiveness when they made mistakes, we would know how to forgive. If we had watched them forgive each other, we would better know how to forgive. If we had experienced being forgiven for our own mistakes again and again, we would not only know how to forgive but would have experienced firsthand the power of forgiveness to transform others.

Because our parents did not know how to forgive, we easily misunderstand what it means. Emotionally, we associate forgiving someone with the realization that what they did was not so bad after all.

For example, let's say that I am late and that you are upset with me. If I give you a great reason or excuse, you are more inclined to forgive me. I tell you, for instance, that my car blew up on the way over. That's why I am late. Surely, you would be more inclined to forgive me. Better yet, let's say a car blew up next to me and I stopped to save a child from dying. With such a "good" reason for being late, I would immediately be forgiven. But real forgiveness is needed when something really bad or hurtful happens and there is no good reason for it.

Real forgiveness acknowledges that a real mistake has been made and then affirms that the person who made it still deserves to be loved and respected.

It does not mean that their behavior was condoned or agreed with in any way.

If forgiveness is required, the implication is that you are acknowledging that a mistake was made that you want corrected or at least not repeated.

Forgiveness contains many of the sixteen messages listed below. Before reading down the list, take just a moment to think about a situation in which you found it almost impossible to forgive. As you verbally or mentally read these phrases, imagine the person who wounded you standing before you.

1. What you did was all your fault and not mine.
2. I am not responsible for what you did.
3. What you did was wrong. I did not deserve to be treated this way.
4. There is no good reason for what you did.
5. There is no excuse, and I am not willing to be subjected to that treatment ever again.
6. It is not OK with me.
7. It was very painful.

AND

8. I do not want to spend the rest of my life punishing you for this.
9. I can reach within my heart and see that even though what you did was "bad," you are still a good person deep inside.
10. I am willing to find the innocent part of you that is doing your best. No one is perfect.
11. I will not withhold my love from you.
12. I will freely give my love, but I will also protect myself from this happening again.

13. It will take time to rebuild trust, but I am willing to give you another chance.
14. It may be that I am not willing to give you another chance with me, but I do wish you well with others.
15. I release my hurt. You are no longer responsible for how I feel. I forgive you and wish you well.
16. I am responsible for how I feel. I am a loving person, and I can be loved just the way I am.

When forgiveness is learned and expressed, a huge weight is lifted. Through saying those three simple words, "I forgive you," lives and relationships have been dramatically saved.

The power to forgive is within us all, but like any other skill we must practice it. In the beginning, it takes time. We work at forgiving our partner, and then suddenly, the next day we are blaming them again. This is par for the course. Mastering the new relationship skill of forgiveness takes time, but with practice, it becomes a natural response.

In the beginning, a helpful phrase you can write out or think is: "Nobody's perfect, I forgive you for being imperfect. What you did was wrong. Nobody deserves to be treated the way you treated me. What you did was wrong and I forgive you. I forgive you for not being perfect. I forgive you for not giving me the love and respect that I deserve. I forgive you for not knowing better. I wish for you the decency and respect that every human being deserves. I forgive you for making a mistake."

The Message of Forgiveness

Christ's message to humanity from the cross was one of forgiveness. To rise above death, beyond pain, one has to forgive. His words were: "Father, forgive them; for they know not what they do." In this simple phrase is contained the secret of how to forgive.

We can begin to forgive our partners and others who hurt us when we can recognize that they really don't know what they are doing.

I remember when I first experienced pure forgiveness. It was when my daughter Lauren was two years old. She was playing with her food. I kept telling her not to, but she went ahead anyway. Within a few moments she was holding the spaghetti in her hands, then dropping it all over our carpet.

I was furious inside because she made a mess and I had to clean it up. At the same time, however, I was completely forgiving of her. I was angry with her, but my heart was completely open and filled with love.

I wondered how this could be and then remembered Christ's words, "Father, forgive them; for they know not what they do."

In that moment it was easy to forgive her because she clearly didn't know what she was doing when she dropped the spaghetti. I suppose she thought she was creating a work of art! What she didn't realize was that she was causing a problem for me.

As a counselor I have repeatedly experienced that people act and react in nonloving ways when they don't know better. People bear grudges out of ignorance and innocence. When they can experience a better way, they go for it. No one in their heart of hearts really wants to withhold and punish. It is merely the only way he or she knows to react when another person disrespects them.

The ideas in this book and my other books about male and female differences have been helpful to people because these insights are based on forgiveness.

No one is being blamed. Your mother and father are not blamed because they didn't anticipate what you would need to know to make your relationships work. Men are not blamed because they are "from Mars"—and don't understand women. Women are not blamed because they are "from Venus"—and don't understand men. We have problems because "we know not what we do." Once we bear this truth in mind and heart, our mistakes and our partners' mistakes are more forgivable.

The angels in heaven rejoice each time you forgive. When you choose to love instead of closing your heart, you bring a little spark of divinity into our dark world of struggle. You lighten the load of others and help them to forgive as well.

When men and women fail in relationships, it is not because they are not loving. We are all born with love in our hearts and a purpose to fulfill. We experience pain in our relationships because we do not know how to share our love in ways that work. We are missing the skills.

Sometimes love is not expressed because it is buried deep inside or locked within the fortress of our hearts. Hiding behind a wall, we are safe from hurt but barred from love.

So many people are imprisoned in themselves. They do not know how to find love so that they can share it. Infinities of love are wasted in a lifetime when we are not taught the basic skills for communicating and relating in a loving manner.

A Time for Hope

Perhaps for the first time in history, we are entering a phase when love can be mastered. This millennial time is one of great hope for relationships and the world. Previously on our planet "survival" was the guiding purpose. Slowly but surely, in the last several thousand years love has become increasingly important. It can become a guiding force within us all. The widespread dissatisfaction between men and women in relationships is a symptom that the world wants more. The pain of nations is the pain we feel when we can't share our love.

We can no longer turn our heads away from our deeper feelings. We hunger deep in our hearts to love. This shift has already taken place. The love is already there.

With this new understanding of what our mothers could not tell us and our fathers did not know, we're now much better prepared to love our partners. With practice, this new, open-ended love can dramatically improve relationships.

It is my hope that in applying the different skills for improving relationships you not only can forgive your partner when he or she forgets to use these skills, but you can also forgive your parents and yourself.

Remember, even if our parents could have taught us more, we still wouldn't have perfect relationships. The most intelligent and successful people around are having problems in their intimate and family relationships. There is no shame in needing to learn and practice. We all need to practice. Although we are born with the ability to love, it is a skill and must be learned.

Making a Difference in the World

Through mastering the secrets of passion and practicing forgiveness, we are not only creating a lifetime of love for ourselves, but we are making a difference in the world.

Practicing new relationship skills and learning to harmonize dissonant values is not only the prerequisite for creating more passionate relationships, but directly contributes to a more peaceful world.

Imagine a world where families are not shattered by divorce or neighbors are not hating each other. This kind of world is possible. Each step you take in your relationship helps actualize that possibility. Peace and prosperity for the world become a reality each time it approaches being your daily reality.

It is naive to assume that we can create peace in the world when we cannot make peace with the people we love. When our leaders are capable of having loving and mutually nurturing family relationships, then they will have acquired the skills to negotiate world peace.

By learning to resolve the differences between men and women, we are, in effect, easing global tensions and allowing ourselves and others to effectively embrace and connect different cultures and races.

As we realize through our relationships that our differences are really superficial and that deep within we are all one, we can transcend conflict and war and approach our problems with a new awareness that respects and harmonizes differences.

As in male/female relationships, the solution is not in denying that differences exist. The potential for conflict is resolved solely through honoring and respecting each other and finding creative ways in which to fulfill our differing needs.

Each time we take the sometimes painful or difficult step to positive resolution in our personal relationships, we are paving the way for harmony in the world. Your every effort and attempt makes it easier for others to follow you.

Thank you for letting me be a part of your journey in this world. May you and your loved ones experience a lifetime of love, and in our lives may we also share the experience of a world filled with love.

MARS & Venus
Counseling Centers®

One-on-One Counseling

To my readers:

Many of my readers phone my office looking for one-on-one counseling to help them build on the principles of communication and understanding in my books. Although I no longer have a private counseling practice, the Mars & Venus Counseling Centers can recommend a counselor to address your unique needs.

Mars and Venus Counseling Centers are a group of experienced therapists and counselors across the country who understand the principles presented in my work.

To be referred to a counselor, please call Mars & Venus Counseling Centers today at 1-800-649-4155!

Dr. John Gray

One-on-One Counseling
Call Toll-Free Today!
1-800-649-4155

A note to counselors: If you want to become part of the Mars & Venus Counseling Center program, please call 1-800-735-6052.

If you like what you just read
and want to learn more . . .

Every day we receive hundreds of phone calls and letters from readers asking for information regarding seminars, books, tapes, and other services. You can now call our representatives, Personal Growth Productions, twenty-four hours a day, seven days a week, toll free, at 1-888-MARSVENUS (1-888-627-7836) for information on the following subjects:

SEMINARS

More than 500,000 individuals and couples around the world have already benefited from John Gray's relationship seminars. We invite and encourage you to share with John this safe, insightful, and healing experience.

Because of the popularity of his seminars, Dr. Gray has developed programs for presentation by individuals he has personally trained and appointed. These seminars are available for both the general public as well as private corporate functions. This broad range of seminar opportunities continues to provide cherished memories and unforgettable experiences for attendees.

Please call for current schedules or booking information.

MARS/VENUS WORKSHOPS

The Mars/Venus Institute was created to offer workshops that bring Dr. Gray's information to local communities around the world. These exciting seminars feature John's favorite video segments and exercises presented by trained facilitators that have completed an in-depth course of study. Participants take home positive, practical experience that allows them to use Dr. Gray's suggestions comfortably and naturally. If you are interested in improving communication and developing more satisfying relationships, just give us a call and ask about Mars/Venus workshops.

MARS/VENUS COUNSELING CENTERS

No matter how helpful the insights in a book, tape, or seminar may be, they cannot replace the value of counseling and therapy. In response to the thousands of requests we have received for licensed professionals that use the Mars/Venus principles in their practice, Dr. Gray has established Mars/Venus Counseling Centers and Counselor Training. Participants in this program have completed an in-depth study of John's work and have demonstrated a commitment to his valuable concepts. If you are interested in a referral to a counselor in your area or information about training as a Mars/Venus counselor or establishing a Mars/Venus counseling center, please give us a call.

THE INTERNET

Visit John Gray's website at:

http://www.marsvenus.com.

Ask questions about *Men Are from Mars, Women Are from Venus*. Chat with other Martians and Venusians. Shop for books, audiotapes, and videos.

Videos, Audiotapes, and
Books by John Gray

For further exploration of the wonderful world of Mars and Venus, see the descriptions that follow and call us to place an order or for additional information.

Personal Growth Productions
P.O. Box 51281
Phoenix, AZ 85076-51281
1-888-MARSVENUS (1-888-627-7836)
or 1-800-821-3033

VIDEOS

Men Are from Mars, Women Are from Venus
Twelve VHS cassettes

This is a complete collection of John Gray's work on video. In this series, Dr. Gray shares the insights and tools necessary for understanding, accepting, and loving our differences. In a positive and uplifting way, couples and singles learn to improve communication and enjoy healthy, happy relationships without sacrifice. Average running time is fifty minutes.

Mars and Venus on a Date
Two VHS cassettes

After years of focusing on couples, Dr. Gray finally answers the thousands of singles and dating partners who asked him, "What about me?" John examines his five stages of dating: attraction, uncertainty, exclusivity, intimacy, and engagement. Find out why women need reassurance and men need encouragement. Increase your understanding of male/female differences and women's most asked question, "Why don't men commit?"

Men Are from Mars, Women Are from Venus— Children Are from Heaven
Two VHS cassettes

Dr. Gray lends his insights to parents trying to understand their little Martians and Venusians. In these cassettes you'll learn the five most important messages to give your children: It's Okay to Be Different; It's Okay to Make Mistakes; It's Okay to Have Feelings; It's Okay to Ask for What You Want; It's Okay to Say No, But Mom and Dad Are the Boss.

AUDIOTAPES

Secrets of Successful Relationships
Twelve 45-minute audiocassettes

This audio series was taped live at Dr. Gray's two-and-a-half-day seminars and features three themes: The Secrets of Communication; Getting the Love You Deserve; and The Secrets of Intimacy and Passion.

Healing the Heart
Twelve 45-minute audiocassettes

The text and exercises contained in these tapes were originally taught as a week-long seminar designed to help individuals understand how and why the past affects the way they respond in relationships today. You will have the opportunity to create your own counseling sessions with the nation's leading expert on relationships and communication, and enjoy the benefits of healing your significant issues any time you choose.